GREAT GOD
OF HEAVEN

Daniel made simple

W0008290

SAM GORDON

Christian Year Publications

'With his typical warmth and wisdom, Sam Gordon peers through Daniel's telescope of future events to show us the clarity of prophecy and, better yet, the glory of our Saviour. You're left whispering under your breath, as the last page is turned, "Even so, come, Lord Jesus" ... we can hardly wait.'

Dr Stephen Davey, Pastor/Teacher, Colonial Baptist Church, Cary NC
President & Professor of Practical Theology, Shepherds Theological Seminary

'The book of Daniel is the perfect blend of prophecy and piety. God shares truths about the "sweet by and by" to give his followers hope, while Daniel and his friends demonstrate the wisdom and faith needed to live for God through the "difficult here and now." Properly interpreted, the book of Daniel helps the reader gain an understanding of God's plan for the future while also learning how to stay faithful today. And in this practical commentary, Sam Gordon gives us that proper interpretation!'

Dr Charlie Dyer, Professor-at-Large of Bible, Moody Bible Institute
Host of *The Land and the Book* radio program

'On several occasions I have enjoyed hearing ministry from the book of Daniel by my brother and dear friend, Sam Gordon. A deep yearning of my heart has been to have this teaching in written form. This dream has come true in the pages of his book. I warmly commend it to you.'

David Logacho, Bible teacher throughout Latin America
Former Director, La Biblia Dice, Quito, Ecuador

'Many people love the book of Daniel, at least the first half. Great stories. Easy to understand. But they skip the second half of the book because it is prophetic and much more difficult to understand. However, Sam

Gordon has a unique way of making understandable what many find puzzling. With his help, you'll enjoy all twelve chapters in Daniel.'

Dr Woodrow Kroll, President & Senior Bible Teacher (retired)
Back to the Bible radio

'What Sam Gordon has done in expounding, exposing, and explaining the message of the book of Daniel in his classic witty and winsome way is nothing short of remarkable. Sam takes one of the most technically challenging books of the Bible and unveils the majesty and supremacy of God in a way that is befitting to both schoolboy and scholar alike. This is an extremely practical, prophetic, and profound guide for living as exiles in our own Babylon today.'

Wayne Sutton, Senior Pastor
Carrubbers Christian Centre, Royal Mile, Edinburgh

'Like he has done in his ministry over the years, Sam Gordon uses his God-given gift of driving the truths of Scripture home beautifully. In the pages of this book, we get to experience God and his workings through lives that are courageously committed to him in a simple, easy-read style, with great depth. This book will admonish, build, and challenge you!'

Dr Bernice Gatere
Director, Trans World Radio, Kenya

'Sam Gordon has done a wonderful job expounding the book of Daniel. He does it in a simplified way thus enabling both lay church members and trained theologians to grasp its timely message. I highly recommend this book to everyone who is seeking to better understand or teach God's Word.'

Rev Connex Saulosi Ijalasi
Former General Secretary of Zambezi Evangelical Church
Founder & Director, J-Life Ministries (Malawi)

'Sam Gordon really brings history alive, which delights me as it was the only subject at which I excelled at school. The book is beautifully written – lively, most intriguing, with liberal use of helpful modern idioms. Most amazing of all, he brings to light the unerring hand of God in history, showing how Daniel's prophecies have been fulfilled to the letter, thus declaring the awesome majesty and uniqueness of the God of Israel.'

Charles Gardner

South African-born journalist and author

'If you've ever longed for a trusted friend to sit beside you and guide you as you read and study the Bible, Sam Gordon is your man. In his characteristically warm and engaging style, Sam unlocks the truths of Scripture. The book of Daniel has inspiring historical narrative and powerful prophetic portions. Like the experienced and trustworthy expositor he is, Sam skilfully guides us through its wonders, while always exalting our great God and Saviour, Jesus Christ.'

Gregg Harris

President & CEO, Thru the Bible

'Sam Gordon accomplishes something special for he helps make the book of Daniel a discipleship manual for daily living. This commentary is a joy to read, and more important, you'll want to come back to it again and again because it speaks so creatively and insightfully into our personal lives and the times in which we are living, all the while drawing you to the great God of heaven.'

Sam Ngugi

Founder & Director, Mission Campaign Network (MCN), Kenya

'In this lovely book, Sam Gordon makes the crooked paths straight, and in his usual compelling way, he explains the more difficult passages in a *manner easily understood. Any serious Bible student, and anyone with a keen interest in prophecy, will benefit greatly from this exposition. It becomes a cherished commentary in my library, as it will be in yours.'*

Alan Parks
Bible Teacher & Gospel Singer, Myrtle Beach, SC

'The complexity of the book of Daniel often deters many believers from accessing the whole counsel of God. Sam Gordon has bridged that gap as he weaves modern imagery with biblical truths thus enabling the Bible student to absorb and understand the mind of God for these end times. This book is a masterpiece that needs to be translated into other languages.'

Rev Patrick Semphere
General Secretary, Word Alive Ministries Intl., Malawi
Chairperson, Malawi Human Rights Commission

'When I began reading Sam Gordon's book my plan was to skim it fairly quickly, but then I was captivated by the constant reminders of the greatness of God. I've never read a commentary with so many footnotes to other scholars and yet so readable and eminently related to our situation today. Thank you, Sam, for reminding me that sound Bible teaching is powerfully practical.'

Dr James E Plueddemann
Retired SIM International Director
Retired Professor at Wheaton College (IL) *and*
Trinity Evangelical Divinity School, Deerfield, IL

GREAT GOD OF HEAVEN

ISBN-13: 978 1 872734 88 0

Cover design by Brian Chalmers Design Services
Typeset by John Ritchie Ltd., Kilmarnock
Printed by Bell & Bain Ltd., Glasgow

DEDICATION

to

the *Truth for Today* Accountability & Advisory Board

Abi, Esther, John, Peter, Ruth, and Wallace

with admiration, affection, and appreciation

and

the most amazing team of ministry partners around the world

to whom I owe an immense debt of gratitude

Check out the Truth for Today website
www.truthfortoday.co.uk

CONTENTS

FIRST WORD

2020 is immortalised in history as the year when the coronavirus struck and brought the world to a standstill. Everything stopped. Non-essential shops closed. Flights were cancelled. Schools and universities shut down. Churches and other religious buildings bolted their front doors. Life as we knew it ground to a screeching halt. New words and phrases popped up all over the place. And so the list goes on, and on.

Gospel work flourished as Bible churches maximised modern technology with sanctified creativity so that weary believers could share together online. Moving forward, we should value and appreciate the joy of warm Christian fellowship when we meet as a gathered company of God's people. There are some things in life we must never again take for granted.

For me, a peripatetic Bible teacher, what was I going to do during these months when I could no longer travel here and there to preach the Word of God? Aside from online ministry (which was a great privilege), my publisher had already asked me to write another commentary. So, after fifteen weeks holed up in my study, the book you now have in your hand is my lockdown legacy. May God bless and encourage you as you read it from cover to cover.

I am deeply indebted to a number of folks who have added so much to this exciting project: to all those wonderful friends from near and far who have endorsed the book, my warmest gratitude … to Dr Julie and Dr Liron whose medical expertise was most helpful in relation to Nebuchadnezzar's experience, a big thank you … to Peter and Patty whose godly insights and editorial comments on every chapter have made a significant difference to the finished manuscript, my heartfelt appreciation … to my wife Lois for granting me leave of absence for almost four months, I am massively grateful … last but not least, to the sovereign Lord, the real hero of the book of Daniel, to him be all the praise and glory forever and ever.

Sam Gordon
Bawtry, South Yorkshire
September 2020

SELECT BIBLIOGRAPHY

Where these books are cited in the notes, it is by author only.

Akin, D L, *Exalting Jesus in Daniel* (Nashville: B&H Publishing, 2017).

Allen, J, *Daniel Reconsidered* (Cookstown: STL, 2013).

Baldwin, J G, *Daniel* (Downers Grove: IVP, 1985).

Boice, J M, *Daniel* (Grand Rapids: Baker Books, 1989).

Davis, D R, *The Message of Daniel* (Nottingham: IVP, 2013).

Duguid, I M, *Daniel* (Phillipsburg: Presbyterian & Reformed, 2008).

Ferguson, S B, *Daniel* (Nashville: Thomas Nelson, 1988).

Gangel, K O, *Daniel* (Nashville: Broadman & Holman Publishers, 2001).

Gordon, S, *All Hail The Lamb* (Kilmarnock: John Ritchie, 2014).

Hawkins, O S, *The Daniel Code* (Nashville: Thomas Nelson, 2016).

Helm, D, *Daniel For You* (Epsom: The Good Book Company, 2015).

Jeremiah, D, *Agents of Babylon* (Carol Stream: Tyndale, 2015).

Jeremiah, D, *The Handwriting on the Wall* (Nashville: Thomas Nelson, 1992).

Lennox, J C, *Against the Flow: The Inspiration of Daniel in an Age of Relativism* (Oxford: Monarch, 2015).

MacArthur, J F, *Daniel, God's Control over Rulers and Nations* (Nashville: W Publishing, 2000).

Olyott, S, *Dare to Stand Alone* (Darlington: Evangelical Press, 1982).

Phillips, J & Vines, J, *Exploring the Book of Daniel* (Neptune: Loizeaux Brothers, 1990).

Showers, R E, *The Most High God* (Bellmawr: Friends of Israel Gospel Ministry, 2017).

Stortz, R, *Daniel, The Triumph of God's Kingdom* (Wheaton: Crossway Books, 2004).

Thomas, G, *Daniel: Servant of God Under Four Kings* (Bridgend: Bryntirion, 1998).

Walvoord, J [revised by Dyer & Rawley] *Daniel* (Chicago: Moody, 2012).

Wiersbe, W W, *Be Resolute* (Colorado Springs: David C Cook, 2000).

THE MAN BEHIND THE HEADLINES

Daniel is my hero. He always has been. The chances are, he always will be. As a young boy growing up in Bangor, Northern Ireland, I learned a wee chorus in Sunday School that was penned by Philip P Bliss away back in 1873. God used it to set my heart on fire, *Dare to be a Daniel, dare to stand alone, dare to have a purpose firm, and dare to make it known.*

There is something special about a man like Daniel. He stands out in a crowd. He has magnetic qualities which are hugely attractive. We are drawn to him with ease. We like what we see and hear. And the good news is, he is made of the same material as the rest of us lesser mortals.

Daniel is one of four eminent Old Testament prophets who share two traits in common. First, each one talks about something which is lost: one, Isaiah, the distinguished evangelical prophet who takes us to the Everest of Christology, is speaking about a lost revelation; two, Jeremiah, the weeping prophet who ploughed a lonely furrow for God, is appropriately talking about a lost joy; three, Ezekiel battled against all the odds as he mimed in open air theatre the message God entrusted to him of a lost glory; and, four, Daniel, the last of this illustrious quartet, addressed the matter of a lost kingdom.

Second, each one refers to the kingly government of God in the affairs of man since God is sovereign. He rules. So, for example, Isaiah spells out the principles of divine government. Jeremiah focuses on the practices which are compatible with such government. Ezekiel gives us a glimpse of the glorious Governor and his government to come. And Daniel addresses the fact that the coming government is one which is permanent and forever.

Like those who preceded him, and many who have followed after, Daniel has not been granted immunity from the critics who cast aspersions on biblical truth. Scholars have scoffed. Doubters have discredited. They see this amazing book as the Achilles' heel of Scripture. Liberal theologians and modernist preachers have waged battle around four main issues, namely, the miracles, predictions, language, and history of the book. W A Criswell writes, 'There is not a liberal theologian in the world, past or present, who accepts the authenticity of the book of Daniel.'

Such voracious lions have not devoured the book, even as they were unable to masticate the man! Here is a gem of a book inspired throughout by the Holy Spirit and saturated with the supernatural from beginning to end. It will ultimately confound the cynic and confirm the faith of the trusting child of God.

This epic book is for adults, not only children. To turn it into a children's thriller is to blunt the seriousness of its message. Within its pages, there are sizzling stories about ruthless political tyranny, civil disobedience, religious persecution, and martyrdom. Bryan Chapell writes, 'Daniel combines classic stories of epic heroism with spectacular revelations of the power of God to orchestrate future events for his ultimate glory.'

The book of Daniel is not a tranquiliser given to those believers who are suffering in order to deaden their pain and alleviate their discomfort. Far from it. To change the analogy, it is more like a bugle call sounding reveille at daybreak to awaken all of us to live wisely as broken people in this broken world.

The question is: What about the man at the centre of the story?

He was a captive

Daniel was forcibly removed from his home in Jerusalem and carried captive by the reigning Nebuchadnezzar (also called Nebuchadrezzar) to Babylon in 605 BC. Presumably, he was in his mid-teens, maybe 15 or 16 years of age. He was born and reared during a great spiritual awakening which swept across the nation in the days of King Josiah who, as Scripture affirms, outshone Asa, Hezekiah, and Jehoshaphat in godly zeal and influence. The historical account in 2 Kings 22-23 shows that Josiah repaired the temple, he recovered the law, he called for repentance, he led reforms, he returned God's Word to the centre of Israel's life, he got rid of ungodly priests, and he restored the celebration of Passover. Josiah's reforms were of immense significance and one of the lessons we learn is that it is never too late to do the right thing.

Unlike many of us, Daniel was privileged to live through times of revival and restoration. Such exposure to a deep work of God stood him in good stead in later life. And without doubt, he was massively influenced by the preaching of the word of the Lord through Jeremiah. God fashioned him during his formative years.

It is clear from the biblical narrative that Daniel knew his God intimately; he came to know and love Yahweh through reading the Torah scrolls and, as a consequence, performed a host of amazing exploits for him. When we consider the significance of his name and its meaning—God is my judge—it casts light on his every move. What God thinks and what God does matters more to him than what anybody else in the whole world thinks or does. That was how Daniel lived! And died.

He was committed

Even a casual overview of Daniel's life leads to one outstanding conclusion, for all that mattered to him was doing the will of God. As a friend said to me, 'Daniel was controlled, compelled, and corralled by the Word of God and the love of God.' Because the will of God is always in sync with the Word of God, for him, in the best of times and worst of times, God was Number One. His long, fruitful life revolved around a conscious awareness of the presence of the sovereign Lord for God was with him. And he knew it! His handle on life was coloured by an appreciation of the sensational power of one who calls all the shots. John Piper notes that 'his life was centred on God, it was built on God. And his way of looking at the world was drenched with God.'

Picture the scene: Daniel was effectively a prisoner in an alien, atheistic land … a hostage to fortune in a pagan, foreign country that was definitely not the land of the free and the home of the brave … home, family, and close boyhood friends are nowhere near, and still, God meant everything to him. He was front and centre in all that he did. *Soli Deo*. Prayer was his habit, faith was his hallmark, and God was his priority.

When some of the refugees were downcast and hung their harps on the poplars, when others lamented their fate and wept on the banks of the River Chebar, when more turned sour and bitterly implored, 'How can we sing the songs of the Lord while in a foreign land?' (Psalm 137:4, NIV), Daniel was content to leave the outcome in the strong hand of a God of gracious providence, because he knew in his heart that God rules and overrules. He may be in exile, his God is not. Our faith is to bloom and blossom wherever God has planted us, be that in Belfast or Baltimore, Beijing or Bogota, Budapest or Babylon.

He was courageous

As a relatively young man, Daniel dared to stand for God and truth. From day one, he unashamedly stood up for what he passionately believed. No one was going to mess around with him and his godly standards. He was no doormat. No pushover. How natural and easy it would have been for Daniel to cave in under intense pressure. Compromise, and the thought of it, may have crossed his mind, but by God's enabling grace he embraced God's plan. When crunch time came, he chose God. I mean, he could have saved himself a lot of hassle if he had reasoned, 'When in Babylon, do as the Babylonians do.' America's first president, George Washington (1732-99), once said that 'few men have the virtue to withstand the highest bidder.' Daniel was such a person.

David Helm notes that Daniel and his friends 'did not prioritise their own pleasures. They did not even prioritise their own promotion. They resolved to prioritise purity.' And principle. He knew where and when to draw the line. He did not isolate himself from the culture around him, but he did insulate himself from it.

When his walk with God in chapter one is challenged, he purposed in his heart. When his witness for God is under serious threat in chapter two, he takes it to the Lord in prayer. When his worship of God is in grave danger in chapter three, he knows that God's way is always the best way. A Christian leader counselled a friend with this wise advice: 'When you are faced with a choice, always choose Christ.' In other words, when God says yes, we say yes, and when God says no, we say no. It has to be said, that resolute, non-compromising mindset takes grit and gumption.

He was commended

The unfolding story of Daniel is a classic tale of rags to riches – about a young Jewish lad, unceremoniously dragged from home and deported 800 miles east, who rose to become prime minister in the imperial government of Babylon. Like Joseph before him, he was elevated to a position of authority and influence in the palace and beyond. In the public sector, the Babylonian Civil Service, Daniel was within touching distance of the top rung of the ladder in terms of plum jobs.

As an incredibly loyal servant of the Most High God, Daniel discovered in his own life and work that the divine promise held true, 'I will honour those who honour me' (1 Samuel 2:30, NLT).

Was Daniel a flash in the pan or a seven-day wonder? How did he fare in the popularity ratings? Ezekiel, a contemporary in exile, describes him as a righteous man (Ezekiel 14:14, 20). The Lord Jesus, in his hugely significant Olivet discourse, viewed him as 'a prophet' (Matthew 24:15). The writer to the Hebrews hints that he was a person of outstanding faith (Hebrews 11:33). God refers to him as someone who is 'highly esteemed' (Daniel 10:11). It is patently obvious from each of these unsolicited character references that they unite to pay fulsome tribute to an aristocrat, one who is both a saint and a seer.

One of the prime reasons for his greatness is because he had the touch of God upon his life. Five times do we read the phrase, 'he touched me' (Daniel 8:18, 9:21, 10:10, 16, 18, KJV). One, God touched him to make him *see* – the touch of *understanding*; two,

God touched him to give him *skill* – the touch of *unction*; three, God touched him to make him *stand* – the touch of *undergirding*; four, God touched him to make him *speak* – the touch of *utterance*; five, God touched him to make him *strong* – the touch of *undertaking*. Lehman Strauss, in *The Prophecies of Daniel*, further notes that the hand of God touched Daniel enabling him to become 'a man of perception, purpose, principle, prayer, purity, and power.'

By way of explanation
The layout and design of the book is most interesting and instructive. There are two facets worth mentioning:

it is bilingual in that two languages are used in its composition. From 2:4b to 7:28 it is written in Aramaic and, therefore, resonates especially with the Gentile peoples. On the other hand, from 1:1 to 2:4a as well as chapters 8-12, it is penned in Hebrew and, therefore, appeals primarily to the Jewish people.

it is bi-literal in that it is a book of two halves. The first six chapters tend to be more historical in nature; the remaining chapters, 7-12, are labelled as prophetic because they focus on the future. As a kind-of disclaimer, there are minor variations within such a broad spectrum of revelation.

In your copy of the Bible and mine, Daniel is found in the section devoted to prophetic books where he comfortably sits alongside the Big Three of Isaiah, Jeremiah, and Ezekiel, and is immediately followed by a dozen so-called Minor Prophets. However, in the Hebrew Old Testament, the Tanakh, with its three divisions – the Law (Torah), the Prophets (Nevi'im), and the Writings (Ketuvim) – Daniel is located in the last of these.

Let me explain: it was placed within the Writings of the Old Testament as opposed to the Prophets because, in the eyes of

Jewish scholars, Daniel was different from Ezekiel, Jeremiah, and Isaiah; he did not hold the office of a prophet, nor was he from the school of the prophets or seen as one of the sons of the prophets, but he was a statesman whom the sovereign Lord endowed with a distinctive prophetic gift.

In terms of the chronology of the book, it goes like this: chapters 1, 2, 3, and 4, are followed by chapters 7 and 8; only then do we come to chapter 5, which is immediately followed by chapters 9 and 6; then it is through to the end with chapters 10, 11, and 12.

The aim of the book

It is an eye-popping illustration of pure dedication and faithfulness to the living God. One man's life is used as a first-class example of what it means to surrender all to God and how we can survive in a pagan, permissive, and perverted culture. He is never a victim of his circumstances. He never bales out no matter how tough it gets. And it does get pretty tough at times. As a result, the blessings and benefits that flow from such a yielded heart are phenomenal. And, indeed, that is what God is looking for among his people in the twenty-first century.

That said, the focus is not exclusively on a man, for overarching the entire journal is the jaw-dropping faithfulness of Daniel's God. As Kenneth Gangel writes, 'This is not a biography of Daniel's life, not a book about the history of Israel, and not a theology of the Hebrews.' The main beam is shining far beyond Daniel to the great God of heaven. This golden thread is woven into the multicoloured fabric of Daniel; the sovereignty, faithfulness, kindness, and integrity of God shine out from every page. Simply put, the book of Daniel is about Daniel's God! Or as Mark Dever succinctly observes in *The Message of the Old Testament*, 'The trumpet choruses of God's promised victory are sounded in chapter after chapter as God displays his sovereign rule over all the mighty rulers of false empires, all of them confessing that he is the true Sovereign.'

Daniel's core conviction is reflected in his reply to Nebuchadnezzar when he acknowledged, *there is a God in heaven* (Daniel 2:28). God is the real hero in the drama. Amidst the inky blackness of world affairs and the murky underworld of Satan and his emissaries, this potent truth is prominent in its appeal. Why? Because it makes a colossal difference. Personally, nationally, globally, the Lord is king. God is in charge. He runs the entire show. Our God reigns!

When life turns sour, God's promises are sweet

The question is often asked by bewildered saints and others who have passed through some devastating experience: Where was God when such-and-such happened? I have asked it and I am sure many of you have too. Did Daniel's mother and father ask that question? Probably. Did Daniel himself voice it on more than one occasion? Possibly. This was certainly not the life that they intended for their beloved son. It was the last thing on Daniel's mind as he entered his teenage years.

For every family in Israel whose lives were forever changed because of Nebuchadnezzar, it was traumatic, tearful, and terrifying. For us, when life takes an unexpected turn from our short-sighted perspective, I think we can do no better than turn to Daniel and see how he came through the other side. Given time and an infusion of God's grace, he emerged a cut above the rest because his trust in his God is the stuff of legend. As Sinclair Ferguson tells us, 'All our trials are important and connected punctuation marks in the biography of grace he is writing in our lives.' For Daniel and his friends, they are all part of the tapestry he is weaving in history.

The book is an eye-opener in that it reveals God's constant, continuing care and compassion for his ancient, covenant people, Israel. When Israel first went into captivity, God ensured that they had a representative to fight their cause right in the middle of the Babylonian government. John MacArthur notes that 'God picked Daniel as Israel's man in the White House.' The sons of Abraham are an integral part of his plan and purpose for the world. Even in exile, they remained 'the apple of his eye' (Zechariah 2:8, NIV). And as Geoff Thomas notes, 'There are thunders in heaven when the apple of the Lord's eye is touched on earth.'

For a Jewish person, the message is one of supreme comfort in that it points forward down the centuries to the advent of the Messiah and far beyond that event to a proposed millennial kingdom. For you and me, Daniel speaks to us as God's exiled people today (1 Peter 1:1) for we are numbered among those who still wait for a better king and better kingdom.

The railway lines of Scripture

It is vital when studying the book of Daniel that we keep in the front of our minds that it runs in tandem with the New Testament book of Revelation. Basically, one explains the other. Both books are apocalyptic, visionary, and eschatological; and both contain important information apropos to the last days in the lead-up to the second coming of Jesus Christ.

As an aside, Bob Stein (former professor of New Testament Interpretation at The Southern Baptist Theological Seminary) concluded that among the millions of persecuted believers around the world the two most favoured books in the Bible are Daniel and Revelation. Why? Because both teach that in the end our God wins!

A *Daily Telegraph* article, penned by Tom Phillips in 2014, said that China was on course to become the 'world's most Christian nation' within fifteen years. Quoting direct from a house church pastor, he intimated that '… the Old Testament book in which the exiled Daniel refuses to obey orders to worship the king rather than his own God is seen as "very dangerous" by the Chinese government in light of the explosion of Christianity in China.'

An interesting thought and a brilliant reminder as we embark on our study of this most enthralling book that Daniel's eternal God is our God. In a world of changing kings, shifting standards, destabilising forces, political turmoil, and crumbling foundations, we, just like Daniel, serve an unchanging God. For us, the question is: Are we up for the challenge, to dare to be a Daniel?

1

NAIL YOUR COLOURS TO THE MAST

The well-known phrase quoted above originated in England towards the end of the eighteenth century. The expression was coined in reference to the exploits of a naval crew at the Battle of Camperdown – an engagement fought between English and Dutch ships as part of the French Revolutionary Wars in October 1797.

The English fleet was led by HMS Venerable, the flagship of Admiral Adam Duncan. Initially, the battle did not go well for the Royal Navy. The main mast of Duncan's vessel was struck, and as a result the admiral's blue squadronal standard was brought crashing down. Not good. This could have been interpreted as meaning that Duncan had surrendered to the enemy.

As the story goes, step forward horny-handed son of the sea and subsequent national hero, Jack Crawford. A young man, in his early twenties, he climbed up what was left of the rickety mast with the standard tucked under his arm and nailed it back to where it was clearly visible to the rest of the fleet. This valiant act of selfless bravery proved crucial in the battle and Duncan's forces were eventually victorious.

Some historians believe that the victory at Camperdown proved to be the end of the dominance of the Dutch at sea and the beginning of an era in which Britannia ruled the waves. Whatever, Crawford returned home to Sunderland to a hero's welcome. And rightly so! More later.

1:1-2

The Lord is sovereign – history affirms it

In the third year of the reign of Jehoiakim king of Judah, Nebuchadnezzar king of Babylon came to Jerusalem and besieged it. And the Lord gave Jehoiakim king of Judah into his hand, with some of the vessels of the house of God. And he brought them to the land of Shinar, to the house of his god, and placed the vessels in the treasury of his god.

The drums of war were beating in the Middle East. Two superpowers, Egypt and Babylon, were jockeying for supremacy in that strategically important region in the late seventh century BC. Above all else, both wanted to be top dog. This was their all-consuming passion. It was, therefore, only a matter of time before they would clash in an epic confrontation that would radically change the face of global politics.

In the summer of 605 BC the inevitable happened when the seemingly invincible Babylonian army, under the brilliant leadership of the crown prince, Nebuchadnezzar, attacked the Egyptian army at Carchemish on the upper Euphrates River. The *Nebuchadnezzar Chronicle*, a cuneiform clay tablet now housed in the British Museum in London, claims that 'he accomplished their defeat, decisively' when the shattered Egyptians beat a hasty retreat south to their homeland, licking their wounds.

That hugely significant and momentous development opened up the land of Judah to domination by the notorious Babylonians. As John Lennox writes, 'There is no contest between peashooters and tanks.' By early August 605 BC, Nebuchadnezzar assumed control of the golden city of Jerusalem. In the middle of that same month, Nebuchadnezzar's father, King Nabopolassar died as a man in his early fifties. When he heard the news, the crown prince rushed home to claim the throne, but he did not go empty handed. Before making a beeline home from Jerusalem, he ransacked the temple and took back with him some of the holy vessels and a contingent of fine young men. Within three weeks, on the day of his arrival in early September, he was crowned king of the rapidly expanding empire.

The stage is set

The principal characters on-stage are Jehoiakim and Nebuchadnezzar. The former was the eighteenth king of Judah (one of two tribes who remained faithful and loyal to the family of David), and the second son of saintly Josiah (1 Chronicles 3:15). He was nothing more than a spineless puppet. His track record left a lot to be desired. For example, he was culpable when he cut and burned Jeremiah's scroll (Jeremiah 36:20-23); he was basically incapable when it came to leadership and squandered state funds to build himself a magnificent new palace (Jeremiah 22:13-17).

After legislating for eleven too-long years, the 'ass' Jehoiakim was 'buried like a dead donkey, dragged out of Jerusalem and dumped outside the gates' (Jeremiah 22:19, NLT). An ignoble end, indeed. And a timely lesson that godly parentage does not necessarily guarantee godly children.

The latter was one of the most impressive rulers of ancient times. A celebrated monarch of forty-three years standing, he governed Babylon in its heyday; a time, according to James Boice, of 'radical secular humanism.' An electrifying leader, he was renowned as a military marksman, a statesman *par excellence*, and a prestigious builder who left behind Babylon's beautiful Ishtar Gate (which has been reconstructed in Berlin's famous Pergamon Museum), the grand Processional Way, and the Hanging Gardens. Barbara Böch, writing in *National Geographic*, said of Nebuchadnezzar, 'A name rich with colour, strength, and prestige belongs to one of the few Babylonian kings known by name today … he left behind a legacy like no other.'

Two kings whose names are etched on the granite of history, for better or worse, are mentioned in verse one. However, there is a third king whose name does not appear in verse one, but whose presence, as we shall see, is evident in verse 2, and throughout the rest of the book as in 2:20-22. Elsewhere, he is acclaimed as 'King of the ages' (Revelation 15:3, NIV) and 'King of kings' (Revelation 19:16, NIV).

God does what he does because he is who he is

There is a telltale statement at the beginning of verse 2, where we read, *And the Lord gave Jehoiakim king of Judah into his hand.* At the outset of this extraordinary book, the message is as clear as daylight: God is in full control. As God, he determines the failures and fortunes of man. He is Lord of all, and because of that, Nebuchadnezzar scored a military victory over his archenemy. He whipped the opposition into submission, but God allowed it to happen. He engineered it from on high. This incident, one of many, is a class example of the active sovereignty of God in the affairs of man and nation. He is involved in human history. Man turns up, God turns down.

All that transpired was not only in line with the flawless character of God, it actually fulfilled the Word of God for the prophet Isaiah predicted it in 39:6-7; Micah, his contemporary, shared the burden (Micah 4:10), and Jeremiah strongly hinted at it in 46:2. So this incident should not surprise us at all; this history in a capsule pays tribute to the unerring faithfulness of our Most High God.

Look at it from another angle: this is a divine invasion of enemy territory. We must not miss what the sovereign God is doing in it all. The city of man is being invaded by the city of God, to draw from Augustine. A nation that opposes the true God of Israel is now being infiltrated by the Lord's army. A small incursion to be sure, but given time and the ripening of God's purpose, one that will accomplish far more than anyone could possibly imagine. Israel will be oppressed and her people scattered, but the nations will have a witness among them to the one true and living God. The so-called 'times of the Gentiles' (Luke 21:24) has now started and continues to this day; it will reach its climax and be consummated with the second coming of Christ.

It is worth noting that the locals in Babylon (lit., Shinar) would be rubbing their hands with glee at this apparent loss of face for the people of Judah. As Dale Ralph Davis notes, 'In the Ancient Near East the fortunes of a god and a people were viewed together. That Judah's king and temple vessels were taken simply meant that the Lord was not able to protect them. If the people were losers, it meant the Lord was a loser.'

The omniscient Lord knew all about it; yes, he did – he knew how it would be perceived in the eyes of the enemy, and how they would milk it for all it was worth, and how the pagans in Babylon would be singing at the top of their voices to their national deity, 'Praise Marduk, from whom all blessings flow' – and still he gave it the go-ahead. Why? Quite simply, to teach his covenant people a salutary lesson that a holy God always judges sin; if they sow the wind, they reap the whirlwind (Hosea 8:7). Like it or not, the harvest is always gathered home. Warren Wiersbe says that 'God would rather have his people living in captivity in a pagan land, than living like pagans in the Holy Land.'

When a nation disobeys the Word of God and departs from the worship of God they are living under the dark storm cloud of imminent judgment. Idolatry, immorality, and injustice toward the poor and needy is a recipe for disaster. Hence, the invasion by marauding armies from the eastern bloc in 605 BC, then later on in 597 BC and 586 BC. In that sense, the curtain fell on Judah for she was erased from the national scene. She was a people and a nation in exile; a people with no temple, no king, and no land.

1:3-5

Nothing but the best will do

Then the king commanded Ashpenaz, his chief eunuch, to bring some of the people of Israel, both of the royal family and of the nobility, youths without blemish of good appearance and skilful in all wisdom, endowed with knowledge, understanding learning, and competent to stand in the king's palace, and to teach them the literature and language of the Chaldeans. The king assigned them a daily portion of the food that the king ate, and of the wine that he drank. They were to be educated for three years, and at the end of that time they were to stand before the king.

Nothing but the brightest and best for Nebuchadnezzar! It was the crème de la crème that he was deporting eight hundred miles east of Jerusalem across the Syrian desert. The skimmed milk he left behind. Historians tell us that between 50 and 75 of these young men were transported. It was those of noble birth, of good heritage, with a respectable family history, even of royal lineage that he wanted to accompany him back to the confines of the royal court in Babylon. For these guys, their credentials are impeccable. These kidnapped teenagers were handsome and healthy, intelligent and innovative. They were top of the class, ticking all the boxes. Any first-rate university would be ready to sign scholarship papers for these four, they really are that good.

For three years they would be students in the local blue ribbon university where they would be instructed, or more likely, indoctrinated in the language and literature of the Chaldeans by some of the world's top scholars. This was the language of Abraham. It reminds me of Moses who 'was educated in all the wisdom of the Egyptians and was powerful in speech and action' (Acts 7:22, NIV). Upon graduation *summa cum laude* from the Oxford of Babylon, they would have a first-class honours degree in arts and science to frame and hang on their apartment wall. In between times, they would be given a makeover and brainwashed with the system in an attempt to remove any vestige of godliness and biblical truth.

On a human level, their future was neatly mapped out. It seemed deliciously rosy. They were under the watchful eye and guiding hand of Ashpenaz, Vice President of Human Resources. They would be employed as advisers in the service of the king and on the payroll of the Babylonian Civil Service. It looked ideal. But as we shall discover later on in the chapter, looks can be deceiving.

1:6-7

A new identity

> *Among these were Daniel, Hananiah, Mishael, and Azariah of the tribe of Judah. And the chief of the eunuchs gave them names: Daniel he called Belteshazzar, Hananiah he called Shadrach, Mishael he called Meshach, and Azariah he called Abednego.*

This foursome from the tribe of Judah were all richly blessed with a godly background and that is reflected in their names which bore testimony in one way or another to the God of Abraham, Isaac, and Jacob. Rabbinic tradition holds that they were descendants of King Hezekiah, based on these words: 'And some of your descendants, your own flesh and blood who will be born to you, will be taken away, and they will become eunuchs in the palace of the king of Babylon' (Isaiah 39:7, NIV). Their captors are fanatically keen to repackage them with a total new identity, more in keeping with the Babylonian culture and worldview with the label sewn in, 'Made in Babylon.' As O S Hawkins says, 'All Nebuchadnezzar had to do now was brainwash these monotheistic boys and transform them into polytheistic leaders.'

Daniel whose name means 'Elohim is my judge' becomes Belteshazzar (*Elohim* is one of the Hebrew names for God); Hananiah whose name means '*Yahweh* is gracious' becomes Shadrach (*Yahweh* is the personal name of the God of Scripture); Mishael whose name means 'Who is what *Elohim* is?' becomes Meshach; and Azariah whose name means '*Yahweh* is my helper' becomes Abednego. The meaning of each of the Babylonian names is tenuous and difficult to suss, but they are more than likely associated with some cultic figure or god. Pharaoh did something similar to Joseph when he chose to call him Zaphenath-Paneah

(Genesis 41:45). Esther, as she is better known, was actually called Hadassah at birth, until her name was changed (Esther 2:7).

This was peer pressure at its very worst. The young men had no say in the matter as it was forced upon them. The new identity suggests they were being groomed for earthly glory and would be at one with their colleagues in the palace or wherever. It was one more attempt to obliterate their past, to treat them as long lost sons who have now found their way back home! A man's name and appearance may change, but that does not alter his nature. Daniel did not *become* Belteshazzar, even though he answered to that name; he is still the same person on the inside. A new home does not have to change your heart. Daniel and his buddies were in Babylon, but they would not let Babylon get into them!

1:8-10

Conformer or transformer

But Daniel resolved that he would not defile himself with the king's food, or with the wine that he drank. Therefore he asked the chief of the eunuchs to allow him not to defile himself. And God gave Daniel favour and compassion in the sight of the chief of the eunuchs, and the chief of the eunuchs said to Daniel, 'I fear my lord the king, who assigned your food and your drink; for why should he see that you were in worse condition than the youths who are of your own age? So you would endanger my head with the king.'

I love those opening words for they show to us the gritty tenacity of this young man. Daniel resolved. When I read those words I was reminded of the preacher Jonathan Edwards (1703-58) who was mightily used by God during the First Great Awakening in

America during the decade of the 1740s. When he was twenty he began composing his list of resolutions. He continued for about a year, writing seventy in all which served as a rudder over the course of his life; for example, 'Resolved, never to do anything, which I should be afraid to do, if it were the last hour of my life. Resolved, always to do what I shall wish I had done when I see someone else doing it.' That is what I would call, the Daniel attitude.

In spite of all that was happening around him and to him, Daniel dug in his heels and would not buckle or bottle it under such intimidating pressure. He has mettle. An unashamed boldness (Psalm 119:46; Mark 8:38; 1 Peter 4:16). Like the ancient Gadites, Daniel has the 'face of a lion' (1 Chronicles 12:8). As John MacArthur says, 'Not too many things intimidate a lion.'

The Babylonians had their rigid agenda of assimilation and they were determined to impose it on Daniel and his friends, but he was having none of it. He is a man of steely resolution, and for him, this was a bridge too far. His approach is easily summed up with these words: where the Scriptures draw a line, he draws a line. We should never cross a line that God has drawn. When you stay on the God side, you will stay on the good side. Daniel was not prepared to sacrifice his honest, sincerely held convictions on the altar of expediency. Not for all the tea in Shinar was he willing to toe their party line. He had had enough of being squeezed into Babylon's mould. Like Jack Crawford in my introductory story, Daniel nailed his colours to the mast!

There is a golden nugget at the beginning of verse 9 (similar to verse 2) which, again, underlines the sovereignty of a gracious God, *and God gave*. The chief was oblivious to it, but the text confirms that he had a soft spot in his heart for Daniel. Unwittingly, unknowingly, the Lord was working in this man's life. So often that is the case, even in our own lives and circumstances. The silent purposes of God are being outworked day after day and it is only when we look back that we can track and trace the guiding hand of God.

Dining in King's College, Babylon

The question is: Why was Daniel not so enamoured with the king's food and wine? To be honest, there is no straightforward answer. Some think the food from the royal table included meats such as pork that were off limits to Jewish people; that is, they were not kosher and were labelled 'unclean' in the long list of banned foods in Leviticus 11:1-23. Others think the food, of Michelin Star quality, may have been offered to idols before being taken to the king's tables for human consumption. Maybe. Maybe not.

It seems to me that this was a key moment in Daniel's development. All that life throws at us, in good times and bad times, is never wasted because ultimately we put it down to experience gained. Life can be a steep learning curve as God is working his purpose out in our lives. So Daniel's aspiration to do what was right at this point actually lays the groundwork for his response when larger upheavals intrude upon his life, such as the raging fire of chapter 3 and the ravenous lions of chapter 6. The timeless principle holds true that the one who is faithful in small things will be faithful in greater things (Luke 16:10).

Dale Ralph Davis suggests that 'sometimes "smaller" commitments made along the way fortify faith to plant its feet when it has to meet more severe threats.' That is powerfully illustrated by the Dutch pastor Herman Veldkamp in his commentary, *Dreams and Dictators*, when he writes, 'We should remember that the devil is an even greater danger in the world's dining rooms than in the den of lions. When we hear the sounds of the king's meal being served, when we hear the glasses clink, we should be even more on our guard than when famished lions open their mouths.'

So far as Daniel was concerned, this was an appropriate time for him to make his move. He showed remarkable wisdom for a young man of his age when he first approached the boss, the chief eunuch. As Ligon Duncan says, 'He does not do this in an obnoxious and a braggadocio way.' He was direct in what he said, he was polite, he was upfront, he did not beat about the bush or fumble over his words.

In spite of the evident warmth in their relationship, Ashpenaz was not overly enthusiastic about Daniel's request; in fact, he blew it out of the water. He torpedoed it. If he acceded to it and the end result had gone pear-shaped, then he himself would have been in seriously big trouble, hence the insightful comment, *so you would endanger my head with the king.*

Fair play to Daniel for he did not throw a tantrum or engage in histrionics. Nothing melodramatic. He kept his thoughts to himself rather than reading the riot act with the chief of the court officials. It would have been so easy, and perhaps understandable, if Daniel had muttered a few choice words under his breath about the heavy-handedness and crass insensitivity of the regime. Daniel's decorum under pressure is most admirable and he deserves a lot of credit for handling himself so terrifically well. Even though Plan A fell at the first hurdle, he was conscious and confident that God would work it all out in his way and in his time.

Here is another commendable trait in Daniel's character for he does not give up easily. He is not one for throwing the towel into the ring too soon. If at first you do not succeed, you try and try again! His next calculated move was to go down a notch on the chain of command.

1:11-20

Daniel's veggie diet

Then Daniel said to the steward whom the chief of the eunuchs had assigned over Daniel, Hananiah, Mishael, and Azariah, 'Test your servants for ten days; let us be given vegetables to eat and water to drink. Then let our appearance and the appearance of the youths who eat the king's food be observed by you, and deal with your servants according to what you see.' So he listened to them in this matter, and tested them for ten days. At the end of ten days it was seen that they were better in appearance and fatter in flesh than all the youths who ate the king's food. So the steward took away their food and the wine they were to drink, and gave them vegetables. As for these four youths, God gave them learning and skill in all literature and wisdom, and Daniel had understanding in all visions and dreams. At the end of the time, when the king had commanded that they should be brought in, the chief of the eunuchs brought them in before Nebuchadnezzar. And the king spoke with them, and among all of them none was found like Daniel, Hananiah, Mishael, and Azariah. Therefore they stood before the king. And in every matter of wisdom and understanding about which the king inquired of them, he found them ten times better than all the magicians and enchanters that were in all his kingdom.

Leave it to Daniel, resourceful as he is, there is always a Plan B up his sleeve. His second attempt for access to a different menu was both reasonable, respectful, and rational – plenty of vegetables, lots of fresh fruit, and litres of spring water. I mean, to the rest of us, it seems ridiculous to turn your back on the luxurious fare of the royal table for daily rations of greens and H2O. It is like eating an iceberg lettuce garnished with strawberries or broccoli and beans when you could be enjoying a sirloin steak with all the trimmings!

Even more remarkable, if that were possible, is that the steward gave it the green light; an answer to Solomon's prayer at the dedication of the temple (1 Kings 8:50), and a beautiful illustration of Psalm 106:46 where we read, 'He caused them to be pitied by all who held them captive.' He was happy to run with Daniel's dietary request. A little token of kindness where and when it was least expected. It may surprise us, but no matter how we look at it, this is grace at work in Babylon's heartland. A reminder, again, that there is nothing parochial about the Lord of time and eternity for he is omnipresent. In Jerusalem. In Babylon. And wherever you are right now, God is there too.

The proof of the pudding is always in the eating. Maybe a vegetarian type diet was not dessert-like, but it certainly worked. After ten days, the four young men looked absolutely amazing. Living on the bare essentials of a meagre and spartan diet, they have flourished. They are a picture of health. Their minds are more alert and they have excelled in their study of language and literature. It is important to note that Daniel alone *had understanding in all visions and dreams*. Visions happen when you are awake and dreams occur when you are asleep, and both were a means of divine revelation, as we shall see. This tidbit of info paves the way for the rest of the book.

Better looking. Better learned. Better liked, because when they came under the rigorous scrutiny of the king he was quite taken aback. He openly acknowledged that they were ten times better in their oral examination than the rest of his courtiers. They are streets ahead of the others. They passed the test without cheating. Only God can do that. Imagine how many employees of Apple or Microsoft, BMW or Chrysler, have been personally chosen by the CEO. Daniel and his buddies were!

Put God first and everything else will fit into place (Proverbs 3:5-6; Matthew 6:33). God is no man's debtor. There are no losers when God's providence is on show. Twists and turns on the path, humps and hollows along the way, yes, but God is merely taking us to a new level in our relationship with himself and in our usefulness to others. Daniel and his friends know all about that!

1:21

There is life after Babylon

And Daniel was there until the first year of King Cyrus.

The Hebrew text of this verse contains only seven words, but they pack a knockout punch. For whatever reason, the writer has pressed the fast-forward button on his keyboard and given us an intriguing piece of information concerning the fate of Babylon as well as the position of Daniel.

At face value, this could be mistaken for one of those statements of fact not worth a second glance. We read it and all too quickly move on to chapter 2 which sounds an awful lot more interesting. A serious error of judgment on our part for Nebuchadnezzar II, a few guys in-between, Nebuchadnezzar III (aka Nabonidus), and Belshazzar are now dead and gone. As the hymnwriter Isaac Watts wisely noted, 'Time, like an ever-rolling stream, bears all its sons away.' Babylon has fallen. Cyrus and the Persians are at the helm and it is 539 BC.

And wait for it, where is Daniel? Daniel is sitting at his desk! The global power of Babylon was snuffed out when Cyrus invaded, but God's faithful servant continues to shine and serve in situ. Perseverance. A few centuries later, when the Magi came from this same region to Bethlehem to worship the Christ Child (Matthew 2:1-12), it was because their forefathers had heard of him from Daniel and passed the account down through the generations.

We see how the tables have turned in chapter 1, and at the same time, we discover the sweet reality of God's continuing faithfulness to his people when earthly kingdoms rise and fall. Dale Ralph Davis hits the nail on the head when he writes, 'Babylon, the hairy-chested macho brute of the world, has dropped with a thud into the mausoleum of history, while fragile Daniel (probably now in his early 80s), servant of the Most High God, is still on his feet.'

2

A ROADMAP FOR THE NATIONS

'I have a dream!'

Washington, DC.
Wednesday, 28 August 1963.

An unforgettable day! That was the day when Martin Luther King Jr. made his historic *March on Washington* speech standing on the marbled steps of the stately Lincoln Memorial. Addressing an estimated quarter million people from all over the USA and teeming millions more on television and radio, civil rights activist King thundered forth with those powerful words that have travelled around the world ever since, 'I have a dream …'

As the 1990s drew to a close, Gary Younge, writing in *The Guardian*, noted that '137 leading scholars of public address named it the greatest speech of the twentieth century' even though it only lasted seventeen minutes. Within a few months, King was recognised by *Time* magazine as their Man of the Year;

and in the following year, 1964, he was honoured to receive the Nobel Peace Prize.

During the protests in Tiananmen Square, China, some university students held up posters of King saying, 'I have a dream.' On the security wall that Israel has built around parts of the West Bank, someone has written, 'I have a dream. This is not part of that dream.' The iconic phrase has been spotted in such disparate places as on a train in Budapest and on a mural in suburban Sydney.

Those four words have spanned the generations, they have criss-crossed every continent. They live on in the third millennium because they are etched somewhere in our memory banks. The Rev Martin Luther King Jr. was fatally shot almost five years later in Memphis, Tennessee, but his legacy continues to this day.

2:1

Another king. Another dream.

In the second year of the reign of Nebuchadnezzar, Nebuchadnezzar had dreams; his spirit was troubled, and his sleep left him.

This is the longest chapter in the entire book, but that is not its only claim to fame for here we come across some of the most amazing prophecies recorded on the pages of Scripture. This is the spinal cord—the nerve centre—of prophetic truth. It is the ABC of prophecy. In his *Lectures on Daniel*, Bible teacher H A Ironside writes that this dream 'contains the most complete, and yet the most simple, prophetic picture that we have in all the Word of God.' Richard Bewes, writing in *The Stone that became a Mountain*, described this chapter as 'a linchpin passage for our understanding of God's rule in history.' It reminds us of an unassailable fact that kingdoms may be here today and gone tomorrow, but our God lives on forever. We watch with bated breath as one world empire after another tumbles and bites the dust: Babylon, then Medo-Persia, followed by Greece, and finally Rome. Daniel 2 takes us back to the future, so to speak.

A year and a bit into the job he always coveted, Nebuchadnezzar seems to be struggling to hold it all together. Sleep deprived. Worrying thoughts. Stressed out. Frayed nerves. All because he is up-tight about the future of his expansive empire. He has a sense of foreboding. Uppermost in his mind is the nagging question of how much longer he can retain his grip on the situation.

Geoffrey King writes, 'As is so often the case, the cares of the day become also the cares of the night.... Nebuchadnezzar did a thing which no believer in God should ever dream of doing: he took his problems to bed with him.' Here we see the restlessness and insecurity in the heart of a man who knows no peace with God. To add fuel to the fire, his fertile mind was working overtime. Any counsellor will tell you that the anxieties we experience after sunrise can become the monsters we encounter after sunset. Unknown to him, God was also working behind the scenes. This was a God-induced problem. So Nebuchadnezzar dreamt a supernaturally engineered dream of destiny!

That should not surprise us for God often used this method before the canon of Scripture was complete and available to men. He used dreams to communicate with believers – thus he spoke to Joseph (Genesis 37:5-8). He used dreams to speak to unbelievers – thus he spoke to Abimelech (Genesis 20:3) and to Pharaoh (Genesis 41:1-8). Radio Bible teacher David Jeremiah, of *Turning Point*, notes that 'this dream was not given to some pious preacher, but to the vilest world ruler at that time. It was like God revealing to Hitler what was going to happen with the Berlin Wall, the demise of the USSR, and the Second Coming.'

An older German Bible commentator, Walter Lüthi, wrote in 1939 that 'when tyrants suffer from bad dreams, God is at work.' The fact is, because of God's grace, mercy, and kindness, he spoke directly to Nebuchadnezzar in his vile wickedness. In the wee small hours, God reached down and out to him when he gave him a glimpse of the present with regard to Babylon and an insight into the future when Babylon was no more. He may wriggle and writhe in bed at night because of his feelings of paranoia, but this was God giving him a vision of things to come in a dream which focused on the dawn, development, and doom of Gentile world powers. Why? Because God has a roadmap for the nations.

No wonder he breaks out in a cold sweat. He is scared stiff because the dream itself was scary. Here is one man who has everything, and yet in the cold light of day, he has nothing. He is like a lost child in the darkness. Geoff Thomas of Aberystwyth makes the point, 'How easy it is to terrify strong men outside of Christ!'

It is important to realise that Nebuchadnezzar is no fool; he sensed in his own spirit that the metallic man in his dream had a message specifically for him. He just did not know what it was. On the face of it, it did not look good and did not sound too promising. As he drank his first cup of coffee on the morning after the night before, the mightiest monarch on the planet was shaking like a reed in the wind. Shakespeare was right when he wrote in King Henry IV, '… uneasy lies the head that wears a crown.'

Sometimes, that is how we feel when God speaks to us one-to-one. When the Lord of heaven and earth deigns to meet with sinful earthlings like us, we are left feeling undone. Intuitively, we know when God has met with us. Not only us, so too men of the ilk and spiritual stature of Isaiah (6:5), Ezekiel (1:28b), and John (Revelation 1:17a).

2:2-11

When wise men are not so clever

Then the king commanded that the magicians, the enchanters, the sorcerers, and the Chaldeans be summoned to tell the king his dreams. So they came in and stood before the king. And the king said to them, 'I had a dream, and my spirit is troubled to know the dream.' Then the Chaldeans said to the king in Aramaic, 'O king, live forever! Tell your servants the dream, and we will show the interpretation.' The king answered and said to the Chaldeans, 'The word from me is firm: if you do not make known to me the dream and its interpretation, you shall be torn limb from limb, and your houses shall be laid in ruins. But if you show the dream and its interpretation, you shall receive from me gifts and rewards and great honour. Therefore show me the dream and its interpretation.' They answered a second time and said, 'Let the king tell his servants the dream, and we will show its interpretation.' The king answered and said, 'I know with certainty that you are trying to gain time, because you see that the word from me is firm – if you do not make the dream known to me, there is but one sentence for you. You have agreed to speak lying and corrupt words before me till the times change. Therefore tell me the dream, and I shall know that you can show me its interpretation.' The Chaldeans answered the king and said, 'There is not a man on earth who can meet the king's demand, for no great and powerful king has asked

*such a thing of any magician or enchanter or Chaldean. The thing
that the king asks is difficult, and no one can show it to the king
except the gods, whose dwelling is not with flesh.'*

Nebuchadnezzar did what he had done so many times before
when he turned to his trusted advisers. John Lennox refers to them
as 'experts mainly from the Imperial Institute of Futurology in
the university.' In modern-speak, they were a think tank, the sort
of group that is common within government circles. A highbrow
bunch of intellectuals who reputedly have all the answers, they
comprised *magicians, enchanters, sorcerers, and Chaldeans.* Rodney
Stortz says of them, 'Using dark magic, mysterious incantations,
and the position of the stars, these men had been trained to
interpret dreams and give the meaning to the dreamer.'

That sounds perfectly reasonable: the dreamer discloses the
dream, and after a period of time, the team of confidantes will
deliver the goods with a well-thought-out interpretation. Child's
play to seasoned campaigners. More often than not, the recipient
will hear what he wants to hear because the message given to him
has been embellished in one way or another.

Quite frankly, Nebuchadnezzar has had enough of that kind of
stuff. His intelligent lackeys fail to appreciate that the king is no
nitwit and he can see through their smoked glass interpretations.
They have conned him in the past when they have pulled the
wool over his eyes. No more! That is why, on this occasion, as
he lowered the axe he upped the ante and demanded that they
tell him the dream followed by a clearcut interpretation. Danny
Akin says that 'the king [threw] a horrifying curveball to the wise
men.' Enough to make any man quake in his sandals because if
they failed they were as good as dead.

A E Steinmann, writing in his commentary, graphically and

gruesomely says they would become 'body parts' (verse 5). Bloodcurdling. To borrow a line from Camelot, 'From fore to aft they would feel a draft.' Even the thought of it sends shivers down our spine, but this was fairly normal practice in the east when the body of a criminal was either hacked to pieces by knives or pulled apart by horses. Allied to that, their homes were completely razed to the ground and ended up being used as garbage dumps or public toilets (2 Kings 10:27).

2:12-13

The butcher of Babylon

Because of this the king was angry and very furious, and commanded that all the wise men of Babylon be destroyed. So the decree went out, and the wise men were about to be killed; and they sought Daniel and his companions, to kill them.

As the story goes, the advisers did not have a leg to stand on when they failed to deliver the goods with regard to the dream and its meaning. The biblical narrative makes it explicitly clear that Nebuchadnezzar totally lost it. He is a royal nut case. He blew his top in a rage of pique and ordered their immediate execution. This guy is autocratic, if ever. Not the last one, sadly, to rule like that in that region of the world! The first name that springs to mind is that of Saddam Hussein whose reign of terror lasted from July 1979 up to his overthrow in April 2003.

Nebuchadnezzar is mystified, manic, and murderous. Behind all the glitz, glamour, and gleaming gold of Babylon, there was lurking in the shadows an irrational monarch who was cruel, barbaric, and inhuman. He is a Jekyll and Hyde with a penchant for brilliance and buffoonery. The old cliché, first spoken by Lord

Acton, is true despite its age and familiarity, 'Power corrupts, and absolute power corrupts absolutely.'

The names of Daniel and his three companions were also on the hit list, even though they were not present when the so-called experts were signing their own death warrant. I suppose this could be seen as Satan's master stroke to eliminate Daniel and his friends. As is often the case, the wily archenemy of the people of God failed to take into account that God always has the last word. Warren Wiersbe writes that 'Satan's servants are expendable, but the Lord cares for his people.' Henry Martyn (1781-1812), missionary to the peoples of India and Persia, said, 'I am immortal until God's work for me to do is done. The Lord reigns.' And for that, we are enormously grateful.

2:14-18

Take it to the Lord in prayer

Then Daniel replied with prudence and discretion to Arioch, the captain of the king's guard, who had gone out to kill the wise men of Babylon. He declared to Arioch, the king's captain, 'Why is the decree of the king so urgent?' Then Arioch made the matter known to Daniel. And Daniel went in and requested the king to appoint him a time, that he might show the interpretation to the king. Then Daniel went to his house and made the matter known to Hananiah, Mishael, and Azariah, his companions, and told them to seek mercy from the God of heaven concerning this mystery, so that Daniel and his companions might not be destroyed with the rest of the wise men of Babylon.

There are times in all of our lives when push comes to shove and we cannot do much else but run to God for mercy. We are overwhelmed with a sense of our personal smallness and helplessness. Events move at breakneck speed around us and we feel as though we are being swept along by a tsunami of forces beyond our control.

Daniel knows the feeling for that is precisely where he is at this juncture. After his rushed tete-à-tête with Arioch the executioner, seeking answers to his questions, Daniel then gains an audience with Nebuchadnezzar himself. That was no mean achievement in itself. In chapter one, Daniel won his way into the heart of Ashpenaz, and now he has disarmed Arioch. Quite a guy!

As prudent as ever, Daniel's humanity shines through when he plays for time. The in-house professionals were classed as wise men; truth be told, from a biblical perspective as defined by God's Word, Daniel is the only wise man among them. Even with so much at stake, his legs are not shaking like jelly when he confronts the head of state. Rather, he is poised and his faith in God is robust as he attests with confidence that the dream can be deciphered and interpreted.

We are not privy to the entire conversation, but whatever was said, the king relented and gave in to Daniel's polite request when he was willing to make some concessions. That gives you some idea of the influence of God's servant in the royal court, and also of the deep-down respect which the king had for him.

As a believer operating in the public square, Daniel had a clean slate; no one could point a finger at him (Daniel 6:4). He is marked by integrity and for every one of us that is where the rubber hits the road. It is worth noting that Daniel has a deep concern for the welfare of those pagan colleagues whose lives were in grave danger. That should serve as a challenge to each of us for his obedience to God's Word sets the standard we should all attempt to live by (Leviticus 19:18).

What a glaring contrast between Daniel and the rest of them: the men of the world were marked by panic and confusion, and the man of God was characterised by prayer and conviction. The other guys are biting their finger nails; the pagan philosophers have no one to whom they can turn in their hour of severe trial; meanwhile, in the royal mews, Daniel and his three friends are having a prayer meeting. I mean, what else could they do? But pray!

For Daniel, this was the norm as prayer was his first port of call, not the last resort, when faced with a challenging situation (Daniel 6:10). For us, a thought-provoking bumper sticker attributed to Corrie ten Boom asks, 'Is prayer your spare tyre or your steering wheel?'

Think about it: on one side of the fence, there is a cluster of ostensible wise men who pretended to have power, but really had none; then there is Nebuchadnezzar who thought he had all power, but really had very little, and the little he had was granted to him by the High King of heaven (John 19:11). On the other side of the fence, there is Daniel and his friends who appeared to have no power, but by virtue of their covenant relationship with Israel's God actually had a gateway to a higher throne and an audience with the omnipotent God. Better to be in their shoes, methinks. As believers in the Lord Jesus Christ, we have the inestimable privilege of open-ended access to the source of all power and ultimate authority (Matthew 28:19-20). That is our entitlement as children of the King of kings! Let us be sure to use it. Lord Tennyson was right when he said that 'more things are wrought by prayer than this world dreams of.'

The God of heaven is the God of history

This prayer quartet is seeking *mercy from the God of heaven* for they cast themselves upon his goodness and implore him to act speedily. Time is of the essence. The best the astrologers could do was get to the stars. Daniel knew the God who made the stars. He went right to the top to get his answer. The God who rules over the nations is the same God who governs the tiniest details in the lives of each of his people. As a group, they desperately long for the God of heaven—*Elah shemayya* (Aramaic)—to step into this critical situation, to intervene, and do what only he can do. Either God acts or they are finished. Game over!

God often creates impossible situations to reveal his greatness and display his glory. Their backs are up against the wall, but their faces are looking up to one exalted and enthroned on high. They were not on a face-saving mission, nor is there any attempt to save their own skin. Their singular desire is for God's name to be honoured and glorified in the mess in which, through no fault of their own, they find themselves.

Just like them, there are moments in all of our lives when all we can do is cling to him and call out to him (James 5:16). The greater our weakness, the greater his glory (2 Corinthians 12:9-10). His best work in us is most obvious when we can do absolutely nothing. Because God is God, he uses all kinds of circumstances and crises to bring us to an end of ourselves, to drive us to our knees. Just like Daniel, when the bottom falls out of our lives, the best thing for us to do is to fall to our knees. We feel a real sense of urgency in such moments. In a strange kind of way, this is the providence of our heavenly Father who always knows best. What a precious treasure it is, when we are disheartened, downcast, and disappointed, to see God's glorious provision in the shop window of our lives.

For the first time in the book we come across a lovely ascription to Daniel's God, when he speaks of him as *the God of heaven*. You will be hard pressed to find this title outside the captivity books in the Bible. For example, it occurs nine times in Daniel, six times in Ezra, and four times in Nehemiah. The first time it is mentioned in Scripture is in 2 Chronicles 36:23 (the last verse in the last book of the Jewish Bible), where Cyrus acknowledged, 'The Lord, the God of heaven, has given me all the kingdoms of the earth …' (NIV).

2:19-23

Moving from prayer to praise

Then the mystery was revealed to Daniel in a vision of the night. Then Daniel blessed the God of heaven. Daniel answered and said: 'Blessed be the name of God forever and ever, to whom belong wisdom and might. He changes times and seasons; he removes kings and sets up kings; he gives wisdom to the wise and knowledge to those who have understanding; he reveals deep and hidden things; he knows what is in the darkness, and the light dwells with him. To you, O God of my fathers, I give thanks and praise, for you have given me wisdom and might, and have now made known to me what we asked of you, for you have made known to us the king's matter.'

They prayed. All four of them in that tiny room poured out their hearts to God in believing prayer. They knew from experience in times past that their God loves to be trusted and that he can be relied upon to come good at just the right moment. So having prayed and petitioned the Most High God (Amos 3:7), they followed the example of Hezekiah and left the matter in God's hand (2 Kings 19:14), and off to bed they went. Daniel knew that his God never sleeps (Psalm 121:4), so there was no point in both of them staying awake all night!

Like a cat on a soft pillow, Daniel must have been refreshed with a good night's sleep for he was ready to face another day as soon as the sun was up. He had a spring in his step because during the night hours 'the mystery was revealed to [him] in a vision' (Daniel 2:19, NIV). More than one biblical scholar has suggested that God let Daniel dream the same dream which Nebuchadnezzar had dreamed. Whether he did, or did not, all that counts is that one more time, God answered prayer. It pays to pray. Always. 'This was,' according to John Lennox, 'the first student prayer meeting recorded in history.' Thank God, it would not be the last!

It is helpful to note that Daniel did not rush from home to the palace to see the king. Sure, he knew all about the dream, but the king could stew in his own juice for another hour or two. More important for Daniel and his friends to engage their hearts in praise and worship and say 'thank you' to the great God of heaven who heard and answered their prayers.

This is a magnificently majestic paean of praise. It is a benediction of unsurpassed worth as he zooms in on the miscellaneous attributes of God. It is a doxology of superlative calibre as he reaches up to the highest heights of heaven. This song is a masterpiece of theology set to music. Joyce Baldwin says 'this little psalm is a model of thanksgiving ... the symmetry and beauty of the poetry make their own contribution to the praise of God.'

In his octave of worshipful praise, Daniel pulls out all the stops with an eloquent tribute to God for who he is and for what he has done. He rejoices because the Most High is eternal, all-wise, omnipotent, sovereign, generous, the revealer of truth, omniscient, and holy. When taken together, these eight qualities are a marvellously full affirmation of faith in God.

Kent Hughes tells of how Spurgeon was in the process of explaining the gospel to a woman who was on the edge of entering the kingdom when she burst out with, 'Oh, Mr Spurgeon, if the Lord saves me, he shall never hear the end of it!' That should be our attitude all day, every day. Lord, help me.

Father knows best

Before we unpack verse 23, take a moment and enthuse over verse 22, where we read: *he reveals deep and hidden things; he knows what is in the darkness, and the light dwells with him*. Speaking personally, those verses mean so much as I have proven the reality of them more times than I care to number. Our God reveals mysteries and that is one of his specialist ministries, but it does not mean we have a God who unveils everything. He only tells us what we need to know and when we need to know it; in his infinite wisdom, some of life's questions will only be answered on the other side in heaven itself.

The sublime truth is that even though we do not know, God knows; whether we find ourselves in darkness or light, it makes no difference to him. At twelve noon or twelve midnight, he knows all there is to know (Psalm 139:11-12). Dale Ralph Davis encourages us when he writes, 'You can walk into the future with a God like that – who shows you that history is going toward his unshakeable kingdom and who assures you that even though you have many personal uncertainties you follow a God who knows what is in the darkness. So you can keep going with hope and without fear.'

For you and me, we have no idea what the future holds, but we know the one who holds the future. The whole wide world is in God's hands, and your small world is there too.

Come, ye thankful people, come

These verses of praise are rounded off in verse 23 with an intensely personal note of appreciation from Daniel himself. He is extremely conscious of his family tree as he speaks of the *God of my fathers*. Here he combines both his lineage and his heritage. When Daniel recalled what God did in days of yore for the patriarchs, Abraham, Isaac, and Jacob, it gave him the impetus he needed to keep going forward.

At the same time, Daniel is quick off the mark to acknowledge the part that his three friends played in all of this for they stood with him, they knelt with him, they prayed through with him; that explains the comment, *for you have made known to us the king's matter*. We all need folks like that in our lives, and when we have them, we should thank God for them.

The answer to their fervent prayer was astounding. Front page news. A world exclusive. The scoop of the century. But Daniel did not get on the phone to the local editor of the *Babylon Evening News* in an attempt to line his own pockets. He was not interested in cheque book journalism. Not at all! That begs the question: What would we have done if we had been standing in Daniel's slippers that morning?

2:24-25

Time to face the music, and the monarch

Therefore Daniel went in to Arioch, whom the king had appointed to destroy the wise men of Babylon. He went and said thus to him:

'Do not destroy the wise men of Babylon; bring me in before the king, and I will show the king the interpretation.' Then Arioch brought in Daniel before the king in haste and said thus to him: 'I have found among the exiles from Judah a man who will make known to the king the interpretation.'

There is a distinct difference between Daniel's attitude and that of Arioch (one Spanish translation calls him 'captain of the cutthroats') in verses 24 and 25. In the first, Daniel is thinking about others; in the second, Arioch is thinking about himself. Daniel's principal concern is the safety and welfare of others within the palace precincts; Arioch, basically, wants to look after the three most important people in his life—me, myself, and I—as well as currying favour with the despotic Nebuchadnezzar.

Daniel, true to form, is happy to give the glory to his faithful God, and in this he reminds us of Joseph when he interpreted Pharaoh's dreams (Genesis 41:16); self-centred Arioch wants to take the credit to himself. As is often the case in the Christian life and in gospel ministry, all that really counts is that the job gets done irrespective of who takes the credit so long as God gets the glory. When God works, there is only room for praise, not pride.

2:26-30

The six million dollar question

The king declared to Daniel, whose name was Belteshazzar, 'Are you able to make known to me the dream that I have seen and its interpretation?' Daniel answered the king and said, 'No wise men, enchanters, magicians, or astrologers can show to the king the mystery that the king has asked, but there is a God in heaven who reveals mysteries, and he has made known to King

Nebuchadnezzar what will be in the latter days. Your dream and the visions of your head as you lay in bed are these: To you, O king, as you lay in bed came thoughts of what would be after this, and he who reveals mysteries made known to you what is to be. But as for me, this mystery has been revealed to me, not because of any wisdom that I have more than all the living, but in order that the interpretation may be made known to the king, and that you may know the thoughts of your mind.'

Nebuchadnezzar wasted no time in going for the jugular when he was straight out with the obvious question, 'Belteshazzar, can you do it ...?' And Daniel did not drag his heels in giving him a straight from the shoulder answer. Having already outfoxed the faculty, his answer is striking both in its honesty and humility, something from which we can all learn. The litmus test: Are we willing to give to God all the glory? Daniel shines the spotlight on his God because he is the only one who can draw back the curtains on the dream and its significance for Nebuchadnezzar and his successors. Not man. Not even Marduk. Only the Most High God. Sinclair Ferguson makes a wonderful point when he says that 'this is the spirit of Jesus before the high priests and Pilate; it is the spirit of Elijah before Jezebel; it is the spirit of John the Baptist before Herod. Daniel is full of the spirit of truth. Even Nebuchadnezzar can recognise that.'

Henry Kissinger—former US Secretary of State under Richard Nixon—said a willingness to speak only the truth to a powerful person was a necessary quality in a subordinate who had the ear of a leader. In that, Daniel excelled. He did not pander to the king in any way; he stood before him, shoulders back, chest out, head held high, and intrepidly delivered a large dose of unpalatable truth to the mightiest man on the face of the earth. David Helm notes that 'the person who trusts in God fears no bad news, and so will boldly proclaim God's good news.'

Daniel was on the verge of disclosing to King Nebuchadnezzar that time was running out for him and his burgeoning empire. The hourglass was slowly and surely emptying. David Jeremiah poses the following scenario: 'If Daniel were alive today, he could very well stand before the ambassadors of all 193 member states of the United Nations and say, "Tell the leaders of your nations that their days are numbered. God has shown me a dream about the future of the kingdoms of this world. His kingdom will be established on earth and will never end."'

Make no mistake about it, God has a plan, a plan for the nations of this world, and that plan has not been rescinded. In fact, it will not be rescinded, it cannot be rescinded (Psalm 33:11). As his story passes into history, we discover with the benefit of hindsight that it is a big, bold, and beautiful plan. This was the key message Nebuchadnezzar had to hear, that the Sovereign Lord has an agenda and everything is under his control; that Daniel and all the exiles needed to hear, and that God's people in every nation and in every age are grateful to hear. As the people of God in the third millennium, we are not pawns in a cosmic chess game; we have a key role to play in the unfolding drama of redemption as God's plan reaches its crescendo with the coming of the King.

The Puritan pastor Thomas Hooker (1586-1647), known as the Father of Connecticut, had a reputation as a plain-spoken clergyman, irrespective of who was in his congregation. One of his contemporaries said of him, 'Hooker, when he preaches seems to grow in size until you would have thought he could have picked up a king and put him in his pocket.' Just like Daniel!

All because, as a servant of the King of kings, he does not really care what any earthly king thinks.

You will notice how Daniel spoke of his God in two different ways by employing two different prepositions in these few verses: first, in verse 19, he is *the God of heaven* – that tells me who he is; and second, in verse 28, he is *the God in heaven* – that tells me where he is.

2:31-33

History viewed through God's binoculars

'You saw, O king, and behold, a great image. This image, mighty and of exceeding brightness, stood before you, and its appearance was frightening. The head of the image was of fine gold, its chest and arms of silver, its middle and thighs of bronze, its legs of iron, its feet partly of iron and partly of clay.'

In this paragraph, Daniel is describing the content of Nebuchadnezzar's dream to the king for he saw what can best be portrayed as a metallic colossus of unendurable brightness. This was no Statue of Liberty; rather, it was a statue foretelling bondage. It was mighty, both in size and structure. It was goliath in stature and something deliberately designed to make a lasting impression on the one who saw it. It was manlike in that it was shaped like a human being and is a fair representation of man's view of the empires of the world. It was majestic for the metals were giving off a gleaming lustre. Its brightness was one of shining excellence and most unusual in its inherent brilliance. Last, but not least, it was motionless for it simply stood there, static and stationary. It was grandiose. Once seen, never forgotten!

David Jeremiah makes the point, 'When Nebuchadnezzar

dreamed this dream, Persia was a Babylonian vassal state, the Greeks were a group of warring tribes, and Rome was a village on the Tiber River. There is no human way he could have seen what God was going to do as those Gentile kingdoms unfolded in the future.'

The statue is broken down into four major components: one, the head was gold; two, the chest was silver; three, the midriff and thighs were bronze; four, the legs were iron and the feet and toes an amalgam of iron and clay. (This is the source of the common expression, he or she has *feet of clay*.)

The key question is: What is the meaning behind it all? A full explanation is given in verses 36-43 which we shall come to in a moment. The eagle-eyed reader will have noticed that I have not mentioned *the stone* up to now, I will come back to it in a few pages. My intention is to look at verses 34-35 when dealing with verses 44-45.

2:36-43

The alphabet of prophecy

'This was the dream. Now we will tell the king its interpretation. You, O king, the king of kings, to whom the God of heaven has given the kingdom, the power, and the might, and the glory, and into whose hand he has given, wherever they dwell, the children of man, the beasts of the field, and the birds of the heavens, making you rule over them all — you are the head of gold. Another kingdom inferior to you shall arise after you, and yet a third kingdom of bronze, which shall rule over all the earth. And there shall be a fourth kingdom, strong as iron, because iron breaks to pieces and shatters all things. And like iron that crushes, it shall break and

crush all these. And as you saw the feet and toes, partly of potter's clay and partly of iron, it shall be a divided kingdom, but some of the firmness of the iron shall be in it, just as you saw iron mixed with the soft clay. And as the toes of the feet were partly iron and partly clay, so the kingdom shall be partly strong and partly brittle. As you saw the iron mixed with soft clay, so they will mix with one another in marriage, but they will not hold together, just as iron does not mix with clay.'

#1 world power

Daniel wasted no time in getting down to business. After he rehearsed the dream to the king, followed by the briefest of comments lasting only a few seconds, I can see him in my mind's eye as he slowly raised his index finger, pointed it directly at Nebuchadnezzar, and then with no quiver in his voice, declared that he is symbolised in the *head of gold* which represented the Babylonian empire (Ezekiel 26:7). Renald Showers notes, 'Orientals regarded kings and their kingdoms as being synonymous with each other.'

The language used by Daniel in his speech is of immense significance for he bravely reminds Nebuchadnezzar that he has what he has and he is where he is simply because God sovereignly granted it to him. He is perched on the throne for no reason other than the great God of heaven placed him there. As Mark Dever, senior pastor of Capitol Hill Baptist Church in Washington, DC, says, 'Daniel celebrates the king's sovereignty, but he celebrates it all as a gift of an even greater sovereign.'

And there was Nebuchadnezzar, as proud as a peacock, thinking he was the bee's knees, the greatest thing the world had seen since manna fell in the wilderness. He reckoned he was God's gift to mankind. A sovereign God thought otherwise. And Daniel did not prevaricate when it came to telling him some unvarnished truth. That should have jolted Nebuchadnezzar into some serious thinking. Alas, as we know from Daniel 4:30, it was like water running off a duck's back.

Babylon was not the most extensive or the most powerful of the global empires, but she was unquestionably the most glorious. She is seen to hold sway from 605 BC to 539 BC which corresponds to the first five chapters, as well as chapters 7 and 8, in the book of Daniel. Not that long for a kingdom to be at its zenith as a world power, a mere sixty-five or so years. And it all came to a sad, speedy, and sorry end, as we know from reading the end of Daniel 5.

Why gold? First, Marduk, the chief god of Babylon, was called the god of gold. Second, ninety years after the reign of Nebuchadnezzar, Herodotus, the Greek historian, visited Babylon and he could not believe what he saw. He had never seen a city so full of gold. It was magnificence everywhere, opulence on every corner. The temples, chapels, shrines, and utensils were all made of gold. Isaiah 14:4 refers to Babylon as 'the golden city' (NKJV), and in Jeremiah 51:7 she is called 'a gold cup in the Lord's hand' (NIV).

Literally, in the original Aramaic language, verse 39 begins with the words, *But after you* (NKJV). That revelation must have been a mega shock to an imperious Nebuchadnezzar as he probably thought he and Babylon were in it for good. The punchline is that his kingdom will not last. All these governments and guys come and go and, ultimately, they enter the landfill of history. Bob Fyall tellingly notes that 'what seems an empire was merely an episode.'

#2 world power

Next up is *another kingdom inferior* to Babylon in its totalitarian rule, as it was more of a partnership empire; the annals of history tell us this was the kingdom of the Medes and Persians, represented by the chest and arms of silver. Her time schedule runs from around 539 BC up to 331 BC. Two arms coming together to form one breast pictured this kingdom perfectly. Two distinct peoples, the Medes and the Persians, were united together in 550 BC, under the same king to form one great power. The choice of silver is fascinating in that it became an area of unprecedented wealth. The Persians had a superbly efficient taxation system which reaped rich dividends in vast hordes of silver being accumulated (Ezra 4:13). The kings of this era had almost unlimited resources at their disposal. Biblically, it stretches from the end of Daniel 5 through to the close of the Old Testament.

#3 world power

Then *a third kingdom* appeared on the global stage of world affairs. With the arrival of Alexander the Great, the kingdom of Medo-Persia was quashed. Greece, represented by the midriff and thighs of bronze, was then in the ascendancy as she reached out towards India and the Far East in an attempt to consolidate her position. She ruled the roost from around 331 BC up to 146 BC. Legend has it that after Alexander conquered the known world he wept because there were no more worlds to conquer. He died at the young age of thirty-three (356-323 BC). Shortly after his death, his kingdom was divided among his four leading generals. However, only two of the divisions played an important role in history. They were headquartered in Syria and Egypt.

The Greeks with their technological expertise developed bronze and used it extensively in their war implements. For example, their soldiers wore bronze armour—bronze helmets, breastplates, shields, and swords. Their contributions to world culture are beyond description: Herodotus stands without peer as the father of historians; Hippocrates is the father of modern medicine; Socrates, Plato, and Aristotle have helped shape philosophy for centuries. Yet again, prophecy is seen to be history written in advance. The prominence of Greece in world government coincided with the so-called four hundred silent years between Malachi and Matthew.

#4 world power

Number four is portrayed as being as *strong as iron* and can refer to none other than the sprawling Roman empire. From the beginnings of the New Testament era she was renowned for her militaristic strength and feared for her destructive power. We can almost hear the tramp, tramp, tramp of marching feet, the iron legions of a hawkish Rome. She crushed and subdued all opposition with an iron heel. In spite of being torn asunder and imploding within because of disunity, moral impurity, and religious anarchy, she was still a force to be reckoned with. No one played around with Rome.

The legs are the longest part of the human body which is a token reminder that irrepressible Rome was in existence longer than any of her predecessors; it lasted by some accounts and in some form from 146 BC to AD 1453 in the East and AD 1476 in the West. Danny Akin argues, and I concur, that 'its influence remains with us today, especially in Western civilisation.' That is evident in America where its government structure, courts, laws, and military all reflect the influence of the ancient Roman Empire; and the monarchies of France, Germany, Spain, and later Great Britain were the result of the western spread of the Roman Empire. There are also two legs which suggest that she was divided, as history confirms in AD 364 to the East, ruled from Constantinople (modern-day Istanbul) where it became known as the great Byzantine Empire, and to the West, ruled from Rome.

The feet and toes are also mentioned in the biblical text as being a mixture of iron and soft clay. As we have already noted, iron represents brawn and strength, but clay represents brittleness and weakness. That was typical of the Roman empire for it was strong in parts and weak in parts. So far as the clay is concerned, the clay cracks easily, then crumbles into dust.

One look at the vast Roman empire and it is ever so clear that there were numerous nations and divisions that made up the whole. The blunt truth is, there was one empire, but the unity was superficial because it was imposed upon the people. The masses are sheltering under one large umbrella, but they are not holding hands with each other; the populace is one in name only, definitely not one in heart and soul. This was fragmentation, big time. That explains the prophetic insight, *they will not hold together, just as iron does not mix with clay.*

The reality is, notes Dale Ralph Davis, that 'this kingdom combines massive strength with disturbing weakness, crushing power with failing cohesion.' That appraisal is serious in and of itself, but Davis continues with his knockout punch, when he writes, 'What a rickety base for the whole monstrosity of human kingdoms to rest upon!'

On a slippery slope

Civilisation is on a downward spiral. The decline is apparent from the metals used in the composition of this august and austere statue. Beginning with gold at number one, it ends with iron at number four. Andrew Hill, writing in *The Expositor's Bible Commentary*, observes of the statue that 'its splendour dissipates (from gold to iron and clay) but its hardness increases (from gold to iron).' That tells the serious student of life that we are plummeting from bad to worse, and still some. There is a deterioration in standards at every level in society and we are presently accelerating downhill on a trend that is irreversible. These verses in Daniel 2 indicate that there will be no golden age when man is at the helm. Utopia is not around the next corner!

From gold to silver to bronze to iron plus clay, there is a diminishing value in the worth of the metals used in the metallic man. The specific gravity moves from gold at 19.32 to clay at about 2.75. It was top-heavy and could topple at any moment. You do not have to be a scientist to understand the implications behind such a message.

Iain Duguid draws a similar conclusion, when he writes, 'What is more ... it is not simply that you can never step in the same river twice, as the Greek philosopher Heraclitus famously pointed out; it is that the river keeps getting more and more polluted as it travels from its source.'

Life is transient. The tide ebbs. The tide flows. People come. People go. Kingdoms rise. Kingdoms fall. Nothing in this life is forever; it is fleeting for 'change and decay in all around I see.' Here is the very shape of history in that the various successive world powers have no permanence. Until ...

2:34-35, 44-45

On the horizon ... #5 the ultimate kingdom

'As you looked, a stone was cut out by no human hand, and it struck the image on its feet of iron and clay, and broke them in pieces. Then the iron, the clay, the bronze, the silver, and the gold, all together were broken in pieces, and became like the chaff of the summer threshing floors; and the wind carried them away, so that not a trace of them could be found. But the stone that struck the image became a great mountain and filled the whole earth. And in the days of those kings the God of heaven will set up a kingdom that shall never be destroyed, nor shall the kingdom be left to another people. It shall break in pieces all these kingdoms and bring them to an end, and it shall stand forever, just as you saw that a stone was cut from a mountain by no human hand, and that it broke in pieces the iron, the bronze, the clay, the silver, and the gold. A great God has made known to the king what shall be after this. The dream is certain, and its interpretation sure.'

Forward to the stone age! This is the wonderful climax of the dream and it comes with an enduring message for God's people. What a gorgeous finale is promised right here in the text. One day, in the ripening purpose of God, it too will come to pass.

Much ink has been spilt over the whys and wherefores of this earth-moving event, but it could not be clearer in Daniel's communication with the king. The question is: When will it happen? Some understand it to be at the end of the age, when Jesus comes again in power and glory to usher in his universal and visible kingdom (Revelation 19:11-20:6). Others believe it is applicable to our Lord's first advent and the inauguration of his kingdom.

It seems to me that both are actually in view (Isaiah 61:1-2). They are pointing to his first coming and the inauguration of his kingdom, and at the same time, also looking to and anticipating his eschatological kingdom. One commentator writes, 'Like twin peaks with a hidden valley between, the kingdom is inaugurated at Christ's first coming and fully realised at his second. Old Testament prophecy often functions in this way.'

All that we have seen in the four global kingdoms of man is brought to nothingness and in time will be consigned to the mists of antiquity. The language used in the interpretation of Nebuchadnezzar's dream is colourful and easily understood, especially so when he speaks of the kingdoms of this world being like *chaff on a summer threshing floor*. One whiff of wind and they are forever gone.

The image disintegrated into millions of tiny pieces that littered the earth; it was smashed into smithereens when the stone did its unique work of judgment. Judgment without mercy. Charles Swindoll, of *Insight for Living*, says it like this, 'As the smiting stone in Nebuchadnezzar's dream, the Lord will not absorb, restructure, or adapt to previous kingdoms; he will totally annihilate them and set up his own monarchy, which will be absolutely perfect politically, morally, economically, and religiously. And he will rule over all the earth as King of kings and Lord of lords (Isaiah 2:2-4; Revelation 19:11-16).'

In the future, a better day is coming. A day when the kingdom of God will be established here on earth by none other than the sovereign Lord himself. That kingdom, unlike the big four in the dream, will be indestructible for *it will never be destroyed*. It 'cannot be shaken' (Hebrews 12:28, NIV). The coming kingdom is marked by uniqueness for the earth will never have seen anything quite like it for it is one where Jesus is ruling and reigning (Isaiah 9:7). Every trace of man's kingdoms will be eliminated for *it will crush all those kingdoms and bring them to an end* – there is a sense of finality about that statement. The kingdom of God is eminently successful because it is international in its reach and influence for *the stone … became a great mountain and filled the whole earth.* There is a real wow factor when we contemplate the future kingdom of God's dear Son.

That thought was in the front of Charles Wesley's mind when he wrote of the magical moment when 'God appears on earth to reign.' Isaac Watts was on the same wavelength when he wrote, 'Joy to the world! The Lord is come. Let earth receive her king.' The final stanza says, 'He rules the world with truth and grace, and makes the nations prove the glories of his righteousness and wonders of his love.'

Meantime, in the here and now, we get on with living life to the glory of God. The bitterness of many pills we swallow this side of eternity are sweetened with the absolute certainty of knowing that one glorious morning we shall 'see the King in his beauty' (Isaiah 33:17, NIV). Our impassioned prayer is, 'May your kingdom come soon' (Matthew 6:10, NLT). Thank God, this dream will come true. 'When that day comes,' writes Iain Duguid, 'what will count will not be our standing in the statue but our standing on the rock.'

2:46-49

Promises are made to be kept

Then King Nebuchadnezzar fell upon his face and paid homage to Daniel, and commanded that an offering and incense be offered up to him. The king answered and said to Daniel, 'Truly, your God is God of gods and Lord of kings, and a revealer of mysteries, for you have been able to reveal this mystery.' Then the king gave Daniel high honours and many great gifts, and made him ruler over the whole province of Babylon and chief prefect over all the wise men of Babylon. Daniel made a request of the king, and he appointed Shadrach, Meshach, and Abednego over the affairs of the province of Babylon. But Daniel remained at the king's court.

In all fairness to Nebuchadnezzar, he kept the promise he made to Daniel. In fact, he went further when he fell at Daniel's feet; that is quite something, and it probably caused Daniel a fair bit of red-faced embarrassment. The king treated him as a kind of mini god and even ordered that a burnt offering and incense be presented to him. I cannot prove this, but I have a hunch that Daniel may have said something to Nebuchadnezzar in between verses 46 and 47 that is not recorded in our text. Why do I say that? Because the king's words turned from looking at Daniel as a god to speaking of Daniel's God.

Nebuchadnezzar also spoke in warm tones to Daniel when he frankly acknowledged that Daniel's God was so incredibly different to Marduk and all the others in the pantheon of gods. Daniel's God is supreme, sovereign, and superior. This is so good to hear, especially when he uttered it in public before those standing around in his inner court. We need to cock our ears and raise our eyebrows and be cautiously wary when pagan politicians use religious language. It is so terribly sad, however, that he does not appear to bow the knee before Daniel's God (more about that in Daniel 3). Like so many in today's world, he had a head knowledge of God, but not a heart knowledge.

Daniel was amply rewarded with gifts generously bestowed

upon him. Both he and his three loyal friends were promoted to enviable positions of influence and authority within the system. Daniel, for example, is elevated to the office of prime minister and is answerable directly to the king. Within the command structure, Daniel is number two. Like Benjamin Disraeli in a much later era, this Jew was to become prime minister in a Gentile country. Kenneth Gangel writes, 'Like Abraham before him and Esther after him, Daniel was elevated to a place of respect by powerful pagan leaders and used in that position by God to care for his people.'

And Daniel did not forget his friends for Shadrach, Meshach, and Abednego were also given responsible managerial roles in the province. By any stretch of the imagination, that is quite a turnaround. Only God can do that. The Rock reigns!

The story is told of the Roman and Christian-hating Emperor Julian (AD 332-363) who was mortally wounded in a war with the Persians. While Julian's expedition was in progress, one of his followers asked a Christian in Antioch what the carpenter's son was doing. The Christian replied, 'The Maker of the world, whom you call the carpenter's son, is employed in making a coffin for the emperor.' Within days news filtered back to Antioch of Julian's death. That is where Daniel 2 leaves us. How glowingly true it is that the Lord Jesus Christ has a coffin for every empire and every emperor; the only true security for any one of us is in the kingdom of the carpenter's Son.

3

KING NEB'S
THREE-LINE WHIP

The *Washington Post* ran a sensational story a few years back about one man and his dissent against the Nazis. In today's climate, people are mostly judged on their actions and by what they do. But, on occasion, what people do not do can be just as revealing, particularly in wartime.

It was Nazi Germany on 13 June 1936 and a crowd of workers and invited guests had gathered at the renowned Blohm+Voss shipyard in Hamburg to watch the launch of a navy training vessel. The 295-foot barque *Horst Wessel* was named to honour the memory of a Nazi activist killed by communists in 1930 and treated as a martyr in the party's propaganda.

The special event was headlined by a rousing speech from Deputy Führer Rudolf Hess with Adolf Hitler at his side. Wessel's mother christened the ship with the customary bottle of champagne, followed by an enthusiastic stiff right arm Nazi salute—Hitler's infamous 'Sieg Heil'—from those assembled. The salute was mandatory for all German citizens as a demonstration of loyalty to the Führer, his party, and his nation.

Except for one! August Landmesser was 26 years old when he stood in the crowd with his arms defiantly and conspicuously crossed. In the ten seconds it took for him to make that decision, his fate was sealed.

He had joined the Nazi party in 1931 with the hope it would lead to a decent job, but he was expelled from the party in 1935 when he became engaged to a Jewish woman, Irma Eckle. They had two daughters, Ingrid and Irene, both of whom survived the war. Irma was killed, along with 14,000 others, at the Bernburg Euthanasia Centre in February 1942. A couple of years after being released from prison, Landmesser himself was drafted into a penal battalion and declared missing in action, believed dead, in the Balkans in 1944.

As a footnote, the *Horst Wessel* ended up in the USA; renamed the *Eagle*, and known as 'America's Tall Ship,' she is the flagship of the US Coast Guard and serves as a training vessel for cadets and officer candidates at the Coast Guard Academy.

3:1

The golden boy of world affairs

King Nebuchadnezzar made an image of gold, whose height was sixty cubits and its breadth six cubits. He set it up on the plain of Dura, in the province of Babylon.

There is no doubt about it, Nebuchadnezzar loves himself. He is on a no expense spared ego trip, like no other. Pride! He was flattered in the metallic man dream to be the head of gold (2:36-38); quite literally, it went to his head. Yankees legend Yogi Berra might have said of him, 'He was a legend in his own mind.' So much so that he has a magnificently grotesque monument built that is all plated of gold! The dimensions are huge, ninety feet high and nine feet wide (60 x 6 cubits, or 27 x 2.7 metres), it was oddly proportioned in that it was tall and thin.

It was a humongous monstrosity you would see from at least fifteen miles away when riding past on your camel. Eye-catching, it dominated the skyline, you simply could not miss it! Resplendent it stood in the noonday sun, like a golden toothpick. Danny Akin says that 'it probably looked like a missile on a launching pad, perhaps something like the Washington Monument.'

Sadly, it was a flat contradiction of what Daniel told him in the previous chapter. It was a blatant denial of the purpose of God in that Babylon would eventually pass away for the head of gold would be superseded by the chest and arms of silver (Daniel 2:36-39). Talk about bullish arrogance and crass big-headedness, the megalomaniac who is Nebuchadnezzar thought he knew better than God. His reaction is reminiscent of the words of the nineteenth-century German philosopher Friedrich Nietzsche, when he said, 'If there is a God, how can I bear not to be that God?' He reckoned he was invincible and could change the course of history to suit his own ends and ulterior motives. As Geoff Thomas reminds us, 'It is an uncompromising beginning to an uncompromising chapter.'

The chosen site for this glittering showpiece was the sun-baked plain of Dura, a flat stretch of land southeast of Babylon, near a small river and mounds bearing the name of Douair or Duair. The name *Dura* simply means 'a walled-in place, a fortress.' A natural arena, it was conveniently located so that its full potential could be exploited. Out in the Mesopotamian desert, there would be no sideshows vying for the people's attention, nothing to distract or disturb. The statue would be centre stage and a money spinner for the local tourist board as it would quickly become a mecca for pilgrims. I wonder, was this image erected on the same site as the Tower of Babel in Genesis 11:2 ...?

3:2-3

By royal command

Then King Nebuchadnezzar sent to gather the satraps, the prefects, and the governors, the counsellors, the treasurers, the justices, the magistrates, and all the officials of the provinces to come to the dedication of the image that King Nebuchadnezzar had set up. Then the satraps, the prefects, and the governors, the counsellors, the treasurers, the justices, the magistrates, and all the officials of the provinces gathered for the dedication of the image that King Nebuchadnezzar had set up. And they stood before the image that Nebuchadnezzar had set up.

This was intended to be the most important day in the calendar year when everybody who was anybody was summoned to be present. One of those red letter days that everyone loves. Quite a guest list that reads like a *Who's Who* of the good and the great, the movers and shakers of the kingdom. An auspicious occasion for high society, an extravaganza of pomp and pageantry.

However, even though this was a big day for the big wigs of high society and anybody else who was fortunate enough to be there, the hard facts are that these men and women were no more than specks of dust in the sands of time. In God's grand scheme of things, they are as impotent as Nebuchadnezzar's ludicrous statue. Both were 'as nothing' before a high and mighty God

(Isaiah 40:15-17, NIV). For you and me (like Shadrach, Meshach, and Abednego), we need to keep this perspective in view when we see what is happening all around us in today's world. We must not allow ourselves to be swept off our feet or wowed at any time by all that this passing world has to offer or even boasts of (Matthew 4:8-10).

A quick read of these two verses will bring a smile to your face – so many words are used to actually say very little! Repetition is the mother of learning, we were told as children. But this is beyond ridiculous. And it is intended to be so. Basically, verse 2 tells us in a long list who was invited *to the dedication of the image,* and verse 3 tells us that *they stood before the image* when they got there. If you were invited, you attended; there was no RSVP in Babylon. (Something similar happens in the next few verses too as the penman highlights the principal players and the musical instruments in the bizarre imperial orchestra.) One commentator remarks, tongue in cheek, that 'the writer turns the pomp into pomposity and coats the dignity with derision.'

It is worth noting that Daniel does not appear anywhere in the chapter; we have no idea where he was, he may have been ill, or he may have been out of town on a diplomatic mission representing the king in some foreign court. Also, this is the last time we come across Daniel's three friends, Shadrach, Meshach, and Abednego, in the book.

3:4-7

Toe the party line

And the herald proclaimed aloud, 'You are commanded, O peoples, nations, and languages, that when you hear the sound of the horn, pipe, lyre, trigon, harp, bagpipe, and every kind of music, you are to fall down and worship the golden image that King Nebuchadnezzar has set up. And whoever does not fall down and worship shall immediately be cast into a burning fiery furnace.' Therefore, as soon as all the peoples heard the sound of the horn, pipe, lyre, trigon, harp, bagpipe, and every kind of music, all the peoples, nations, and languages fell down and worshipped the golden image that King Nebuchadnezzar had set up.

The presidential edict was read out loud by the town crier so that everyone was left in no doubt as to what was expected of them and, indeed, demanded of them. No matter how they felt or where their loyalties lay, they were required to toe the party line and vote with the ayes; that is, they were obligated to bow down and worship the golden image. It was, in British parliamentary speak, a three-line whip. Failure to comply with this mandatory and explicit instruction, for whatever reason, would mean being tossed into a fiery inferno. And these Babylonish kings have history (Jeremiah 29:22).

The image was a subtle attempt by Nebuchadnezzar to deify himself as one of the gods. He yearned for the worship and adulation of his people because he saw himself as a messiah who brought salvation to many through his feared war machine. Allied to that is the religious element. He is welding together politics and religion in a shrewd, calculated move to woo and win his subjects. He knows if he can conquer their hearts then he has captivated their imagination. Talk about being conceited, this autocrat epitomises it at every twist and turn. I mean, who does he really think he is? He has delusions of grandeur!

Before his death, Mao's statue dominated China, just as the image of Lenin was pervasive throughout the former Soviet Union, and that of Saddam Hussein in Firdos Square, Baghdad. Similar could be said of Enver Hoxha in Albania and the revolutionary Fidel Castro in Cuba.

Around the world today, there are many of our brothers and sisters in the family of God who are suffering persecution because they chose to disobey the powers that be. They are languishing in cramped prison cells, are assigned the dirtiest and most menial jobs in society, endure the unthinkable horror and heartbreak of their children forcibly taken from them, scream under brutal torture and die horrible deaths—all because they would not renounce their faith in the Lord Jesus. For some of us, we have not walked that thorn-strewn path, that Calvary-type road. Yet, to quote Stuart Olyott, the words of saintly Samuel Rutherford (1600-61) remain true for us too, 'You will not get leave to steal quietly to heaven in Christ's company without a conflict and a cross.'

In a pagan pressure cooker

Someone has estimated that the head count at this assembly may have been as many as three hundred thousand, with people coming from near and far. An impressive convocation. At the appointed hour, the ragtime band strikes up something akin to *Hail to the Chief*. The atmosphere is electric. The temperature rises. The sand stirs. To a man, the vast representative gathering falls down as one in obeisance to the golden statue. Like a bunch of rubber ducks ready to quack the same way, they did not disappoint. Dale Ralph Davis writes that 'the praise band plays, and the crowd gets its backsides in the air and its noses in the sand and enjoys job security.' Truth be told, however, not every man bowed down!

There were three notable exceptions who refused to follow the three-line whip and back the king. Shadrach, Meshach, and Abednego are guilty of treason. They defied the orders of the king. Bravely, they stood their ground and stand out as plain as three pikestaffs. These three are worth their weight in gold. In gospel-speak, these shining lights were able to do what they did because they had a dynamic relationship with their God. Their faith had been tested many times before in their professional lives, and on each occasion, they came through with flying colours. The abiding principle of 1 Peter 3:15 was evident in their daily lives and it showed in their determination to honour God even when the dominoes were falling all around. Warren Wiersbe notes that 'the crowd had credulous faith, but the Jews had confident faith.'

Like August Landmesser in my intro, their well-honed principles were not up for auction. Shadrach, Meshach, and Abednego were not prepared to sell their birthright or ditch their set of godly core values. They were not being foolhardy or fanatical, but they were faithful to the God in whom they trusted. They were unflagging in their commitment to honour him in all that they did. Sure, they were all resident in Babylon and holding down top jobs, but they were still not willing to trash the first two commandments (Exodus 20:3-6). Why? Because they never forgot *who* they were and *whose* they were; they were sons of the covenant, redeemed by the outstretched arm of Yahweh.

Don Stephens in *War and Grace* tells the story of Paul Schneider. He stood lined up with other prisoners at Buchenwald Concentration Camp. It was 20 April 1938, Hitler's forty-ninth birthday and, in tribute, the prisoners were ordered to remove their berets and venerate the Nazi swastika flag. At once all whipped off their headgear. But guards noticed one man who would not 'bow' to the swastika – Paul Schneider. They beat him, twenty-five lashes with an ox-hide whip. Because he refused to worship the idol.

3:8-12

The finger pointing starts

Therefore at that time certain Chaldeans came forward and maliciously accused the Jews. They declared to King Nebuchadnezzar, 'O king, live forever! You, O king, have made a decree, that every man who hears the sound of the horn, pipe, lyre, trigon, harp, bagpipe, and every kind of music, shall fall down and worship the golden image. And whoever does not fall down and worship shall be cast into a burning fiery furnace. There are certain Jews whom you have appointed over the affairs of the province of Babylon: Shadrach, Meshach, and Abednego. These men, O king, pay no attention to you; they do not serve your gods or worship the golden image that you have set up.'

In no time at all the secret police were on to the three of them, probably all in their mid-thirties at this point in the narrative (according to the Septuagint—the Greek translation of the Old Testament—there was a time lapse of between sixteen and twenty years between the end of chapter two and the beginning of chapter three). This was real. It actually happened. This is not a fairy tale. These men, our spiritual ancestors, because of their unblemished devotion to God found themselves in a life threatening situation. The founder of Operation Mobilisation (OM), George Verwer, says, 'We who have Christ's eternal life need to throw away our own lives.'

This highlights the fact that standing up for God and truth will often be a lonely activity, as illustrated for believers in our day in 1 Peter 2:19-23. Just because others are doing it does not make it right for you to do it. More often than not, you will be in the minority, and at times even in a tiny minority of one. Not unlike Martin Luther when he stood before the church authorities at the Diet of Worms in 1521, and said, 'My conscience is captive to the Word of God, I cannot and will not recant anything, for to go against conscience is neither right nor safe. God help me. Amen.' These men with the very real possibility of cremation staring them in the eye had embraced the attitude of Luther when, according to tradition, he said, 'Here I stand; I can do no other.'

Their refusal to bow down to the image was an act of civil disobedience. But they did what they did with their eyes wide open; they knew the consequences were not to be laughed at and they also knew that a snubbed Nebuchadnezzar was not the kind of person to back down. He was the high priest of political correctness and he did not suffer fools gladly.

You can imagine the volatile atmosphere as the trio were surrounded by a baying lynch mob of officialdom calling for their blood. They wanted to smell the seared flesh of Shadrach, Meshach, and Abednego. Solomon said, 'Jealousy ... burns like blazing fire, like a mighty flame' (Song of Songs 8:6, NIV). The agitators were having a heyday as they whipped the seething multitude into a frenzy. All too quickly it could have escalated out of control as some folks probably wanted to take the law into their own hands. These three guys were living dangerously.

Within a matter of minutes, Shadrach, Meshach, and Abednego were denounced in the presence of the king by a handful of astrologers who should have known better. These Chaldeans have incredibly short memories! That is the way it often is at the coalface where men tend to look after themselves and it does not really matter how it impacts others. Bent on revenge and driven by malice, a plot was hatched to oust the three of them and get rid of them once and for all (Proverbs 14:30). We read they stepped forward and *maliciously accused the Jews*. Literally, like rapacious animals 'they ate their pieces!' In other words, they sank their teeth into them like cannibals.

A triple charge with heavy anti-Semitic undertones was levelled against them: one, they disregarded the sovereign; two, they disobeyed the statement; and, three, they disapproved of the statue. As Dale Ralph Davis notes, these three men 'thumb their noses at the king's order.'

3:13-15

A second chance

Then Nebuchadnezzar in furious rage commanded that Shadrach, Meshach, and Abednego be brought. So they brought these men before the king. Nebuchadnezzar answered and said to them, 'Is it true, O Shadrach, Meshach, and Abednego, that you do not serve my gods or worship the golden image that I have set up? Now if you are ready when you hear the sound of the horn, pipe, lyre, trigon, harp, bagpipe, and every kind of music, to fall down and worship the image that I have made, well and good. But if you do not worship, you shall immediately be cast into a burning fiery furnace. And who is the god who will deliver you out of my hands?'

To put it mildly, the king is hot under the collar. He is livid. The gloves were off. The Babylon bully demanded that the impertinent trio be brought before him. Taken by the scruff of the neck, they were frogmarched to stand before an outraged Nebuchadnezzar, the most powerful man on earth. His voice was breaking with intemperate fury as he interrogated them. In spite of his vehement manner, he was prepared to give them the benefit of the doubt and offer them an exit route from the furnace. He was happy to let bygones be bygones. How conciliatory of him. Not!

He stokes the proverbial fire by cynically and caustically reminding them of their fate if they remain intransigent and do their own thing. He is oozing arrogance from every pore in his body as he challenged them with a sniggering sneer on his lips, *and who is the god who will deliver you out of my hands?* And that question gets right to the nub of the matter for the whole emphasis is on Nebuchadnezzar's hands, not on a god who delivers. Such is his smugness.

This comes over to every one of us as a huge personal challenge for the same pride that is in the heart of the king is often lurking in our own hearts. It is so easy for us to draw attention to who *we* are, whom *we* know, and what *we* have done. The God who misses nothing is the same God who sees our pride and he does not like what he sees, for we read that 'God opposes the proud' (Proverbs 3:34; James 4:6; 1 Peter 5:5, NIV). The question for us is, according to Danny Akin, 'Who will deliver me from me?'

It was a *set up* job, as the text repeatedly points out no fewer than nine times, and these three had the temerity to challenge his power and his authority. The bottom line: Nebuchadnezzar is affronted by their effrontery.

3:16-18

A matter of life or death

Shadrach, Meshach, and Abednego answered and said to the king, 'O Nebuchadnezzar, we have no need to answer you in this matter. If this be so, our God whom we serve is able to deliver us from the burning fiery furnace, and he will deliver us out of your hand, O king. But if not, be it known to you, O king, that we will not serve your gods or worship the golden image that you have set up.'

This is one of the greatest statements of faith recorded in the Bible. This might be called Applied Theology 101. It thrills me and humbles me to read the response of these heroic men to the king. They were not disrespectful in any way when they answered Nebuchadnezzar. Technically, he was their boss for they were employed by the Babylon Civil Service, but they made it clear to the king that they are actually serving God when doing their day jobs (Ephesians 6:5-7). Men of the world do not understand God's people when they talk like that!

There was no need for Shadrach, Meshach, and Abednego to think twice in relation to his kind offer of clemency. Their minds were made up before they arrived at the intersection of Peer Pressure Corner. No U-turn for them. They would never, never, never bow down to a false image, an image made by human hands; to do so would be to defy and defile the almighty God. Not for a moment are they willing to entertain the notion of worshipping a foreign god; for them, this is not a grey area, it is a no-go area. Now that is backbone! They have the courage of their convictions. People talk about the Moral Majority, this is God's Moral Minority.

And that is where their principled stance is a continual challenge to those of us who name the peerless name of Christ in the third millennium. In fact, even before us in the twenty-first century, their single-minded decision to stand firm on biblical truth would have impacted on the likes of Ezra and Nehemiah and their contemporaries, and on all those who have followed suit.

Such a spirited stance reminds me of a theologian named Athanasius of Alexandria (298-373) who was fighting the heresy of Arianism in his day. The Roman emperor summoned Athanasius to appear before him so that he could put pressure on him to relinquish his stand against Arianism. He failed, for Athanasius would not compromise. Finally, he said, 'Athanasius, don't you understand? The world is against you!' Athanasius looked back at him and said, 'Then Athanasius is against the world.'

The three men offer no defence. They tender no apologies. They make no excuses. They are guilty, as alleged. And second time around they will do the same again. This was their finest hour. Like Athanasius, they will not give an inch despite the unrelenting pressure upon their shoulders. Right is right and wrong is wrong. They remained unbendingly faithful to the true Sovereign just like their mentor and friend Daniel did in chapter one. They were absolutely convinced that God was well able to set them free. When all is said and done, he performs miracles and he has a dazzling track record of successful rescue missions. God can!

However, in a statement of breathtaking courage and stellar confidence in God, they placed their faith in God and God alone. They told the king that they had taken into account the possibility that God might not deliver them. There is more than a hint of realism in their faith; a faith not averse to taking risks. In his sovereignty and for the outworking of his eternal purposes, God may choose not to intervene and they are totally relaxed about that option. As Rodney Stortz writes, 'We need to understand that faith is not a rabbit's foot, and God is not a genie who is bound to do for us whatever we want.'

The same holds true in our lives, as many of us can testify that life is not a bed of roses, but the prick and pain of every thorn is cushioned with the grace of our faithful God. Our prayers are not always answered the way we would like them to be, we do not always get the promotion that we were hoping for, our children do not always turn out the way we had planned; but, whatever is our lot this side of heaven, we know that one day the *if not* of God's plan will be fully understood. This is the beautiful attitude of the Lord Jesus in the garden of Gethsemane a few centuries later when he prayed, 'Father, if you are willing, please take this cup of suffering away from me. Yet I want your will, not mine' (Luke 22:42, NLT).

So far as the three men are concerned, God is God, he has a mind of his own, and they know that his way is always the optimal way. Not necessarily the easiest route to traverse, but always the best path to wander down. H C Leupold writes, '... these three men display one of the noblest examples of faith fully resigned to the will of God. These men ask for no miracle; they expect none.' Their loyalty to him is in death as well as in life. Job expressed something similar many years earlier, when he pluckily wrote, 'Though he slay me, yet will I hope in him' (Job 13:15, NIV). Remember, the same God who gave so much to Job also took so much from him. The same God who miraculously delivered Simon Peter from prison allowed James to be martyred by Herod's sword. Esther's classic pronouncement says something similar, 'If I must die, I am willing to die' (Esther 4:16, NLT). For them, they would either know the joyous grace of deliverance or they would be given the grace to die well for God's glory.

As believers in the Lord Jesus, we would do well to follow their noble example. Jim Elliot and his four companions certainly did when they ventured out to reach the savage Auca (or Huaorani) Indians in the steamy jungles of Ecuador. On 8 January 1956 they were all martyred, having been speared by those whom they were seeking to reach with the gospel of grace. Elliot penned in his journal a few years previous a one-liner that has challenged many of us, 'He is no fool who gives what he cannot keep to gain what he cannot lose.'

Cassie Bernall was a 17-year-old teenager who was martyred on 20 April 1999 at Columbine High School, just outside of Denver, Colorado. Several reports of the fatal shootings suggest that one of the murderers, Eric Harris, asked Cassie if she believed in God, to which she said yes. He immediately shot and killed her because of her faith. Cassie's courageous act to stand for Jesus was not a spur of the moment decision. It was something she had already settled in her heart sometime earlier, as is evident from this letter sent to a friend, 'When God doesn't want me to do something, I definitely know it. When he wants me to do something, even if it means going outside my comfort zone, I know that too. I feel pushed in the direction I need to go … it can be discouraging, but it can also be rewarding … I will die for my God. I will die for my faith. It's the least I can do for Christ dying for me.'

3:19-21

The madness of the monarch

Then Nebuchadnezzar was filled with fury, and the expression of his face was changed against Shadrach, Meshach, and Abednego. He ordered the furnace heated seven times more than it was usually heated. And he ordered some of the mighty men of his army to bind Shadrach, Meshach, and Abednego, and to cast

them into the burning fiery furnace. Then these men were bound
in their cloaks, their tunics, their hats, and their other garments,
and they were thrown into the burning fiery furnace.

The king got his answer, probably not the one he was expecting. It was a firm refusal on the part of the threesome, Shadrach, Meshach, and Abednego, to do his bidding. Within seconds, he changed colour as his contemptuous anger reached boiling point. His face became distorted with rage. The balloon of his pride was punctured. He was like a raging bull. If looks were enough to kill, the three men would drop dead on the spot. He had been humiliated by three Jews and that was more than he was prepared to take.

Since the three of them were not prepared to play ball with him, he upped the stakes when he raised the temperature of the burning furnace seven times hotter. Geoffrey King writes, 'He lost his temper! That is always the mark of a little man. The furnace was hot, but he himself got hotter! And when a man gets full of fury, he gets full of folly. There is no fool on earth like a man who has lost his temper. And Nebuchadnezzar did a stupid thing. He ought to have cooled the furnace seven times *less* if he had wanted to hurt them; but instead of that in his fury he heated it seven times *more*.'

The men offered no resistance when they were manhandled and tied up by the king's elite guard. Faithful in life. Faithful in death. We cannot help but admire these young men for they took their faith in God seriously and were willing to take the rough with the smooth. As they discovered, the path of life is undulating, but there is a constant in God, and we are grateful for that. Samuel Rutherford said, 'Duties are ours, events are the Lord's.' In other words, it is our job to be faithful; it is the Lord's job to deal with the outcome. These men are trusting God, no matter what. It could be said of them, as was said at the grave in Edinburgh of the Reformer John Knox, that they feared the face of no man, because they had learned to live in the fear of the Lord.

We know from archaeological evidence that this was a smelting furnace, comparable to a modern-day limekiln, a substantial pot-bellied structure with an open top on the roof through which materials were deposited. There was a sizeable opening down below, a few feet off the ground, from which the ore and other materials could be removed. There were holes all around the walls through which bellows were inserted and operated to increase the heat. And there was an inclined plane, usually made of earth leading up to the opening on the roof.

3:22-27

From the frying pan into the fire

Because the king's order was urgent and the furnace overheated, the flame of the fire killed those men who took up Shadrach, Meshach, and Abednego. And these three men, Shadrach, Meshach, and Abednego, fell bound into the burning fiery furnace. Then King Nebuchadnezzar was astonished and rose up in haste. He declared to his counsellors, 'Did we not cast three men bound into the fire?' They answered and said to the king, 'True, O king.' He answered and said, 'But I see four men unbound, walking in the midst of the fire, and they are not hurt; and the appearance of the fourth is like a son of the gods.' Then Nebuchadnezzar came near to the door of the burning fiery furnace; he declared, 'Shadrach, Meshach, and Abednego, servants of the Most High God, come out, and come here!' Then Shadrach, Meshach, and

Abednego came out from the fire. And the satraps, the prefects, the governors, and the king's counsellors gathered together and saw that the fire had not had any power over the bodies of those men. The hair of their heads was not singed, their cloaks were not harmed, and no smell of fire had come upon them.

Up the ramp the three foreign upstarts went, still dressed in their flammable finery and bound with rope. When the Army Rangers reached the top, they somehow tipped the three men in to the blazing cauldron like logs being thrown on to a fire or like chips of wood into a glowing Vesuvius. For them, though, the surging gust of hot air from the furnace was so powerful that they were burned to cinders there and then. They made it up; tragically, they did not make it down. An utter waste of innocent lives just to appease the whim of an angry king. Typical dictator. So far as a swashbuckling, self-serving Nebuchadnezzar was concerned, life is cheap.

If it was like a scorching-hot incinerator on the outside, what must it have been like on the inside? Shadrach, Meshach, and Abednego plummeted to the bottom of the furnace. Truth is, within a fraction of time—milliseconds—they should all have been burned alive. Cremated. Ashes. But God's ways are not our ways.

The inquisitive, yet capricious king cannot resist the temptation to look through the aperture into the furnace. He wanted to get the last laugh. Alas, he is shocked with what he sees. It is almost too much for him to get his head around. He is baffled and bewildered. He tried to reconcile what he saw with his own two eyes with what he knew to be true. Three men were thrown in to the flames, but he saw four ...! Perhaps he and his advisers looked a second time, and counted out loud, 'One. Yes. Two. Yes. Three. Yes. Four. Hmm?'

Tied up, but not tied down

Sometimes truth is stranger than fiction and that is certainly the case right here on the plains of Dura. The three men found liberty in the flames as they were unbound. They found freedom and fellowship in the fire as they were able to walk around as normal, except it was warmer in there than it was outside. In a miraculous manner they were kept from suffering any injury or being harmed in any way by a caring, compassionate, covenant-keeping God.

Writing many years later, it is not without significance that when Peter penned his first epistle to those living in an alien culture—first century asylum seekers—he reminded them of the fiery trials that all of us as believers face (1 Peter 1:6-7, 4:12-13, KJV).The apostle would have been familiar with the story of Daniel 3 and the lessons we all need to learn from it, so he exhorted God's people to be vigilant and wary of the tactics of the adversary of our souls (1 Peter 5:8).

Can we identify the fourth person in the furnace? I think we can! From the king's perspective, he said he was *like a son of the gods*. That was his pagan way of saying that this individual looked like a divine or supernatural being. He was rational as he tried to explain this unusual incident within the confines of his own religious framework. Thankfully, this side of Calvary, we know better.

He wasn't merely *like* a Son of God, he *was* the Son of God. He wasn't *a* god, he was *the* God. An occurrence like this is what we call a Christophany—a manifestation of the Lord as the pre-incarnate Christ in the Old Testament. David Jeremiah makes the valid point, 'Amazing as it may be, some 580 years before the virgin birth, Nebuchadnezzar saw Christ in the fiery furnace.'

Yes, the Lord was watching over them, just as he said he would do. In fact, he was in it with them, as the prophet promised when he penned, 'When you walk through the fire, you will not be burned; the flames will not set you ablaze' (Isaiah 43:2, NIV). C H Spurgeon, preaching in the Metropolitan Tabernacle, said it so well, 'Beloved, you must go into the furnace if you would have the nearest and dearest dealings with Christ Jesus.'

Seeing is believing

The king and his band of merry men must have been gobsmacked. This had never happened before. It never happened again. They were spectators to a miracle and they never knew it. When the three men responded to the king's request to come out of the still burning furnace, was there a stunned silence of disbelief from the crowd or was there a rapturous round of applause?

Shadrach, Meshach, and Abednego would not budge or bend or bow in the desert heat, and they did not burn in the furnace. Unmarked. Unscathed. No scars. No sores. No smell. Nothing was singed. Simply because God undertook for them and delivered them. The God who did not deliver them *from* the fire was the God who met them *in* the fire and delivered them *out of* the fire. The unmistakeable fact that Nebuchadnezzar did not end up with the blood of three innocent men of utmost integrity on his hands is a clear token of God's kindness and undeserved grace to him. God was trying to get through to him again, but there are none so deaf as those who refuse to hear.

I think it is most important for us to realise that life does not always turn out like that. He is our shield and our protector, but that does not mean we will not face trials and tribulation down here, but it is in those moments when we are at wits' end corner that the Fourth Man comes and walks with us and talks with us. On Calvary's cross, the Lord Jesus was abandoned by God so that we might never be. He willingly endured the red-hot fury of God's just and righteous anger. Alone. That is why 'in every pang that rends the heart, the Man of Sorrows has a part' (Michael Bruce).

Yes, the Lord looks after us as his cherished possession, and he deeply cares for us night and day, but when things go pear-shaped as they sometimes do, it does not necessarily guarantee a dramatic deliverance for us before the sun goes down. We may not live to tell the tale this side of heaven. But we shall recount it on the other golden shore. No doubts there.

3:28-30

From trial to triumph

Nebuchadnezzar answered and said, 'Blessed be the God of Shadrach, Meshach, and Abednego, who has sent his angel and delivered his servants, who trusted in him, and set aside the king's command, and yielded up their bodies rather than serve and worship any god except their own God. Therefore I make a decree: Any people, nation, or language that speaks anything against the God of Shadrach, Meshach, and Abednego shall be torn limb from limb, and their houses laid in ruins, for there is no other god who is able to rescue in this way.' Then the king promoted Shadrach, Meshach, and Abednego in the province of Babylon.

Nebuchadnezzar saw a lot in his life, but he never saw anything like this before; there is a first time for everything. And now at the end of the episode, he is saying a lot of good things about the God of Shadrach, Meshach, and Abednego. Their God is a God who comes close to his children in their hour of greatest need. Their God is one who rescues his servants when they find themselves in a tough place. I mean, he is impressed, *most* impressed. But he is not converted. He has a few notches to come down before that happens.

He waxed eloquent when he spoke of the sheer dedication of the three men who were willing to die for a cause rather than dishonour their God and Saviour. He knows deep down in his heart that these men are different from all the hangers-on in the royal court. They know that their God is untouchable and unbeatable – but, now, even Nebuchadnezzar is willing to tolerate their beliefs and ultimately reward them for sticking by their principles. Solomon's wise words are still true, 'When a man's ways are pleasing to the Lord, he makes even his enemies live at peace with him' (Proverbs 16:7, NIV).

For them, it was a journey from trial to triumph. As the saying goes, man's extremity is often God's opportunity. It shows beyond any doubt that when we are at the end of ourselves, only then are we at the beginning of God. He is not at work in your life creating circumstances that you want; he is at work in your circumstances creating in you what he wants. When that transpires, we become in the words of Joni Eareckson Tada, 'an audio visual of the power of God.'

Today, on the plain of Dura, there is no glittering golden statue for men to see and take a selfie alongside; but all around the world, the people of God are marching onwards and upwards, inspired and encouraged by the faithful testimony of Shadrach, Meshach, and Abednego. Like them, because we are kept by God's power, he will hold us fast until we come to the end of the road, and then on in to Glory (1 Peter 1:4-5). The precious truth is, when you stand for what is right, you never stand alone. God always stands with you.

The writer may have been thinking of these three valiant individuals when he wrote in God's Hall of Fame, 'who through faith ... quenched the fury of the flames' (Hebrews 11:33-34, NIV). These men could testify, 'You have tested us, O God; you have purified us like silver melted in a crucible.... We went through fire and flood. But you brought us to a place of great abundance' (Psalm 66:10-12, NLT).

4

PUT OUT TO PASTURE

On a horrible day – Sunday, 18 June 1815 – Emperor Napoleon Bonaparte, commander of the French army, squared up to a coalition of European armies formed against him at Waterloo: an Anglo-Allied force led by Field Marshal the Duke of Wellington, and the Prussians led by Field Marshal Gebhard von Blücher. Portrayed as the most influential battle of its age, it concluded a war that had raged for twenty-three years, ended French attempts to dominate Europe, and destroyed Napoleon's imperial power forever. Simon Worrall penned in *National Geographic*, 'At stake was world dominance.'

As dawn broke on that fateful day, Napoleon described to his senior officers his strategy for that day's campaign. He said, 'We'll put the infantry here, the cavalry over there, and the artillery in that spot. At the end of the day, England will be at the feet of France, and Wellington will be the prisoner of Napoleon.'

The commanding officer listened attentively to the proposed battle plan, then responded with a famous one-liner, itself a paraphrase of Proverbs 16:9, 'Your Imperial Majesty, we must not forget that man proposes and God disposes.' Napoleon, boastfully arrogant as ever, pulled his body to its full five-feet-two and sardonically replied, 'I want you to understand, sir, that Napoleon proposes and Napoleon disposes.'

The French novelist, Victor Hugo, wrote, 'From that moment, Waterloo was lost, for God sent rain and hail so that the troops of Napoleon could not manoeuvre as he had planned, and on the night of battle it was Napoleon who was the prisoner of Wellington, and France was at the feet of England.'

'How the mighty heroes have fallen!' is a triple refrain in David's song of lament for the passing of Saul and Jonathan (2 Samuel 1:27, NLT). So apt for a big-headed emperor who perfectly epitomised the sayings that 'pride goes before destruction' (Proverbs 16:18, NIV) and 'when pride comes, then comes disgrace' (Proverbs 11:2, NIV). He was too big for his boots. The annals of history confirm that Napoleon knew both when he met his Waterloo!

4:1-3

Open confession is good for the soul

King Nebuchadnezzar to all peoples, nations, and languages, that dwell in all the earth: Peace be multiplied to you! It has seemed good to me to show the signs and wonders that the Most High God has done for me. How great are his signs, how mighty his wonders! His kingdom is an everlasting kingdom, and his dominion endures from generation to generation.

This chapter is an official state document—an imperial proclamation—that is addressed to mankind and comes with a sincere desire that his subjects may know peace and find prosperity in abundant measure. It is comparable to a State of the Union Address delivered by the President of the United States or a speech from a serving Prime Minister. Unusual for such, it is compulsive reading; it is sitting on the edge of your seat stuff. Riveting. A jolly good read. It is one of those chapters that when you start it, you feel as though you want to keep on going to the end!

David Helm writes, 'In short, we could say that this proclamation presents us with a song, sung by a worldly but religious king who decided to lift his voice in public (like a tenor rising solo above the choir), testifying to his new-found personal faith in the God of Daniel, and with the aim of instilling peace in all who hear his melody.'

Basically, most of it is written in the first person and is best seen as an autobiography of Nebuchadnezzar. An evangelistic tract where he tells it like it is. It makes the hair stand on the back of your neck. It would bring tears to a stone as it highlights the lengths to which God is prepared to go so that he may savingly draw someone to himself. It is a gentle and timely prompt that none of us are beyond the reach of a God of extravagant grace and magnanimous mercy. To quote the words of Matt Papa's song, 'Our sins they are many, his mercy is more!'

You will recall there was a similar intro in the previous chapter (Daniel 3:4), but this time it seems a tad different for this one is cut from a different cloth. Then Nebuchadnezzar was totally immersed in himself; now he is enthusiastically extolling the wonders of God. Then he ardently wanted to be the centre of attention; now he joyfully magnifies the Most High God as he 'declares the praises of [the] God who called' him (1 Peter 2:9, NIV). Then he wanted to be in the limelight; now he gladly 'proclaims the excellencies of [his] God' (1 Peter 2:9, NASB). Talk about transformation, this is it! As a new man, he wants to tell of the amazing things the amazing God has done in his life to the glory of God.

This 'primitive press release,' as Geoff Thomas called it, is a personal reflection of God's dealings with him up to the moment of his dramatic conversion experience. He pulls no punches. It is unprecedented. He is honest, frank, and open. He provides us with a before and after account of all that transpired between him and his God. It is one man's spiritual journal where no stone is left unturned as he traces his quest for peace with God. John Walvoord claims, 'It may well be that this chapter brings Nebuchadnezzar to the place where he puts his trust in the God of Daniel. Even merely as a lesson in the spiritual progress of a man in the hands of God, this chapter is a literary gem.'

Nebuchadnezzar was determined that his message would reach out to those *who live in all the world*. And why not? Think of the impact it would have in the world of his day. Danny Akin reflects, 'If Nebuchadnezzar were alive today, he would have called a primetime news conference for TV and radio, live-streamed online. He would have used Twitter, Instagram, and Facebook. He wanted as many people as possible to know what God did.'

I think we all appreciate hearing a true life story and especially so when it is one like this: from riches to rags to riches. For Nebuchadnezzar, it is a different kind of riches at the finale for these are the inestimable 'riches of grace' (Ephesians 1:7, 2:7). Living as we are in a post-Christian culture we need to do what he did and tell the world. As believers, we must take the great commission seriously and seize every God-given opportunity to spread the good news globally of a Saviour who is 'mighty to save' (Isaiah 63:1; Zephaniah 3:17, NIV). We have, in the words of the hymn, 'a story to tell to the nations.'

As far as I am aware, this is the only recorded testimony of a Gentile king in Scripture. When we reach the last few lines in his story, it appears that we are confronted with a new Nebuchadnezzar. Paul, no stranger himself to a high drama turnaround in life (Acts 9), when writing to the saints in the church at Corinth, referenced those who came to know Jesus Christ personally when he declared that 'not many of noble birth' (1 Corinthians 1:26-29, NIV) find their way to Calvary. Thanks be to God, there are exceptions! And that is why God's grace is so utterly amazing.

Starting with the ending

Nebuchadnezzar's parting shot actually becomes his opening salvo when he gives us his conclusion in the introduction. Editorial licence, I presume. It is highly unusual, but not unique in the Bible for another instance of this literary ploy is found in Psalm 73, where Asaph writes in verse 1, 'Truly God is good to Israel, to those who are pure in heart.' Then, in the following twenty-seven verses, he tells the story of how he reached that epic ending. That is precisely what Nebuchadnezzar does here: verses 1-3 declare where he came out, and verses 4-37 are his memory in overdrive as he relates how he arrived at that conclusion.

Dale Ralph Davis summarises the emphases in chapters two to four, when he writes that 'the stress in Daniel 2 is that God reveals, in chapter 3 that he rescues, and in chapter 4 that he rules.' Like a carpenter hammering nails in a piece of wood, the message is repeatedly affirmed that 'the Most High is sovereign over the kingdoms of men and gives them to anyone he wishes' (Daniel 4:17, 25, 32; see also 26, NIV).

One man's pleasure

World leaders in the West do not usually 'do God,' as former prime minister Tony Blair's top spin doctor (director of communications)

Alastair Campbell famously declared on British television. King Nebuchadnezzar did, and in the course of his opening remarks, he makes four pulsating statements that heighten our awareness of who God is.

As a transcendent God, he is the God of the impossible and the God who revolutionises for *signs and wonders* are all in a day's work for him; he is the God who always will be for his *eternal kingdom* outlasts and outshines all flimsy and fragile earthly kingdoms; and he is the God who never changes since he is famed for his immutability from one *generation* to another. The words of this doxology echo the truths found in Psalm 145:13 that no God is like this God in what he does, and no God is like this God in what he has.

Nebuchadnezzar is saying to all within earshot, 'Hey, listen to this: God has worked in my life. *Really* worked. He has done a miraculous thing, and it has had many wonderful spinoffs. The end is not yet. Watch this space!'

Kenneth Gangel writes, 'Quite remarkable in their direct praise of God, these two verses could form part of a worship service in any evangelical church.' Indeed, for that is what authentic praise and worship is all about: it is God-focused and God-saturated.

4:4-9

Blissfully content until …

I, Nebuchadnezzar, was at ease in my house and prospering in my palace. I saw a dream that made me afraid. As I lay in bed the fancies and the visions of my head alarmed me. So I made a decree that all the wise men of Babylon should be brought before me, that they might make known to me the interpretation of my dream. Then the magicians, the enchanters, the Chaldeans, and the astrologers came in, and I told them the dream, but they could not make known to me its interpretation. At last Daniel came in before me—he who was named Belteshazzar after the name of my god and in whom is the spirit of the holy gods—and I told him the dream, saying, 'O Belteshazzar, chief of the magicians, because I know that the spirit of the holy gods is in you and that no mystery is too difficult for you, tell me the visions of my dream that I saw and their interpretation.'

Life was hunky-dory for Nebuchadnezzar at this point in his life. For the best part of forty years the warrior king was undefeated on the battlefield. He was in a good place in terms of personal contentment and national prosperity. He had the people under his thumb. To all intents and purposes, the garden was rosy, the sky was blue, and he was living on cloud nine. He ticked all the boxes and seemed to have life by the tail. He was a man at the very top of his profession, sitting on the pinnacle of power. He was master of all he surveyed.

The biblical narrative paints an optimistic picture of the golden years of his reign, days of serenity and satisfaction. It intimates that Nebuchadnezzar was 'flourishing in [his] palace' (Daniel 4:4, KJV), and in so doing employs a word that is used for plants and trees, quite an appropriate metaphor for this chapter (Psalms 52:8, 92:12-14, NIV). The Aramaic word can be understood literally as, 'I was growing green.' That has nothing to do with environmental issues, but it has everything to do with a luxuriantly luscious lifestyle.

The unease and discomfort returned with a vengeance when he dreamed yet another one of those nightmarish dreams; upwards of thirty years have lapsed since his last major vision when he saw the statue of the metallic man in chapter two. By his own admission, he was in a cold sweat for he was *terrified*. Been there, done that, he certainly has. How easily one man's peace can be splintered. How quickly one mighty man's feathers can be ruffled by the Almighty.

Again, this was the sovereign Lord pulling all the strings as he sought to interrupt the rhythm of Nebuchadnezzar's melodic life. He has run all of the red stop lights, and now he is caught and arrested. This was God banging on the front door of his life, one more time. Stuart Olyott says that this time around 'God is going to knock in such a way that the door will come right off its hinges.' God had spoken loudly to him in chapter two, and again a few years later in chapter three. Now he speaks again in a way that is reminiscent of Elihu's speech to Job, where we read, 'For God does speak—now one way, now another—though man may not perceive it. In a dream, in a vision of the night, when deep sleep falls on men as they slumber in their beds, he may speak in their ears and terrify them with warnings, to turn man from wrongdoing and keep him from pride' (Job 33:14-17, NIV).

Such is the astoundingly infinite patience of a grace-loving, sinner-seeking God. John Calvin rightly concludes, 'When God, therefore, wishes to lead us to repentance, he is compelled to repeat his blows continually, either because we are not moved when he chastises us with his hand, or we seem roused for the time, and then we return to our former torpor. He is therefore compelled to redouble his blows.'

Confronted with the harsh realities of life and death, his calloused heart was shell-shocked and shattered. Needless to say, he did not like what he saw with every passing image. The carpet was pulled out from under his feet and he felt as though things were crumbling in his own life and, potentially, on the verge of crashing. Another wake-up call from the Most High. Deep down, he knew it. It is no exaggeration to say that Nebuchadnezzar is a desperately worried man. One look at his furrowed brow and flushed face is enough to confirm that diagnosis.

As before, driven by quivery fear, the first port of call is his group of paid pagan professionals, so we are not in the least surprised to see the march of the wizards into the inner sanctum of the royal palace. The motley crew of *magicians, enchanters, Chaldeans, and astrologers* filed in to see the king and timidly waited for him to do his bit. In all probability, their pulses were racing and their stomachs churning as they vividly recalled the monarch's shenanigans on previous visits.

Kenneth Gangel makes the valid point that 'we should not view these men as some group of pseudoscientific crackpots who pronounced incantations over the entrails of a slaughtered animal. One could call them the savants of the ancient world, scientists of a type, and certainly university-level philosophers and professors.'

It was the same old rigmarole. These veterans have trundled down this well-worn path on numerous occasions. They know the drill. And again, as before, they flunk the test. The text clinically states, *I told them the dream, but they could not make known to me its interpretation.* To quote the preacher, 'History merely repeats itself. It has all been done before. Nothing under the sun is truly new' (Ecclesiastes 1:9, NLT).

Exasperation. Tenseness. The sheer folly of practical atheism is exposed right here. He petitioned Daniel, his go-to guy, but he had not yet learned to plead with Daniel's God. When all else fails, read the directions. One detects a palpable feeling of relief when the king sighs, *at last Daniel came in before me.* The king's face lights up with Daniel's arrival. Dale Ralph Davis refers to him as

'God's gift to the pagan king … a light in the midst of his darkness and fears. Daniel is the kindness of God to Nebuchadnezzar.'

If nothing else, he knows that Daniel will tell him the truth, like it or not. God communicates, God speaks, Daniel is simply a conduit. His track record on such matters is exemplary and the king recognises that commendable trait in his prime minister. He knew by Daniel's lifestyle and personal godliness that he was a man full of 'the Spirit of the Holy God' (verse 9, NKJV), and because of that, *no mystery [was] too difficult for him* to handle. At the same time, he quickly acknowledges that it is not just Daniel on his own who can do it, it is actually his God speaking through him.

It is always refreshing when a man of the world is quick off the mark to genuinely applaud a faithful servant of God for services rendered. People on the outside intuitively know when God's people have a warm relationship with their heavenly Father; in normal circumstances, they can tell the gaping difference between synthetic saints and spiritual saints, even before we open our mouths to talk about Jesus. There is something delightfully attractive and personable, as Daniel displayed, about a Spirit-filled life. So often we are the butt of cynical jokes and derogatory comments, but when life falls apart for the unbeliever, we tend to be the ones to whom they turn. Why? Because they know that we care, and pray, and that our God answers prayer, and we sing the Lord's song in a strange land.

4:10-18

Learning the hard way

'The visions of my head as I lay on my bed were these: I saw, and behold, a tree in the midst of the earth, and its height was great. The

tree grew and became strong, and its top reached to heaven, and it was visible to the end of the whole earth. Its leaves were beautiful and its fruit abundant, and in it was food for all. The beasts of the field found shade under it, and the birds of the heavens lived in its branches, and all flesh was fed from it. I saw in the visions of my head as I lay in bed, and behold, a watcher, a holy one, came down from heaven. He proclaimed aloud and said thus: "Chop down the tree and lop off its branches, strip off its leaves and scatter its fruit. Let the beasts flee from under it and the birds from its branches. But leave the stump of its roots in the earth, bound with a band of iron and bronze, amid the tender grass of the field. Let him be wet with the dew of heaven. Let his portion be with the beasts in the grass of the earth. Let his mind be changed from a man's, and let a beast's mind be given to him; and let seven periods of time pass over him. The sentence is by the decree of the watchers, the decision by the word of the holy ones, to the end that the living may know that the Most High rules the kingdom of men and gives it to whom he will and sets over it the lowliest of men." This dream I, King Nebuchadnezzar, saw. And you, O Belteshazzar, tell me the interpretation, because all the wise men of my kingdom are not able to make known to me the interpretation, but you are able, for the spirit of the holy gods is in you.'

It was a fairly straightforward vision as visions go and the king had little or no difficulty recounting it for Daniel's benefit. John Lennox notes that 'the main contours are clear.' Initially, it is all about a cosmic tree that was big, beautiful, and bountiful; it stood like a bastion in the middle of the land. Then an angel, *a watcher*, appeared and the order was given to cut down the tree, leaving only a stump in the soil. In itself, that was harsh, but hopeful. The postscript did not sound too promising either when it suggested that the person represented in the vision would act like a beast for an extended period of time. Overall, the message is: you have never had it so good, then crash, bang, wallop, and you go from boom to bust within hours. Sinclair Ferguson notes that 'a superhuman empire would be reduced to subhuman proportions.'

The heavily underlined baseline—repeated a few times in the chapter (verses 17, 25, 32; see also 26)—is to affirm that *the living may know that the Most High rules the kingdom of men and gives it to whom he will and sets over it the lowliest of men*. Have a look at this key verse through the creative pen of Eugene Peterson in *The Message*, '… so that everyone living will know that the High God rules human kingdoms. He arranges kingdom affairs however he wishes, and makes leaders out of losers.'

Come what may, God gets his man. Always. He is relentless in his pursuit of individuals, irrespective of who or where they are. Ask Nebuchadnezzar! This arboreal vision is permeated throughout with the age-old truth that the Lord is sovereign. Nebuchadnezzar needed to learn that his tenure on the throne was only at God's pleasure; the same holds true for every human ruler of men, be they good, bad, or indifferent. The principle is that God crowns whomever he chooses (Romans 13:1-5). The God who reigns over all is the one who puts them up, he puts them down and, ultimately, he puts them out. How essential it is for us to humble ourselves before God does it for us. The sooner we lesser mortals learn that lesson the better for God has his way of teaching us, and sometimes it is in the school of hard knocks.

The Babylonian dendrophile

Before we lift the lid on the vision and its interpretation, it is interesting to note that Nebuchadnezzar was an original tree hugger.

That is why the vision of the tree is so apt and relevant for the green-fingered king. Kenneth Gangel says, 'He not only dreamed about large trees, he also spent a lot of his time and money working with them.' Ancient manuscripts tell us about his love for the renowned stately cedars of Lebanon. He imported beautiful cedar logs for the cosmetic decoration of Babylonian buildings and skilfully transformed the sun-kissed landscape with all types of vegetation.

Trees have great significance in Scripture. There is a tree on the first page of Genesis and on the last page of Revelation. At the beginning, we read of one tree that represented knowledge and another life (Genesis 2-3). The first psalm informs us that people who are blessed by God are like trees planted by refreshing streams of water. Assyria takes the form of the majestic cedar of Lebanon (Ezekiel 31:1-9). Jesus told parables about trees (Matthew 24:32-35; John 15:1-17). Paul compared Israel to an olive tree and the Gentiles to a grafted branch (Romans 11:17-24). The rugged, accursed cross on which the Lord Jesus died had been a living tree (Galatians 3:13; 1 Peter 2:24). Finally, the Apocalypse refers to the tree of life (Revelation 22:1-2).

W A Criswell reminds us how important this symbol had become in Nebuchadnezzar's culture, when he writes, 'Often the tree of paradise can be seen in Assyrian and Babylonian culture. The people carved it on gems, on ornaments, and on great buildings. It was seen everywhere and signified the power and regal authority of the monarch himself.'

4:19-27

The truth, the whole truth, and nothing but the truth

Then Daniel, whose name was Belteshazzar, was dismayed for a while, and his thoughts alarmed him. The king answered and said, 'Belteshazzar, let not the dream or the interpretation alarm you.' Belteshazzar answered and said, 'My lord, may the dream be for those who hate you and its interpretation for your enemies! The tree you saw, which grew and became strong, so that its top reached to heaven, and it was visible to the end of the whole earth, whose leaves were beautiful and its fruit abundant, and in which was food for all, under which beasts found shade, and in whose branches the birds of the heavens lived—it is you, O king, who have grown and become strong. Your greatness has grown and reaches to heaven, and your dominion to the ends of the earth. And because the king saw a watcher, a holy one, coming down from heaven and saying, "Chop down the tree and destroy it, but leave the stump of its roots in the earth, bound with a band of iron and bronze, in the tender grass of the field, and let him be wet with the dew of heaven, and let his portion be with the beasts of the field, till seven periods of time pass over him," this is the interpretation, O king: It is a decree of the Most High, which has come upon my lord the king, that you shall be driven from among men, and your dwelling shall be with the beasts of the field. You shall be made to eat grass like an ox, and you shall be wet with the dew of heaven, and seven periods of time shall pass over you, till you know that the Most High rules the kingdom of men and gives it to whom he will. And as it was commanded to leave the stump of the roots of the tree, your kingdom shall be confirmed for you from the time that you know that Heaven rules. Therefore, O king, let my counsel be acceptable to you: break off your sins by practising righteousness, and your iniquities by showing mercy to the oppressed, that there may perhaps be a lengthening of your prosperity.'

This confrontation between Daniel and Nebuchadnezzar is epic when set alongside similar showdowns in biblical history. It ranks with the encounters between Moses and Pharaoh, Elijah and Ahab, John the Baptist and Herod, Jesus and Pilate, and Paul and Agrippa. Ligon Duncan sees it as 'one of the great contests between a man of God and a man of this world recorded in the Bible.' That, it most certainly is.

For Daniel, the thought of having to divulge the precise meaning of the dream to Nebuchadnezzar sent him into an emotional tailspin. He was visibly affected to such a degree that the swell-headed king even noticed; it took its toll on God's servant, now a man in his early fifties. He was psychologically challenged, to put it mildly. Perplexed. Perturbed. The more Daniel thought of the serious implications—short term and long term—of the interpretation, the more he recoiled within. He was to be the bearer of bad news, terribly bad news.

Daniel's compassion, care, and concern for the king shine through in the narrative. He was known as a man of believing prayer (Daniel 6:10) and there is no doubt that Nebuchadnezzar was probably up there at the top of his prayer list. He must have often prayed for the king's salvation and longed for him to turn in repentance to his God. His passionate pleading with God in the secret place for the conversion of his earthly boss caused him, on this occasion, to be overwhelmed with the gravity of the message he was about to deliver. Not unlike Paul when he declared, 'For when I preach the gospel, I cannot boast, since I am compelled to preach. Woe to me if I do not preach the gospel!' (1 Corinthians 9:16, NIV). When it comes to you and me reaching people with the truth of the gospel, vulnerability, tears and pleading go a very long way. It is good for us to feel the impact of the message in our own hearts before we open our mouths and speak of mercy and judgment to others. John Calvin says, 'Daniel displays both a reticence of love and a compulsion of truth.'

In spite of the bruising tenderness of his heart, Daniel was truthful, loyal, and faithful. 'And that is the proper balance one meets in the Lord's true servants: a love-driven sadness that cringes to speak the hard Word of God, yet a God-honouring obedience that speaks it anyway,' notes Dale Ralph Davis. He exhorted Nebuchadnezzar to do what was right and to do what he knew to be right. It was an unpalatable message which the king did not want to hear, but it was one that he needed to hear. Daniel implored him to forsake his sin and turn from his wicked ways. Basically, in gospel-speak, he urged him to get right with God (Isaiah 55:7; 2 Corinthians 5:20).

The first tree-man

In the space of twelve to fourteen lines in the average Bible – 3 verses – Daniel unfolds to the king the significance of the first part of his vision. After waxing eloquent about its height and its foliage and its fruitfulness, he continued to highlight that it provided shelter for the animals and nesting places for the birds. Pictorial language, sure, but when taken at face value, it is quite an exhaustive list of accomplishments and achievements.

Without pausing for breath, Daniel then quipped, '… you, O king, are that tree!' (Daniel 4:22, NIV). These sound like the words spoken by Nathan when he confronted David with his sin (2 Samuel 12:7). In other words, he equates the impressive pictorial language with a person, namely Nebuchadnezzar. It is as if Daniel was saying to the king, 'All very nice, all very pretty, all very safe and secure, all very grand, and it is all about you! And, oops, I nearly forgot, it is all very big ...!'

When we look at the three occasions when God revealed himself to the king, the focus is always on something big: a colossal metallic man in chapter 2, a colossal golden statue in chapter 3, and a colossal dream tree in chapter 4. Each of them is ginormous in their own right and certainly eye-catching for one reason or another. The lasting impression is that Nebuchadnezzar was a big man in every sense of the word. As Daniel says, *it is you, O king, who have grown and become strong. Your greatness has grown and reaches to heaven, and your dominion to the ends of the earth.*

Nebuchadnezzar was a larger-than-life character in charge of an extensive empire whose capital city was a wonder of the ancient world. John Lennox writes that it was 'a city originally engineered to reflect human achievement, symbolised in its famous ziggurat whose top pierced the heavens.' Daniel, with one final push in this paragraph, makes sure that Nebuchadnezzar joins all the dots – it is now the emperor whose *greatness has grown and reaches to heaven.* Simply put, Nebuchadnezzar had succeeded in making a name for himself. If there had been a Fortune 500 list in those days, he would have been first on the list.

The divine lumberjack

Unbeknown to Nebuchadnezzar, he would soon make a name for himself for a very different reason. On reflection, it is frighteningly scary how fast a man in his prime can be so humbled and, indeed, humiliated, to become a man in a trough. From the peaks of glory to the pits of despair (Isaiah 2:11). Pride puffs us up, God brings us down. Because God hates pride (Proverbs 8:13). That is where the sovereignty of God wins every time. God is God; who are we to argue with him? Such hard-nosed reality in man's experience is a ringing endorsement of Paul's words, when he spoke of 'the kindness and severity of God' (Romans 11:22, NASB).

Daniel speaks of 'a messenger, a holy one, coming down from heaven' (Daniel 4:23, NIV); the ESV refers to *a watcher*. Three different expressions are used to portray an angel who is despatched from the throne room of the Most High to ensure that the Sovereign's orders are fully carried out. The heavenly lumberjack calls out, 'Timber!' and in no time at all the giant tree topples to the ground. When God is on the move he does not drag his heels. Dale Ralph Davis describes it thus, 'A thorough job it is – branches whacked off, leaves stripped, fruit scattered, while beasts and birds skedaddle (Daniel 4:14, 23).'

The stump and its roots is a classic example of judgment tempered with mercy. The banding of the tree may suggest that he was marked by God and protected by him until his purposes for him were fulfilled. This was a warning shot across his bow. Nebuchadnezzar, having been abandoned to the forces of nature and exiled to seven years of detention in the open field, will have an opportunity to make amends and seek God. If he does, then God will recompense him and his sunset years will be his best years. So all is not lost, there is a ray of hope, but only if and when he finally submits to the sovereign purposes of God. As the original prodigal son, he must learn that ultimate power did not rest in Babylon or in his own hands but in heaven in God's hands. The promise, like the punishment, was conditional; he needs to come to a point in his life where he openly acknowledges that *Heaven rules*.

We catch a glimpse of Daniel's heart for Nebuchadnezzar when he went off-piste and pressed the conscience button in the king's heart and mind. The king did not anticipate this bit in Daniel's oration as it was not in the original script, but Daniel grasped the God-given grace-opportunity to tell him a few home truths. He faithfully warned the king that if he would not break from his sin, he would be broken by that sin. 'Unlike some preachers,' writes Warren Wiersbe, 'Daniel did not divorce truth from responsibility. There was a *therefore* in his message.'

His impassioned appeal to the king in verse 27 is akin to that of an old-time gospel preacher extending an invitation to lost souls, when he says without stutter or stammer, *break off your sins by practising righteousness, and your iniquities by showing mercy to the oppressed*. Nebuchadnezzar had three principal fault lines in his character and two of them are referred to here: one, a serious lack of moral integrity and, two, a dearth of humanitarian mercy. That is why Daniel pours out his heart and pleads with him to stop sinning and do what is right, and to stop treating his people with callous disregard. The third is the glaringly obvious one of overweening pride where he would think nothing of riding roughshod over all and sundry so as to stamp his name on the entire empire. On that point, Renald Showers confirms that 'most of the bricks recovered from ancient Babylon have had stamped on every one this inscription: "I am Nebuchadnezzar, King of Babylon."' He was renowned for doing his own thing and for ruthlessly getting his own way.

Having used the big stick, Daniel then dangles a carrot in front of the king when he offers to him the tantalising prospect of light at the end of the tunnel for there is a divine *perhaps* at the end of his message. There is a way out, a way back. Judgment can be averted, but only if he gets things satisfactorily sorted between himself and the God of heaven.

With that, Daniel has done his bit. He walks out from the

royal court with a heavy heart, leaving behind an unconverted Nebuchadnezzar alone with his thoughts.

4:28

A gap year – a missed opportunity

All this came upon King Nebuchadnezzar.

In a clinical, matter-of-fact, one-line report—six words in English—we read all that had been prophesied came to pass in the life of Nebuchadnezzar. There was, however, a delay of twelve months before anything actually happened. An unbelievably patient God gave him a decent breathing space to gather his thoughts, sort out his life, and repent of his sin. 'Mercy loves delays,' notes Dale Ralph Davis. God was not in a rush or in a particular hurry to teach the king an advantageous lesson he would never forget; that said, stubborn Nebuchadnezzar was ludicrously foolish and barmy to presume on the generosity of God's grace and kindness.

Just because the Most High did not slam the door in his face there and then did not mean that a righteous God had forgotten all about it. Unlike us, the omniscient Lord of time and eternity has no problems with amnesia. God goes well beyond the third mile in his gracious workings in the life of the king by giving him sleepless nights, sending Daniel into his inner court as his trusted right-hand man, and by granting him many months of leeway to turn from his sin. Grace at its finest when man is at his foulest.

As the weeks slipped by, the chances are Nebuchadnezzar thought he had got off scot-free. No doubt, he put the whole experience down to a bad dream with nightmarish vibes. He dropped his guard and gradually returned to some semblance of routine normality, doing whatever autocratic kings do on a daily basis. Sinclair Ferguson writes, 'Nebuchadnezzar made the most fatal mistake an individual can make. He assumed that he would interpret God's activity by his own plumb line.'

John Elias (1774-1841), a Welsh firebrand evangelist who laboured mostly in Anglesey, once used a vivid illustration of the conscience-silencing that took place in Nebuchadnezzar's life. He recalled the time when the local blacksmith had bought a new dog. Shortly afterward, when Elias visited the blacksmith's shop, the dog could be heard barking fiercely as the blacksmith's hammer beat rhythmically on the metal of the horseshoes. As time went on, however, the barking became quieter and less frequent until one day Elias looked into the smithy to catch the blacksmith hammering away at the anvil and saw the dog, asleep by the fire, silent at last.

Such was the self-inflicted experience of Nebuchadnezzar. At one point, twelve months earlier, he was scared out of his wits but, alas, that fear and dread has given way to a complacency fuelled by a sense of pride that he firmly believed he was untouchable. In his heart, he really felt that he was bigger and brighter than the great God of heaven. Sadly, and tragically, he is not the last man to feel like that for there are many in today's world who feel exactly the same. Given time, the Spirit's promptings become less frequent and such individuals feel a sense of immunity from the wrath of a holy God. They no longer hear with clarity the hammering voice of a redeeming God on the anvil of their hard hearts. Blind eyes. Deaf ears. A silent conscience. Not a good place for any man to be! Like one of old, my thankful heart is able to say, 'There but for the grace of God go I.'

4:29-30

A one-sided conversation

At the end of twelve months he was walking on the roof of the royal palace of Babylon, and the king answered and said, 'Is not this great Babylon, which I have built by my mighty power as a royal residence and for the glory of my majesty?'

Twelve months have slipped into eternity. One morning Nebuchadnezzar is out on the palace roof getting some fresh air and exercise. He is prancing around on top of the palace and on top of the world. Alone, in the hanging gardens (one of the seven wonders of the ancient world) he is talking to himself. Most of us have done that at one time or another!

He proudly surveys the landscape as far as the eye can see and he starts gloating over his magnificent achievements down the years. He had every reason to believe his own press releases. He is immersed in the art of self-admiration, the knack of patting oneself on the back. He rants and raves about his accomplishments and ambitions. His narcissistic world revolves around himself and all that he has done. To be fair, and to give credit where it is due, that was an amazingly long list! All the archaeological evidence gathered to date supports that claim.

The city and its environs were aesthetically pleasing. Nebuchadnezzar and his team of architects had a strong eye for detail. And it showed. I mean, this city was definitely well worth a visit for any traveller on a Middle Eastern itinerary. Babylon was listed on most people's bucket-list as somewhere they longed to explore.

Aside from the hanging gardens which he had built for his wife, there was the outer perimeter wall of the city, which was wide enough to enable a chariot driven by four horses to turn around on the top. Josephus wrote these words of Nebuchadnezzar, 'So when he had thus fortified the city with walls ... and had adorned the gates magnificently, he added a new palace to that which his father had dwelt in, and this close by it also, and that more eminent in its height, and in its great splendour. However, as prodigiously large and magnificent as it was, it was finished in fifteen days.' The stunningly attractive Ishtar Gate was forty feet high and on the north side of the city; it led into Procession Street (62 feet wide, 1,000 yards long) paved with imported stone. A bridge (400 feet long) spanned the Euphrates between the east and west sectors of the city. Nebuchadnezzar enjoyed the luxury of at least three palaces within the city.

No wonder he is crowing about his own greatness. We hear him say in triumphalist tones in verse 30, 'I did it. I built it by *my* mighty power. I built it for the glory of *my* majesty.' Every syllable drips with self-glorification. There is one word to best describe such a swaggering utterance of personal pronouns, pride. Did you notice the middle letter in pride? I! The symptoms are spelled out. The diagnosis summed up, pride. Like the king, we need to remind ourselves that we have nothing that God in grace has not given us. That is why we are exhorted to guard our hearts (Proverbs 4:23), knowing that God knows all there is to know about us (Psalm 139:1-4, 23-24). Even the mightiest among us are 'frail children of dust, and feeble as frail' to quote the hymnwriter, Robert Grant (1779-1838). We are not in control; God is. Nebuchadnezzar forgot that fundamental truth.

All appears to be going swimmingly in our lives, then with no advance warning, a pandemic such as Covid-19 arrives on the scene and everything changes faster than the batting of an eyelid. This coronavirus was no respecter of persons for it entered royal palaces and also infected heads of state. Major cities were under lockdown. There were no planes in the sky. Citizens were obligated to adhere to social distancing. Global economies shrunk, pension funds took a massive hit, and stock market gains were quickly wiped out. The global death toll of hundreds of thousands was worryingly high. All of this conveys one robust message: we are not in control of our destinies. God is. A message some of us, along with Nebuchadnezzar, leave on the back burner.

4:31-33

A man out standing in his field

While the words were still in the king's mouth, there fell a voice from heaven, 'O King Nebuchadnezzar, to you it is spoken: The kingdom has departed from you, and you shall be driven from among men, and your dwelling shall be with the beasts of the field. And you shall be made to eat grass like an ox, and seven periods of time shall pass over you, until you know that the Most High rules the kingdom of men and gives it to whom he will.' Immediately the word was fulfilled against Nebuchadnezzar. He was driven from among men and ate grass like an ox, and his body was wet with the dew of heaven till his hair grew as long as eagles' feathers, and his nails were like birds' claws.

Nebuchadnezzar's few minutes of pompous self-adulation on his lofty perch came to an abrupt end when God interrupted the one-way conversation. God broke into his life like a thunderbolt and spoke directly to him; in as many words, he told him that his time was up (Proverbs 29:1; Ecclesiastes 9:12). He was going out to pasture, with immediate effect. No comments. No questions. No more chances.

Nineveh had only forty days, and their king did not waste a moment (Jonah 3:3-10), but a longsuffering God gave Nebuchadnezzar one year to repent. He frittered that away. None of us knows if we have forty minutes, never mind forty days or more. Hence the urgency of the situation. He then gives him a further seven years to rethink and refocus, to come to his senses and acknowledge that the sovereign Lord is bigger than he is and that he alone rules and reigns. John Piper says that 'God bends our stiff necks and pushes our face to the ground because that is where the streams of life are flowing.' Nebuchadnezzar has no one to blame but himself.

The biblical text is a sad and sorry tale of wasted opportunities and foolish choices. For a proud king with, literally, the world at his feet, he made the grass bed he now lies on. One man's reversal of fortune (Galatians 6:7). The one who thought he was superhuman became subhuman. It is pathetic. Even tragic. Sinclair Ferguson writes, 'The one who refused to honour God's glory loses his own glory. Refusing to share what he has with the poor, he becomes poorer than the poor. He becomes outwardly what his heart had been spiritually and inwardly—bestial.'

Nebuchadnezzar was smitten with an illness which resulted in him walking on all fours, eating grass like an ox, living with animals in an open field, alienated from society, and abandoned to the elements of high and low temperatures in summer and winter. Within a period of time he was unkempt and unrecognisable for his matted hair and non-manicured nails were bird-like. Kenneth Gangel says, 'He looked like an ox, and he ate like an ox; the grand and glorious king became a repulsive animal.'

There has been much speculation among commentators about the nature of what afflicted Nebuchadnezzar's mind. In preparation for this chapter, I was in email communication with a couple of friends, Julie and Liron, both of whom are psychiatrists. They attribute this illness to God's intervention in Nebuchadnezzar's life and describe it, in medical terms, as 'an extremely serious delusional (psychotic) disorder.' An analysis of the biblical facts corresponds with their specialist diagnosis and explains the bizarre behaviour of Nebuchadnezzar when he believed himself to be an animal. On that hugely significant note, the prophecy of his dream was thus fulfilled (Daniel 4:15-16).

The narrative does not tell us who stepped up to the plate and ran the show when Nebuchadnezzar was sidelined for seven years. Presumably, it was the first secretary of state or prime minister who stood in the breach and that points to God's faithful servant, Daniel. We know that Nebuchadnezzar's son, Evil-Merodach, did not take command during that time. You see, God has his people in the most unlikely of places for the most unusual of times.

4:34-37

Sanity restored

At the end of the days I, Nebuchadnezzar, lifted my eyes to heaven, and my reason returned to me, and I blessed the Most High, and praised and honoured him who lives forever, for his dominion is an everlasting dominion, and his kingdom endures from generation to generation; all the inhabitants of the earth are accounted as nothing, and he does according to his will among the host of heaven and among the inhabitants of the earth; and none can stay his hand or say to him, 'What have you done?'

At the same time my reason returned to me, and for the glory of my kingdom, my majesty and splendour returned to me. My counsellors and my lords sought me, and I was established in my kingdom, and still more greatness was added to me. Now I, Nebuchadnezzar, praise and extol and honour the King of heaven, for all his works are right and his ways are just; and those who walk in pride he is able to humble.

The first thirty-three verses of Daniel 4 illustrate that God resists the proud, but these last four verses demonstrate that he also gives grace to the humble (Proverbs 3:34; James 4:6). For Nebuchadnezzar, hubris must give way to humiliation. A total of eight years since he first dreamed that dream, the king is now in a much better place. His eyes are opened. The mental fog has lifted. In the palace he was looking around like a fool, then he spent seven years in the field looking down like an animal, and now he is looking up for salvation (Psalm 121:1-2). His reason was restored; his reputation was restored; and his reign was restored. As an aside, this is a parable of God's covenant people who at first were blessed by him with the promised land, then exiled for seven decades because of their unfaithfulness and then, because of his grace and power, were once more restored to their homeland.

He learned the lesson he needed to learn, and in the process, he discovered that the God who disciplines is the same God who delivers. 'We have a choice between being humble and being humbled,' writes C H Spurgeon. That is what Nebuchadnezzar proved (Jeremiah 9:23-24). The king does justice to the sovereignty of God because he sings about it. He first ponders this magnificent truth, then bursts forth in eloquent praise for it. His soul delights in it, he is resting on it. His ascription of joyous praise to the Most High is breathtakingly beautiful in every way as he acknowledges the Godship of God. God does what he does because he is who he is. *Heaven rules* is his anthem of worship.

He recognised the eternality and covenant faithfulness of God. He respected the ongoing sovereign rule of God on earth and in heaven for God reigns down here, not merely up there. He realised the nothingness of sinful man and his total dependence upon God. He rejoiced in the matchless grace of God to salvage every situation to his glory. He found out to his enormous pleasure that there was stability in God's truth and ability in his higher throne.

The closing words of his most moving testimony show the reality of what he actually experienced. With more than a sprinkling of undiluted joy in his God and King, he realises that the God whose works and ways are perfect is the same God who gets it right first time, every time (Deuteronomy 32:4).

He continues without hesitation to affirm that God gets what he wants when he humbles all those who are consumed with pride—an application of the Peter principle, where we read, 'Humble yourselves, therefore, under God's mighty hand, that he may lift you up in due time' (1 Peter 5:6, NIV). That, in itself, is a sovereign work of grace and a ministry in which our God is the divine specialist. God did it, not by boosting him up, but by knocking him down. The way up is down (Luke 18:14; Philippians 2:5-11).

The God who felled him, flattened him, and floored him, is the same God who freed him, and forgave him. As Stuart Olyott says, 'If he can crack a nut like Nebuchadnezzar, who will prove to be too difficult for him?'

These words of praise were not culled from Isaiah, David, Jeremiah, or even Moses. They came from the lips of a pagan king who at one time fancied himself as the true king of the world. Now, because of God's intervention in his life, he worshipped

God as the True King. Think about it: in today's world, such an affirmation would be comparable to the G7 (the Group of Seven world leaders), at the end of their annual summit, singing a hymn of praise to the triune God, acknowledging that he is the True King over all things. Not them. But God!

Chuck Colson (1931-2012) tells how he climbed the ladder of power and prestige to become the Special Counsel to the President of the United States of America. He was filled with pride as he walked in and out of the office of the most powerful man in the world any time he wanted. That most powerful man was seeking advice from him, and Colson's heart swelled with pride. He was known as Nixon's hatchet man.

That was when he became involved in the Watergate affair of the Nixon administration. John Dean blew the whistle in 1973, and Colson soon found himself a convicted criminal doing time in a federal penitentiary. He was so humiliated that he lifted up his eyes to the King of heaven and gave his life to Jesus Christ. He admitted that the worst, most humiliating experience in his life was the best thing that ever happened to him. Can it be that when we realise God is so big, we finally see how small we are?

Nebuchadnezzar knows what he means and would say an ebullient amen to that. One of the biggest challenges we all face as the people of God is to finish life's race, and to finish well. Nebuchadnezzar did. Thank God. Graham Scroggie writes, 'There is nothing ... more sublime than this testimony of Nebuchadnezzar's. To him light came at eventide, and he turned his throne into a pulpit, and his State papers into sermons.' What an exit for Nebuchadnezzar! The final words recorded on the pages of Scripture from this Babylonian king give praise to the God of Israel. May we be found to do the same.

5

GRAFFITI ON THE WALL

From the year dot or time immemorial, public walls, motorway bridges, underground train stations, toilets, billboards, and wherever else, have been used to communicate various ideas ranging from political dissent to love messages to purely artistic endeavours. Some of it is eye-catchingly beautiful and we smile when we see it—it is appealing; sadly, there is a dark side for some of it is obscenely vulgar which we find disgustingly awful—it is appalling. Next time you are out and about, take a walk or drive through an average-size town, and before you have travelled too far, you will be introduced to an alfresco art exhibition without ever setting foot in a gallery.

'Our own culture,' writes O S Hawkins, former senior pastor of First Baptist Church, Dallas, 'has expanded and enhanced this age-old art form we commonly refer to as graffiti.' The word *graffiti* finds its origin in ancient Rome. It is the plural of *graffito*, which means 'to scratch.' It traces its roots away back to various inscriptions and drawings found on the walls of the ruins of ancient Pompeii and Rome around 50 BC.

In a culture where communication is at a premium, graffiti is a worldwide phenomenon with the internet its playground. It is global in its influence. Who of us can forget the tearing down, one brick at a time, of the Berlin Wall on 9 November 1989? That was only a beginning before it was fully demolished, paving the way for Germany to be reunited on 3 October 1990. As we watched events unfolding on our television screens, it was amazing to see the graffiti on the western side of the wall. For years, this 13-feet high, 96-miles long wall bore messages of aspiration to the world of a long hoped-for freedom.

A divine graffiti artist is actively at work in this chapter. In order to see what he wrote, we must retrace our steps beyond Pompeii and Rome and keep going a further five centuries back on our timeline to walk inside the marble-floored banqueting hall of the royal palace in Babylon. The writing on the plaster wall—a message of doom and gloom—prefaced the historic moment when the curtain came down for the last time on a global empire and Babylon, to quote Dale Ralph Davis, 'dropped through the trapdoor into the nether regions of history.' The end. Period. Just like the prophets said it would be (Isaiah 21:1-10; Jeremiah 51:34-37, 54-57).

5:1-4

Monarchical meanderings

King Belshazzar made a great feast for a thousand of his lords and drank wine in front of the thousand. Belshazzar, when he tasted the wine, commanded that the vessels of gold and of silver that Nebuchadnezzar his father had taken out of the temple in Jerusalem be brought, that the king and his lords, his wives, and his concubines might drink from them. Then they brought in the

golden vessels that had been taken out of the temple, the house of
God in Jerusalem, and the kings and his lords, his wives, and his
concubines drank from them. They drank wine and praised the
gods of gold and silver, bronze, iron, wood, and stone.

The previous chapter ended on a thrillingly high note of worshipful praise with King Nebuchadnezzar rejoicing in God's extraordinary grace in his life. Twenty-three years later and this chapter is diametrically opposite; it is a culture shock as it reveals what often happens in the upper echelons of high society, a place where God is neither welcomed nor wanted and, indeed, where God is totally excluded and left out in the cold. As David Pawson says, 'The message of Daniel 5 is very simple: God has no grandsons. Godliness cannot be inherited from generation to generation.' Correct. This chapter is, therefore, both a rude and crude awakening.

And the man at the helm is Belshazzar, someone we have not come across before in the Daniel narrative. He comes out of nowhere. As Sinclair Ferguson points out, 'The drama of God's dealings with Belshazzar (Bel-sar-usur) is heightened by the fact that he appears and disappears in the space of a single chapter.' The questions are: Who was he? How did he arrive on the scene? To be honest, it is a rather convoluted storyline, fascinating nonetheless.

The famed and famous Nebuchadnezzar died in 562 BC after ruling an expansive empire for forty-three years. His son, Evil-Merodach (562-560 BC), followed his father on the throne. He is mentioned in 2 Kings 25:27-30 and Jeremiah 52:31-34 as one who released Jehoiachin from prison and gave him a place of privilege in the Babylonian court. He reigned until he was assassinated in a coup in August 560 BC by his brother-in-law,

General Neriglissar. I cannot imagine what their family reunions looked like! He is mentioned in Jeremiah 39:11-14 under the name of Nergal-Sharezer. He was an official under Nebuchadnezzar, who apparently was involved in helping Jeremiah be released from prison. He had a shortish tenure of around four years and was succeeded by his son, Labashi-Marduk. Babylonian folklore would tell you that the gods were not smiling on him as he was savagely beaten to death by his friends within nine months and one of the key conspirators, Nabonidus, then became king (556-539 BC).

It seems that Nabonidus was not overly enthusiastic about kingship being foisted upon him; the chances are he was planted there as a compromise candidate by the plotters. Some think that his eldest son Belshazzar was the real mover and shaker behind the wheeler dealers and that he was pulling all the strings. When Nabonidus was invited to relocate (to coin a phrase) to Tema, an oasis in the North Arabian desert, five hundred miles from Babylon, because of his religious beliefs, as he worshipped a rival god to the supremo, Marduk, his son Belshazzar became his co-regent, a kind-of proxy king. We cannot be sure, but in all probability his mother was a daughter of Nebuchadnezzar; and according to John Walvoord, 'this explains why Belshazzar in the lineal descent from Nebuchadnezzar was honoured as a co-ruler under Nabonidus.' He operated as *de facto* king in Babylon for over a decade and that is why we bump into him in the manner we do without any formal introduction or personal bio in verse 1.

Chapter chronology

Before we unpack the teaching in chapter 5, it is important for us to realise that between chapters 4 and 5 Daniel has been busily occupied with affairs of state as well as receiving and writing prophecies. Even in advanced years, the pensioner Daniel is active in the work to which God has called him. The lesson is, we are never too old to serve the Lord. The hymn is spot-on when it says, 'There's a work for Jesus none but you can do.' For example, the vision of the four beasts was revealed to Daniel *in the first year of Belshazzar* (Daniel 7:1), and the vision of the ram and male goat occurred *in the third year of the reign of King Belshazzar* (Daniel 8:1).

Wine, women, and worship

The story of Belshazzar's feast is one of the most famous parts of the book of Daniel. It is one that the majority of us are familiar with since childhood or teenage years. Over the years many evangelistic sermons have been preached from it and they have often been connected with the foolish farmer in the gospels, where the parting shot is, 'You fool! This very night your life will be demanded from you' (Luke 12:13-21, NIV). It has been painted by no less a star than Rembrandt in the late 1630s and can be viewed in London's National Gallery; it was set to music in a cantata by the English composer William Walton and first performed at the Leeds Festival on 8 October 1931. Much later in 1957, country singer Johnny Cash, the man with a gravelly voice, sang *Belshazzar* as his first gospel song on an album recorded in Memphis.

The state banquet, full of pomp and circumstance, was held in the magnificent banqueting hall of the royal palace with its hanging candelabra in a special tiered alcove, marble pillars carved into the form of elephants, and a variety of paintings and artefacts gracing the room. Trained peacocks dressed in a gold and silver trimmed harness drew miniature chariots around the room filled with goblets of wine. When archaeologists excavated the site in modern times they discovered that the huge ballroom where the party was held was some 60 feet wide and 172 feet long.

It was probably a valiant attempt on the king's part to bolster the flagging morale of his cronies by reminding them of his perceived invincibility and the city's impregnability, as well as a psychological ploy to give the impression that life was going on as normal even though Cyrus and his troops were lurking at the back door. Why worry if the city is under siege? There was enough food stored away to feed the population for twenty years. To make matters worse, as Jerry Vines portrays, 'Like a sleeping lion with a spider weaving its web around him, he was oblivious to his imminent danger.' He was indifferent to the danger posed by the enemy army and insensitive to the emotional needs of his people. This last night of an empire is a haunting reminder of the poignant scenes garnered from the sinking Titanic where the band goes on playing while the ship is sinking.

The occasion was outlandish in many respects—in ceremony, content, and celebration this was the night of all nights, the party of all parties. This one promised to outshine and outdo every other party in living memory in the kingdom. And it did! For all the wrong reasons.

A night on the town

Take one look at the guest list for it was one VIP after another. They would jostle each other just to be near the king at the top table. This was a black-tie event for the upper crust of high society. These were the top brass, the gentry, and the well-heeled among the people. A sizable complement, one would think. However, according to archaeological records, this was small-time stuff. It pales into insignificance when compared to some of the Persian monarchs who dined daily with 15,000 guests at a meal. When Alexander the Great was married there were 10,000 invited guests to the marriage dinner. One more and this guy beats them all hands down: it involves Ashurnasirpal II in 879 BC who threw a banquet for 69,754 guests when he dedicated his new capital city of Calah (Nimrud).

Thirty-six-year-old Belshazzar, royal party animal that he is, led the way when it came to alcohol consumption or, perhaps, alcohol abuse might be a better expression. This was no wine and cheese party for we read that *he drank wine in front of the thousand*; there is more to that detail than initially meets the eye. It means that he was acting like a showman hogging the limelight and loving every minute. He drinks himself under the table as a sign of his bravado. No doubt, the nobility egged him on, and playing to the gallery from his elevated platform, he responded inappropriately as we shall see (Proverbs 31:4-5).

Having drunk himself into a woeful state of inebriation, this scum of a man barked an order for the holy vessels to be brought into the hall. These were the sanctified goblets that had been taken from the temple in Jerusalem and brought back to Babylon to be put on display in the king's cabinet of priceless items from afar (Daniel 1:2). Herman Veldkamp offers a modern metaphor, when he writes, 'We might compare it to a group of drunks stealing the church's communion set in order to drink from its glasses at their favourite bar. It's a wonder that Belshazzar and the other revellers didn't choke on the wine, that no one was struck dead.'

The wine flowed freely. The revellers gorged with food. The music stirred the emotions. Passions were high. And it was not too long before the evening turned into a drunken orgy of debauched excess where anything and everything of a sensual nature took place. Unquestionably, there was lewd sexual behaviour as a bevy of most beautiful women, aka high-dollar concubines, from the royal harem were conspicuous by their presence (in the East, women were usually in strict seclusion). Their presence was actually a violation of royal protocol (Esther 1:2-3, 9).

There was sacrilege as they blatantly and defiantly drank alcohol from the holy vessels which represented the presence and power of God, thereby mocking the Holy One of Israel (Exodus 30:26-29). That is when the cocky, hard drinker Belshazzar, smirking with insolence, led the guests in drinking toasts to their deities. Sinclair Ferguson perfectly sums him up when he notes that 'his heart was a factory of rebellion against God.' Irreverent profanity was prevalent.

It was a few hours of sin, more sin, and much more sin. Raucous revelry, bombastic blasphemy, and carousing carnality, and they really believed they were having a fantastic time in this upmarket night club. Pride. Perversion. Promiscuity. A great night out at a sinkhole of indulgence, they thought! At someone else's expense too. Little did they know what awaited them.

Unlike Nebuchadnezzar whose long list of achievements is legendary, it seems that the only thing Belshazzar is renowned for is that he throws a jolly good party. The playboy prince comes out of this night of shame looking like a crazy, arrogant fool. A monarch by name, he is acting here like a stupid moron who is marked by intemperance, impropriety, impiety, and idolatry; a man of very few inhibitions especially after a drinking bout. As Dale Ralph Davis writes, 'Belshazzar was not simply a drunken slob but a profane slob.' We can be assured that he has done himself no favours and earned himself no brownie points in the all-seeing eyes of a thrice-holy God. No person, be they king or pauper, can sin and win (Ezekiel 18:20).

Enough is enough

Belshazzar who was headstrong in his rebellion had ample scope to sort his life out, but he dug his heels in and spurned every God-given opportunity. He chose not to humble himself before a holy God, and paid a high price for his crass arrogance where he reckoned he was one better than God. In so doing, and he has only himself to blame, he was written out of God's saving plan for God had had enough of him (Genesis 6:3). Instead of tip-toeing around sin, he went for it like the proverbial bull in a china shop. He repeatedly spits in the face of God. The decadent and dissolute Belshazzar stepped over the line with his in-your-face disregard for the worship, works, and Word of God. The hymnwriter Joseph Alexander (1809-60) penned these words, 'There is a time we know not when, a point we know not where, That marks the destiny of men to glory or despair; There is a line, by us unseen, that crosses every path, The hidden boundary between God's patience and his wrath.'

God deals with us as individuals; with him, there is no one size fits all. That is why we dare not presume upon the grace and mercy that God has shown to others and think he will do the same for us. Scary thought. The wisdom of Solomon is apt, 'Disaster will overtake him in an instant; he will suddenly be destroyed – without remedy' (Proverbs 6:15, NIV). When that happens to any man or woman who does not have a personal relationship with Jesus Christ as their Lord and Saviour, there is no way back, as Esau found out too late in Hebrews 12:17.

We are confronted here with the twin towers of justice and judgment, both attributes of a sovereign God. As Rodney Stortz says, 'As Yahweh got the attention of the Philistines by knocking the god Dagon off his pedestal (1 Samuel 5:7), he got the attention of Belshazzar and knocked him off his pedestal too.' Bryan Chapell is right when he says, 'There is no human wall so high, no human fortress so secure, no activity so hidden that it can protect sin from the wrath of God.' A timely reminder that from Nebuchadnezzar to Nero of Rome and on to the killing fields of Pol Pot of Cambodia, from Belshazzar to Mao of China and to Idi Amin of Uganda, pagan rulers have defied God. But the Lord of heaven always wins. His plan is unstoppable.

5:5-6

A hand from heaven

Immediately the fingers of a human hand appeared and wrote on the plaster of the wall of the king's palace, opposite the lampstand. And the king saw the hand as it wrote. Then the king's colour changed, and his thoughts alarmed him; his limbs gave way, and his knees knocked together.

One minute, Belshazzar has a golden goblet in his hand filled with the best Babylonian red wine and he is raising a toast to little gods; next minute, he is sobered up when he sees what looked like a human hand writing four words on one of the white plastered walls, illuminated by a lampstand. Once again the God of heaven offered a kind-of PowerPoint presentation in public. This was a Keynote presentation like no other, before or since. Stuart Olyott says that 'the royal wall resembles a gravestone, and the whole company has seen the epitaph being engraved upon it.'

This same finger of God had written before and will do so again. When God sent the plague of gnats upon Egypt, Pharaoh's counsellors recognised that 'this [was] the finger of God' (Exodus 8:19). It was the finger of God that wrote the Decalogue for Israel on the two tablets of stone (Exodus 31:18). Jesus said that he drove out demons 'with the finger of God' (Luke 11:20), referring to the power of the Spirit of God (Matthew 12:28). Another incident is when Jesus dealt with the woman taken in adultery, and we read that 'Jesus bent down and started to write on the ground with his finger' (John 8:6, NIV). Right here, the same finger of God is writing a warning to Belshazzar and Babylon that judgment was imminent (Job 20:4-7). As David Helm writes, '… strange fingers appear. They prepare to answer his toast with text.'

To this day, in the course of conversation we often use the cliché—the handwriting on the wall—to refer to unchangeably bad news. Sometimes sinister. Always negative. This is where that colloquialism originated.

The biblical principle is that 'God is not mocked' (Galatians 6:7, NASB). There is only one winner in such a face-off, and it is not sinful man. It is God! The timing of the divine response to Belshazzar's provocation is immaculate and designed to cause maximum discomfort to the king and his drinking pals. It succeeds! No one affronts or insults the Most High. A holy, righteous, angry God is determined to set the record straight. And he does!

Shocked to the core and shaken out of his wits—in a state of apoplexy—Belshazzar's countenance changed colour to a pallid shade so that he was ashen and anaemic looking. He was drained. His mind goes into overdrive as he tries to rationalise all that he sees in front of him, but he struggles to make any sense of it. His arms go into limp mode and his legs go from under him (Nahum 2:10). He buckles. Even his knees are banging against each other. In fact, the Aramaic conveys the idea that he lost control of his bodily functions, with a wet patch appearing under his chair. How embarrassing! Belshazzar is so terrified he is like a rabbit caught in the glare of a car's Xenon headlights. His heart was beating so fast that his chest was heaving up and down. His blood pressure has rocketed. His pulse is racing. He is rattled. Unnerved. Belshazzar is petrified and completely undone. Paranoia has gripped him and is leaving him in a state of paralysis where he just feels so helpless. And he is.

The monarch, who just happens to be a man made of the same material as the rest of us, is a total nervous wreck. This is serious. Extremely serious. Ligon Duncan says that 'this man goes from a break with reality to a check with reality.' Unbeknown to him, Belshazzar has become the latest victim of the divine 'gotcha' as is clearly implied in Psalm 2:4-5, where we read, 'The One enthroned in heaven laughs; the Lord scoffs at them. Then he rebukes them in his anger and terrifies them in his wrath' (NIV).

5:7-9

All the king's men

The king called loudly to bring in the enchanters, the Chaldeans, and the astrologers. The king declared to the wise men of Babylon, 'Whoever reads this writing, and shows me its interpretation, shall be clothed with purple and have a chain of gold around his neck and shall be the third ruler in the kingdom.' Then all the king's wise men came in, but they could not read the writing or make known to the king the interpretation. Then King Belshazzar

was greatly alarmed, and his colour changed, and his lords were
perplexed.

The nineteenth-century German philosopher Hegel once said that the only thing we have learned from history is that we have learned nothing from history. So, like Nebuchadnezzar many times before him, Belshazzar's holler for help reaches the ears of the wise men. The same old losers. They are like broken cisterns that hold no water (Jeremiah 2:13). As John MacArthur says, tongue in cheek, 'These guys couldn't put Humpty Dumpty together again.' We have been down this well-worn path so often before and their track record, according to the biblical text, is nothing to write home about. I think, for many of us, if we had been paying their salary we would have shown them the exit door long ago!

These first responders who were prominent in their time are repeatedly dragged into the high-octane drama of chapters one thru five, only to be shamed and shown as utterly impotent and unreliable. They are hugely influential on many fronts but, in the final critical analysis, they are inconsequential men of the world who can never explain the mind and will of God (1 Corinthians 2:14). Not all are wise who are labelled as such! A lesson we need to learn is echoed by the psalmist, when he advises, 'Don't put your confidence in powerful people; there is no help for you there.... But happy are those who have the God of Israel as their helper, whose hope is in the Lord their God. He is the one who made heaven and earth, the sea, and everything in them' (Psalm 146:3, 5-6, NLT).

In an act of sheer desperation, Belshazzar offers no threats, but a threefold reward of honour, wealth, and status to the person who could accurately decipher the writing on the white gypsum wall. One, they would be clothed with purple, the symbol of royalty and power among Babylonians, Medes, Persians, and Greeks; two, a chain of gold would be placed around their neck as a symbol of high office in government; and, three, they would be promoted to third ruler in the kingdom, bearing in mind that Nabonidus was first and Belshazzar was second.

This was God speaking directly to Belshazzar and he did not understand a word of what was written. He racked his brain but, worryingly, it did not make any sense at all. A silent, supernatural message that spoke so loud and so clear was Double Dutch to the king. Neither was anyone in the banqueting hall able to decode the hieroglyphics. They were all baffled.

And, not surprisingly, the wise men with all their expertise and experience were in the same boat as they failed to deliver the goods. Even though the rewards were high, they just could not unravel the mystery on the wall. All his props are gone. No more crutches to lean on, and in the words of Dale Ralph Davis, Belshazzar 'is reduced to a shivering, sniffling mess with no supports whatever.' Never, never trifle with God. Now, Belshazzar is really frightened and his face turns whiter than a white Egyptian cotton sheet with a look of stark terror. His reaction is contagious for the assembled partygoers are bemused, bewildered, and befuddled too. God scared the living daylights out of them!

5:10-16

Enter Daniel the octogenarian

The queen, because of the words of the king and his lords, came into the banqueting hall, and the queen declared, 'O king, live forever! Let not your thoughts alarm you or your colour change. There is a man in your kingdom in whom is the spirit of the holy gods. In the days of your father, light and understanding and wisdom like the wisdom of the gods were found in him, and King Nebuchadnezzar, your father – your father the king – made him chief of the magicians, enchanters, Chaldeans, and astrologers, because of an excellent spirit, knowledge, and understanding to interpret dreams, explain riddles, and solve problems were found in this Daniel, whom the king named Belteshazzar. Now let Daniel be called, and he will show the interpretation.' Then Daniel was brought in before the king. The king answered and said to Daniel, 'You are that Daniel, one of the exiles of Judah, whom the king my father brought from Judah. I have heard of you that the spirit of the gods is in you, and that light and understanding and excellent wisdom are found in you. Now the wise men, the enchanters, have been brought in before me to read this writing and make known to me its interpretation, but they could not show the interpretation of the matter. But I have heard that you can give interpretations and solve problems. Now if you can read the writing and make known to me its interpretation, you shall be clothed with purple and have a chain of gold around your neck and shall be the third ruler in the kingdom.'

Here we have a time-honoured scenario: when all else fails, listen to the advice of a woman, even more so if she is your mother or grandmother or some other matriarchal figure in the family tree. The text refers to her as the queen, but Belshazzar's wives were all accounted for as they were at the big bash in the palace, partying with everyone else. It is likely a reference to the Queen Mother who was the widow of the late Nebuchadnezzar. In this drama she has a walk-on role to play, but no less important for that. She is similar to Nabal's unnamed servant in 1 Samuel 25:14-17 and Mrs Naaman's Israelite servant girl in 2 Kings 5:2-3. Anonymous in the biblical record she may be, but known to the Author of the book she definitely is.

As the dowager queen she would have lived in one of the state apartments, probably fairly close to the banqueting hall. Whatever, in the late night air, she must have heard the commotion and the hullabaloo from within, but she sensed with a sixth sense that something was not just quite right. Because of who she was, and the esteem with which she was held, she had free access to the banqueting hall and everywhere else within the palace precincts.

After giving the king a firm but cordial talking-to, she got straight down to business and informed him all about Daniel with the paraphrased words, 'I know a man you don't know, but whom you ought to know, who can tell you what the writing on the wall is all about!' Based on her intimate experience, she proceeded to fill in the blanks in his mind as to who Daniel was. She may have had her physical limitations because of age, but there is nothing wrong with her memory.

Others forgot all about Daniel, his name was barely mentioned now in the corridors of power, but one person remembered and deeply appreciated what he did in days past. She called him by his Jewish name, his real name, not the Babylonian name. A small but sweet blessing in itself. In a lot of ways he is like Mordecai in the book of Esther. You will recall he uncovered a plot to kill Xerxes, the king. He duly brought it to the attention of the authorities and they saved him (Esther 2:21-23). Mordecai did what he did because it was right in the eyes of God. That act by one man was buried in the minutes of the royal court records and he went unappreciated and unnoticed for many years (Esther 6:1-

3, 10:2-3). And that is so similar to what we read of right here in the book of Daniel.

In our life and ministry, it is essential that we thank God for that one person because they do make a mega difference. Even surpassing that, God knew where he was and knew where to find him when he was needed. How encouraging that is for us too, that the ageless God never forgot his elderly servant. The God who fashioned him did not look at his date of birth and conclude that Daniel had outlived his usefulness. No! He did not cast him off as though he were a worn out garment. As we shall see, Daniel's bit part has ginormous consequences for one man and his kingdom.

She knew all about Daniel having seen from close quarters how God used him during the long reign of her husband. She has a fond recollection of him as he frequently revealed and interpreted Nebuchadnezzar's dreams and made sense of his visions. She knew him to be a person of utmost integrity as he loyally served alongside her husband as his right-hand man. She was also very aware of the positive influence he had on her husband in his later years and especially in the lead-up to his conversion experience. His reputation goes before him. Thank God, he was all that he was reputed to be. The question is: Are we? It is fascinating to note that Daniel was not invited to the banquet, but when a crisis hit, he was the one summoned to save the day. We must never underestimate the power of a godly life and a life lived to the glory of God.

David Jeremiah makes the point that in her eyes, Daniel 'was significant, spiritual, superior, and skilful.' The queen believed Daniel had three virtues: one, he knew God personally; two, he was one to whom God often spoke; and, three, he was one through whom God communicated to others. With a glowing commendation like that, Belshazzar would be downright crazy not to take on board her sound advice. Sure, but Josephus, the first century historian, wrote that Belshazzar did not want to consult Daniel and the queen had to literally beg the king to send for him. And he did.

William Barclay tells a story about T E Lawrence, the archaeologist, diplomat, and writer, dubbed *Lawrence of Arabia* for his part in leading the Bedouin tribes in a successful revolt against their Turkish oppressors during the First World War. He was a close personal friend of Thomas Hardy, the poet, and would frequently visit Hardy and his wife. During the time Lawrence was serving as an aircraftsman in the Royal Air Force he sometimes came to visit the Hardy home wearing his aircraftsman's uniform. On one such occasion his visit overlapped with a visit of the Mayoress of Dorchester. The latter took it as an affront that she had to meet a common aircraftsman; she had no idea who the aircraftsman was. In French she told Mrs Hardy that never in all her born days had she had to sit down to tea with a private soldier. No one said anything, until T E Lawrence responded in perfect French, 'I beg your pardon, Madame, but can I be of any use as an interpreter? Mrs Hardy knows no French.' Someone she had looked down upon was the only one who could help her. Dale Ralph Davis writes, 'That is the case in Daniel 5: the only help for Belshazzar was a cast-off Jew whose God he despised.' Here we are today and the message that changes lives and eternal destinies remains the same, that Christ is the answer to our every need (1 Corinthians 1:22-24). Jesus saves.

'Ah, you must be Daniel ...!'

Reading between the lines of Belshazzar's opening comment, it appears that Daniel has been sidelined during his term of office and that he was like a minor royal with a minimal role to play (Daniel 8:27). The same tale has been repeated over and over again for many of us when a change of management follows the dictum of 'a new brush sweeps clean.' However, that is only one half of the popular maxim; the second half says, 'but an old brush knows the corners' meaning that experience is invaluable and cannot be bought online from Amazon or straight off a shelf in a High Street hypermarket. Belshazzar implemented the first with zeal and enthusiasm; now he needs to swallow his pride, eat humble pie, embrace the second, and bring Daniel out of semi-retirement.

When Daniel arrived, as cool as a cucumber, it seems to me that the king did not give him the respect which he deserved. Belshazzar comes across in his opening remarks as someone who is cynical and condescending in his tone of voice to the Lord's servant. He did not waste much time as he related the events of the evening to him in relation to the writing on the wall, being careful to mention that the wise men could not help out. Maybe Daniel managed a soft smile at that point and thought to himself, 'I could have told you so!' He offered Daniel the same reward package he had previously offered to all and sundry. God's man, Daniel, brusquely told him to forget his bag of goodies, that he was not in the least bit interested. So far as Daniel was concerned, *quid pro quo* was a non-starter. He worked for God, not gold.

Such a firm refusal on Daniel's part is reminiscent of the prophet Elisha's response to Naaman in 2 Kings 5:1-19. Daniel and Elisha, like every true servant of God, were not interested in lining their own pockets or making a name for themselves; all that mattered to them was the honour of God's name and the furtherance of his kingdom. Along with these two giants, there is Moses (Numbers 16:15), Samuel (1 Samuel 12:3), and Paul (Acts 20:33), among others, who have not bowed the knee to this god. Such principles should colour every aspect of our life and ministry in the twenty-first century.

I mean, what does a man of Daniel's vintage want with a purple robe and a golden chain? Furthermore, when Nebuchadnezzar was on the throne, Daniel was second in command, why would he now accept a demotion to third place? Once again, the godly character of Daniel shines through; in the real-world politics of power and sleaze, the white-haired Daniel is a person of real, refreshing integrity. He could not be bought with any bribe, at any price, at any time. We need men of his calibre—Spirit-filled men who are fearless, courageous, and truthful in their allegiance to God—in our society.

5:17-23

Preach it, brother

Then Daniel answered and said before the king, 'Let your gifts be for yourself, and give your rewards to another. Nevertheless, I will read the writing to the king and make known to him the interpretation. O king, the Most High God gave Nebuchadnezzar your father kingship and greatness and glory and majesty. And because of the greatness that he gave him, all peoples, nations, and languages trembled and feared before him. Whom he would, he killed, and whom he would, he raised up, and whom he would, he humbled. But when his heart was lifted up and his spirit was hardened so that he dealt proudly, he was brought down from his kingly throne, and his glory was taken from him. He was driven from among the children of mankind, and his mind was made like that of a beast, and his dwelling was with the wild donkeys. He was fed grass like an ox, and his body was wet with the dew of heaven, until he knew that the Most High God rules the kingdom of mankind and sets over it whom he will. And you his son, Belshazzar, have not humbled your heart, though you knew all this, but you have lifted up yourself against the Lord of heaven. And the vessels of his house have been brought in before you, and you and your lords, your wives, and your concubines have drunk wine from them. And you have praised the gods of silver and gold, of bronze, iron, wood, and stone, which do not see or hear or know, but the God in whose hand is your breath, and whose are all your ways, you have not honoured.'

Unlike the queen in her greetings to Belshazzar in verse 10, Daniel is radically different in what he has to say. He nowhere says, 'Long live the king' for he knows there is no point in giving him a false sense of security. Our friend Daniel does not believe in leading people down the garden path with sugar-coated niceties. He also confirms to the king what he can do with his well-intentioned gifts of bling and a shawl and a wee bit of power, they are not for him. I reckon you could hear a pin drop in that vast company when he turned down the king's reward. Wow. No matter how we look at it, that was probably the biggest snub the king had ever known. Fair play to Daniel, he said what he had to say, then he moved on ... but not to the writing on the wall, that could wait a few minutes longer. For the king, the clock seemed to be ticking too slowly.

John Lennox says that Daniel 'took the trembling potentate on a damning journey through the labyrinth of his mind, and showed him what the physical light of the lampstand ... had been unable to reveal.' Basically, Daniel gave Belshazzar a history lesson spanning a few decades as far back as one of his predecessors, Nebuchadnezzar. He traced his rise and fall and mentioned his sensational comeback after his time of humiliation. It was a career of many twists and turns, highs and lows. Nebuchadnezzar chose to ignore the fact that his power and authority were God-given. He selfishly took all the praise and credit to himself. He paraded himself before his citizens as if he was the be-all and end-all of God's creation.

For many long years he refused to bow his knees before the Most High. Ultimately, judgment fell, but because of the kindness of a merciful God it led to his conversion and a personal relationship with God. He had one of those light bulb moments near the end when he recognised that *the Most High God rules the kingdom of mankind*. One of those life stories which, thank God, ended well. It is not how we start the race that counts, it is how we finish and, sadly, too many fall out on the last lap. Not Nebuchadnezzar.

As thick as two short planks

Then boom, boom, boom and Daniel targeted Belshazzar with a salvo of truth which he did not want to hear. His rhetoric ratchets up now that the king is in the dock. 'I have no doubt that he meant to speak roughly to the ungodly Belshazzar, a man beyond hope,' writes John Calvin. Nebuchadnezzar was notoriously bad. No one argues with that assessment. Belshazzar, though, was a million times worse. This is a reminder of words once spoken when Dan Quayle was running as George H W Bush's vice-presidential candidate after he had alluded in a speech to John F Kennedy. 'Sir, I knew John Kennedy and I knew him well, and you are no John Kennedy.'

Certainly Belshazzar was no Nebuchadnezzar. No doubts there, because his condition was arguably more serious. He was acting like an upstart, guilty of being puffed up with self-important smugness. So patronising that, in his jaundiced opinion, he was at least ten or twelve feet above contradiction. He was implicated for wilfully sinning against revealed light and knowledge. In a spirit of daredevil, suicidal defiance Belshazzar rode roughshod over the law of God, treasured truth, when he engaged in idolatrous sacrilege and used the holy vessels for a booze-up. An example of premeditated sin. No fewer than a dozen times is Belshazzar accused of one thing or another with the words *you* and *your* heard like a rat-a-tat-tat from an Uzi submachine gun (Daniel 5:22-23).

All the time Belshazzar knew exactly what he was doing and would be held accountable for his barefaced actions. He should have known better and learned the salutary lessons from yesterday, but he failed. Acute, selective amnesia was his problem most of the time. It could be what C S Lewis called 'chronological snobbery' because the current generation always knows better than the past. Or they think they do! He knew the truth that might have saved him, but he stubbornly chose not to obey it. He did not take God seriously enough. He is dense. His conscience is silent. He did not ask for a history lesson, he got one. 'Those who cannot remember the past are condemned to repeat it,' wrote Spanish philosopher George Santayana, and Belshazzar ticked all the boxes.

Joe Kennedy, oldest son of Joseph P Kennedy and older brother of JFK, was slated for a bombing run on 12 August 1944. He was to fly a PB-24 Liberator, a plane designed to be loaded with high explosives then directed to its target via remote control after the pilot and co-pilot had bailed out. Before the time to depart, an electronics officer warned Joe that the remotely controlled electronic device that was to detonate the explosives was faulty. That meant that almost anything – radio static, a jamming device, turbulence – could set off an explosion before the crew could bail out. The officer urged Joe to abort the mission. Kennedy ignored the warning and flew anyway. The plane blew up at 6.20 p.m. over England. Both Kennedy and his co-pilot were blown out of the sky. As Dale Ralph Davis concludes, 'He knew, he was told, but it made no difference.' Sounds too close for comfort to Belshazzar.

I tell you, it was a powerful 'preach' as Daniel reminded this consummate hedonist of some vitally important issues; he did not mince his words in any shape or form when it came to confronting Belshazzar with the senseless folly of his ways. He nailed him more than once and left him squirming in the swirling sea of his own stupidity. Nothing milquetoast about that. As John Walvoord notes, 'He did not fear man, he feared only God.' Well done, Daniel.

We need men like that in our pulpits today; men who will stand tall and call sin for what it is and men who will faithfully proclaim that God has his finger on every man's pulse and who, as sovereign Lord, determines issues of life and death (Job 12:10). The God who holds the whole world in his hands is the same one who gives us every breath that we breathe. The message is that we ought to number our days (Psalm 90:12), lest God number them for us.

5:24-28

Heavenly hermeneutics

'Then from his presence the hand was sent, and this writing was inscribed. And this is the writing that was inscribed: Mene,

Mene, Tekel, and Parsin. This is the interpretation of the matter: Mene, God has numbered the days of your kingdom and brought it to an end; Tekel, you have been weighed in the balances and found wanting; Peres, your kingdom is divided and given to the Medes and Persians.'

David Helm writes, 'So Belshazzar has moved from wine in gold to blood run cold; and the preacher old and bold reaches a verdict to be told.' Four words on a wall. That was all. And even one of them was repeated! When God speaks, there is no need for verbosity or pious platitudes. He goes for the jugular with a straight-to-the-point message. God has plenty to say in that we have his mind revealed in Scripture from Genesis 1 to Revelation 22; but here in a Babylonian palace, he is a God of few words.

Mene. Mene. Tekel. Parsin. In Aramaic, no vowels, only consonants. Less than a handful of words from God and the party is over. The nation is on her last legs. The sun is about to set for the final time on a once great empire, just as predicted in the metallic statue dream (Daniel 2:36-39). No exaggeration, these are the closing hours of Belshazzar's life and he does not seem to grasp the gravity of a worsening situation.

Mene, the first word, is repeated so as to emphasise the salient message that it is. If it did not sink in first time, they would surely get it second time around. It means 'numbered' as in Leviticus 23:16 and Psalm 90:12. That is, the days of Belshazzar's Babylon were numbered by God and they were rapidly drawing to a close. No gloriously golden finale is promised, just an ignominious end. Within hours, his life's work and the legacy of Nebuchadnezzar would collapse like a pack of cards around his feet. Their number was up. Repeat. They are finished!

Tekel, the second word, means 'weighed' as in 1 Samuel 2:3 and Job 31:6. In that sense, Belshazzar had been weighed on the scales of divine justice and found lacking. The balance was the normal device used for measuring values of payment in that day. The amount of silver a person paid had to balance a designated standard weight. (Those of us of a certain vintage will recall something similar happening in the local greengrocer's shop.) The thought here is that Belshazzar was found too light in moral and spiritual worth to balance out God's gauge of holiness and righteousness. He was a liability to God. When measured against the searching light of God's critique, he is shallow, unconvincing, and flimsy!

Parsin, the third word, means 'divided.' That is, the entire kingdom would be taken from Belshazzar and given to the conquering Medes and Persians (Daniel 5:30-31). It does not imply that it would be split in two parts with one part for the Medes and the other part for the Persians. Rather, they would take all that was Babylon and absorb it into their still larger portfolio of annexed nations. As we shall see in the opening verse of the next chapter, a divided Babylon is inevitable when Darius implements his plan to carve it up into a number of administrative regions.

The handwriting was on the wall in a palace far away in Babylon, and it is inscribed on our wall today. It is not yet too late for us, even though time is fast running out. God is articulating his message loud and clear in the third millennium. He is not suffering from laryngitis. He has not lost his voice. He is still speaking right now at this moment of time, through his inspired Word proclaimed from the lips of his faithful servants. The challenge for us is: What do we do with what we hear from God?

5:29-31

And it came to pass

> *Then Belshazzar gave the command, and Daniel was clothed*
> *with purple, a chain of gold was put around his neck, and a*
> *proclamation was made about him, that he should be the third*
> *ruler in the kingdom. That very night Belshazzar the Chaldean*
> *king was killed. And Darius the Mede received the kingdom,*
> *being about sixty-two years old.*

In spite of the hard message he heard from God's servant, Daniel, the king kept his word and honoured Daniel, even though he did not want it at all. This was the last thing on his mind; in fact, truth be told, it was not even in his mind. His elevation to Number Three in the hierarchy was probably one of the shortest promotions in history, lasting only a matter of minutes. For Daniel, there was no mileage in causing a fuss; better to take the paraphernalia and be done with it, it was much ado about nothing for he knew that Belshazzar and Babylon were as good as gone.

On Wednesday 19 March 2003 Saddam Hussein and his sons, Uday and Qusay, invited a few of their close friends and advisors to have dinner with them in an exclusive restaurant in downtown Baghdad. They did this despite the fact than an invasion seemed imminent from the US forces that were amassing across the border in Kuwait. Saddam and his sons were used to the good life and they were not about to let the threat of war ruin an opportunity to party with their friends. But someone tipped off some of the American Special Forces troops who were already operating in the area and President Bush ordered a strategic strike. Saddam's dinner party came to an abrupt end when cruise missiles slammed into the building and completely demolished it. They survived this initial attack, but it was the beginning of the end for a brutal dictator who had ruled Iraq for thirty years.

Sound familiar? It should! For that is what happened on a larger scale in Babylon in October 539 BC. Cyrus knew from reconnaissance information that the defences of Babylon were as good as impregnable. Conventional means of warfare would never secure victory. There was just no way in to the city and no way over the top. So he deployed another action plan. He ordered his sappers to use a diversionary manoeuvre by rerouting the flow of the Euphrates River which went under the massively thick walls of the heavily fortified city. Once the water was shallow enough to be forded, his soldiers entered the river channel and walked underneath the walls straight into the unsuspicious city. Clever thinking. Smart tactics. Brilliant military strategy. And that was long before the world ever heard of such elite military training establishments as West Point in the USA and Sandhurst in the UK.

Needless to say, the Babylonians were caught napping. They were totally surprised. Before many of them knew what was happening, their beloved city had fallen to the enemy. The Medes and Persians gained control without a major battle being fought. Some of the storm troopers of the advancing army made directly for the royal palace to get their plum target, Belshazzar. As they dealt with the guards outside the palace gates, a great deal of noise ensued. Curiosity caused the king to order some of the internal sentries to go outside and investigate. As these men unwittingly opened the palace gates, a handful of elite soldiers rushed past them, through the open gates into the palace itself. They made a beeline for the banqueting hall. And they got their man!

When the music stops ...

Scripture records in a brief obituary, *That very night Belshazzar the Chaldean king was killed.* He died a gruesome and horrible death. What a last night for any man. He learned the hard way that God is the Most High. He never saw another sunrise. To spend your closing hours with the finger of God pointing directly at you is not the best way for any person to be launched into an eternity where there is no wine, no women, and no worship. A place of aloneness, consciousness, darkness, and separation. He died the way he lived, without God (Proverbs 29:1). Like King Saul (1 Samuel 28:25b), and Judas Iscariot (John 13:30), and the rich man (Luke 12:20). No sin goes unpunished, but when the sinner knows better, the punishment will be greater. Solemn stuff.

The hymnwriter expressed it well, when he wrote, 'How long might I go on in sin, How long will God forbear; Where does hope end and where begin, The confines of despair? The answer from the skies is sent – "Ye who from God depart, While it is called today, repent, And harden not your heart."'

These words are most instructive to every one of us and enormously challenging too. There is a last night for every nation and there is a last night for every individual. People need the Lord in today's world – our family and circle of friends, our neighbours and colleagues. We have a responsibility to share the gospel of God's grace with them, one person at a time, bearing in mind that there is a colossal difference between the endings of chapters four and five for Nebuchadnezzar repented of his sin and was wonderfully converted whilst Belshazzar refused to get right with God and died in his sins (Psalm 9:17).

Bishop J C Ryle of Liverpool wrote some perceptive words about the two men who died at Calvary alongside the Lord Jesus that are so applicable here, when he said, 'One was saved, so that no one need despair; and one was lost, so that no one dare presume.' That reflects a serious truth penned by Paul, when he wrote, 'Therefore God has mercy on whom he wants to have mercy, and he hardens whom he wants to harden' (Romans 9:18, NIV).

The chapter ends with an important historical observation for the *head of gold* was toppled by the *inferior chest and arms of silver* (Daniel 2:39), with a 62-year-old man at the helm. The end of an evil empire. Extraordinary. God said it would happen (Isaiah 13:17-22). And it did!

6

PRAYING BIG PRAYERS TO A BIG GOD

SIM (Serving in Mission) is an international mission with upwards of 4,000 people serving in gospel ministry in more than 70 countries around the world. It has a rich history of founders who journeyed to hard places to share the good news of Jesus Christ with people who were unreached, and in some cases, almost unreachable. These early pioneers blazed a trail for God in the regions beyond and God has spectacularly blessed their efforts in his name.

SIM began in 1893 when Canadians Walter Gowans and Roland Bingham along with American Thomas Kent had a vision and heavy burden to evangelise the 60-million least reached people of sub-Saharan Africa. No established mission at that time was willing to take the trio on board, so they set out by faith trusting God to get them there and then use them mightily.

It was not too long before illness overtook all three men. Gowans and Kent died of complications in 1894, and Bingham returned to Canada. On his second attempt, Bingham caught malaria again and was forced to return back home. Unable to return to Africa, Bingham sent out a third team who under God successfully established a ministry base about 500 miles inland at Patigi, Nigeria in 1902. From there, the work of SIM began in Africa.

The rest is history as SIM is now operating globally and is, in every sense, a ministry from everywhere to everywhere. For them, the 'mustard seed' principle holds true (Matthew 13:31-32). Speaking personally, it was a real honour and privilege for me to serve on the UK Board of Directors for thirty years and to also sit for two four-year terms on the international Board of Governors.

One of the distinctive marks of SIM from the earliest of days is their total commitment to prayer. Believing prayer. It is not just a statement of intent written on a paper document which is brought out every so often and dusted down; I am delighted to acknowledge that it is a daily practice at every level of the organisation. The strapline of SIM is crisp and concise, *By Prayer*. The third bullet point on their list of Core Values affirms: 'Prayer is foundational in our life and ministry. "By Prayer" we praise God, seek his direction, request resources, and call upon the Holy Spirit to empower our ministries.'

Sounds like something Daniel would write! He did not only talk about it, he did it. The children's chorus says it all, 'Daniel was a man of prayer, daily he prayed three times....' Here is one man who modelled prayer at all times and who faithfully led by example. He lived by prayer. Sure, he served in government, but prayer was his bread and butter. Unlike some of us who are like spiritual jellyfish, bobbing around on a tide of emotionalism, praying a little here and a little there as the waves of emotion rise and fall. Not Daniel. John Piper says, 'For Daniel, that meant a life of daring, defiant, and disciplined prayer.' We have so much to learn from God's servant on this vital matter.

6:1-3

A squeaky-clean politician

It pleased Darius to set over the kingdom 120 satraps, to be throughout the whole kingdom; and over them three high officials, of whom Daniel was one, to whom these satraps should give account, so that the king might suffer no loss. Then this Daniel became distinguished above all the other high officials and satraps, because an excellent spirit was in him. And the king planned to set him over the whole kingdom.

Babylon has fallen. Nations wax and wane, kingdoms rise and fall. Kings come and go. They all have their day until God has his say. God rules! And Daniel had a front row seat. In the unfolding purpose of a sovereign God we now come face to face with a brand new dynasty, the Medo-Persian empire, the second of four great world powers mentioned in the metallic statue image of Daniel 2:31-35 (still to follow in this timeline are Greece and Rome). This empire stretched all the way to the Atlantic Ocean past modern-day Libya, east towards India, and north towards Turkey.

Nebuchadnezzar's rule in Babylon was one of absolute monarchy for he was an autocrat. Power sharing was not even countenanced. He was boss, and everyone knew that. Woe betide anyone who thought different. End of story. Darius, however, a tad more amenable and reasonable and not as power-hungry, made some noticeable changes at the top. Perestroika and glasnost were around long before the 1980s and the arrival of Soviet leader Mikhail Gorbachev. It is clear that this is a well-organised, structured administration where, in modern-speak, there are 120 regional governors, who reported to three deputy ministers, who reported to one chief minister or prime minister with overall responsibility and oversight and answerable directly to the king. This is the Medo-Persian equivalent of decentralisation.

Accountability is important in every sphere of life. We are all ultimately answerable to God, but it is vital that we as believers have a band of individuals around us to whom we are personally accountable. Men and women who are not afraid to ask hard, searching questions of us. That is a safeguard for us, and when properly implemented, it certainly does not shackle or threaten us in any way. It frees us up to be the kind of people that God wants us to be so that we might effectively do what he wants us to do.

Right here, Darius is determined to eradicate bureaucratic bungling and waste at every level; it is also a bold attempt on his part to ensure that no one is siphoning off funds to their own bank account. Corruption is endemic in all cultures (to a greater or lesser degree) and is often prevalent among senior government officials. Darius is resolute in his commitment to wipe it out with his root and branch reform. Whether or not he succeeds is a matter up for debate, as we shall see in a few verses.

And veteran Daniel is there as well, occupying one of three deputy minister roles in the triumvirate within the government. Aside from anything else, it proves that there is a life that is fulfilling after turning 80 and even when, like Daniel, you are closer to 90 – Enoch, Abraham, Joseph, Moses, Joshua, Caleb, Simeon, Anna, and John, to name a random few from Scripture, would all concur with that assessment (Ruth 4:15; Isaiah 46:4). Indeed, sometimes our sunset years can be our most fruitful and flourishing years (Psalm 92:12-15). C S Lewis says, 'You are never too old to set a new goal or dream a new dream.' We thank God for seniors who serve faithfully and grow old gracefully in the church of Jesus Christ.

When 83, William Gladstone, for the fourth time, became Prime Minister of Great Britain. Michelangelo, at 89, executed his *Last Judgment*, perhaps the most famous single picture in the world. John Wesley preached with almost undiminished eloquence at 88, closing at that remarkable age the most exceptional career of his time, having travelled a quarter million miles in an age that knew neither electricity nor steam, and delivered upwards of 4,000 sermons and written volumes of books. The richness of age.

Such men and women are often wiser than the younger set who may have amassed a wealth of knowledge on their journey of faith and discovery. One look at Daniel and we quickly observe that he is a man of great wisdom. What is the difference between knowledge and wisdom? Knowledge is always giving the right answer to a question, wisdom is having the right attitude; knowledge is being parrot-like as it repeats back the truth, wisdom is being able to live out the truth on a daily basis; knowledge is knowing what to say, wisdom is knowing when to say it.

An elder statesman

In a modern democracy, a change of government from one ruling party to another is challenging because of all the stuff that is marked urgent sitting in the ministerial in-tray; most decent politicians in their less-guarded moments would admit that. Imagine what it must have been like in Daniel's day when it was a transition from one world power to another! That is a totally different ball game which calls for a different game plan.

Darius had it all worked out as to what he was going to do and featuring high on his agenda was the appointment of Daniel to a very senior role within government. Even here, the unseen hand of God is guiding Darius. Leon Wood writes that 'his appointment can only be explained on the basis of God's direct superintendence.' In fact, the king's eventual aim is to elevate Daniel from being one of three, to being number one—prime minister—over the entire kingdom.

In the midst of all that was going on around him in the corridors of power, Daniel conducted himself in such a way that he was without reproach in every area of his private and professional life (1 Timothy 3:2). He was equipped and enabled by the Most High to keep himself untainted and unspotted. Having learned to live as a pilgrim, Daniel's track record both at work and home was unblemished and unsullied. A faithful man (1 Corinthians 4:2), he had a sense of history as he had been in the upper echelons of power in the previous empire.

He comes across as someone whose disposition is bright and cheery and whose personality is warm and winsome. He gets jobs done and is happy to delegate responsibility to capable people around him. His attitude is upbeat and exemplary at all times. Daniel was a glowing example of a person with an upright character, unimpeachable honesty, and untarnished integrity. He is marked by transparency for he knew it was never right to do wrong and never wrong to do right. He holds down a high-pressured job near the top of government because of the help of God on a daily basis. Daniel is the ideal employee, he is every employer's dream. The unbelieving Darius recognised that. As O S Hawkins says, 'Not bad for a boy who started out as a captive and was plopped into a new world with a different language and an entirely different culture.'

Even though Daniel was a committed believer in the God of Abraham, Isaac, and Jacob, Darius did not appear to hold that against him in any way; if anything, it may have worked in his favour when the king overlooked the others and instead promoted Daniel. He knew he could trust him implicitly; he would not fiddle the books or endorse any clandestine deals, nor would he engage in any underhand behaviour which could potentially undermine the state and his leadership. Ligon Duncan says that 'Darius trusted Daniel from beginning to end, and even when Darius was caught in the trap of his own satraps, he never questioned the integrity of Daniel.'

6:4-5

Green-eyed colleagues

Then the high officials and the satraps sought to find a ground for complaint against Daniel with regard to the kingdom, but they could find no ground for complaint or any fault, because he was faithful, and no error or fault was found in him. Then these men said, 'We shall not find any ground for complaint against this Daniel unless we find it in connection with the law of his God.'

So much for Daniel's Civil Service workmates who are fanatically keen to pool their wits and resources in order to bring him down. They set aside their personal rivalries and dislikes in order to unitedly gang up on him, all 122 of them. Shame on them. The Puritan Thomas Brooks (1608-80) said, 'An envious heart and a plotting head are inseparable companions.' But that is the way it often is in the real world of employment where petty jealousy, envy, and resentment can rear its ugly head. Someone said that jealousy is the tribute that mediocrity pays to genius. So true in this instance. Iain Duguid writes, 'Daniel knew that we live in an exceedingly dangerous world, a world filled with lions, not all of whom are caged in pits.'

You can tell a lot about a person by the quality of his enemies; Daniel was a good man because he had the right kind of enemies. They do not like Daniel. They do not value or appreciate the truth that he stands for and the lifestyle that he follows. They have no respect for his faith and no admiration for his God. In their hearts, they know he is miles better at his job than they are at theirs for he out-performs them all the time, as the annual appraisals reveal. Maybe they see him as an unrelenting whistle-blower? It is the strongest warrior who is the target of the enemy's arrows. It is the ripest fruit that is pecked by the birds.

John MacArthur asks the questions, 'How could anybody hate Daniel? How could anybody despise a man who has done them no injury and caused them no harm?' But they did, on both counts. The world hates God's people and our enemy, a roaring lion, will do all in his power to bring us down (John 15:19; 1 Peter 5:8). Similar happened to preacher-man Paul when he found himself in a prison cell through no fault of his own (Philippians 1:12-18). Jesus knew all about it too for the same crowds who welcomed him and cheered for him on Palm Sunday cursed him and wanted him killed a few days later on Good Friday (John 12:12-15, 19:1-16).

Charles Schulz's very first *Peanuts* cartoon shows a boy and a girl sitting on some steps by a sidewalk. Another boy approaches them in the distance and boy says to girl, 'Well! Here comes ol' Charlie Brown!' Charlie passes in front of them and the same lad says, 'Good ol' Charlie Brown – Yes, sir!' After Charlie passes beyond earshot both boy and girl look after him, and boy says,

'Good ol' Charlie Brown … how I hate him!' Liked and loved one minute, loathed next minute. As God's people we cannot expect any different in this world; persecution is always on the cards (2 Timothy 3:12).

In spite of their ferocious and frantic efforts, they cannot nail anything on Daniel; his character and service is one hundred percent impeccable. The guy is innocent. No matter how hard and long they searched, there was nothing; they drew a blank every time. On every point, Daniel the bachelor emerged with a spotlessly clean sheet: they tailed him, they hacked into his computer, they checked his mail, they tracked his credit cards and business expenses, and it yielded nothing. The unauthorised internal inquiry conducted by his peers unearthed no scandal, nor even a hint of one. They could not dig up anything from his past or present. No skeletons in his closet. No bugs on Daniel! 'No disappointing omissions, no tainting commissions,' remarks Dale Ralph Davis. He is one of a rare breed, a virtuous and honourable man.

One day some men came to see Charles Haddon Spurgeon, one of the finest preachers in the world. They were trying to blackmail him. They walked into his study and threatened him, saying that if he did not meet their demands they would publish things that would ruin his reputation. Mr Spurgeon said, 'Write all you know about me across the heavens.' That is the power and purity of a clear conscience. And Daniel is just the same.

Then some bright spark in officialdom suggested they go after him because of his prayer life. They reckoned this was their one and only chance of success. They smelled the aroma of victory in their nostrils. You see, Daniel stood in the way of these twisted officials in their quest for personal gain. They wanted to feather their own nests. He was an insuperable barrier so they had to frame him. So far as they were concerned, there was no viable alternative but for them to move into top gear and eliminate their target.

6:6-9

Cunning conspirators

Then these high officials and satraps came by agreement to the king and said to him, 'O King Darius, live forever! All the high officials of the kingdom, the prefects and the satraps, the counsellors and the governors are agreed that the king should establish an ordinance and enforce an injunction, that whoever makes petition to any god or man for thirty days, except to you, O king, shall be cast into the den of lions. Now, O king, establish the injunction and sign the document, so that it cannot be changed, according to the law of the Medes and the Persians, which cannot be revoked.' Therefore King Darius signed the document and injunction.

The crooked caucus hatched their cunning plan and went straight to the king to get him on their side. The sheer subtlety of their scheme is glaringly obvious as it is a flagrant breach of God's law, a religious ruse, and they know that Daniel will not turn aside from worshipping his God. They knew that Daniel would sooner go to the lions and die than give up his practice of daily prayer. Since they could find no dirt to dish on Daniel, they decided to work on a weakness in the character of Darius and encourage him to hold in the words of Dale Ralph Davis, a 'Darius Appreciation Month.' Plainly put, they stroked his ego.

It began with flattery when they wished the king a long and

prosperous life. Then they resorted to falsehood when they brazenly suggested to the king that all those whom he appointed were unanimous in their agreement of what they were about to share with him. It was hogwash. The blunt truth is that Daniel was not aware of where they were nor even of the consultations carried out beforehand. He was not privy to their discussions and he was not in any way associated with their proposal. They pulled the wool over the eyes of a gullible Darius. He fell for it, hook, line, and sinker.

They requested that the king issue a decree for a period of thirty days banning all citizens from praying to any god or man in private and public. If prayers were offered, they should only be directed to the king, and he alone. In so doing, they were deifying the king, making him into a kind of mini-god for a short time. And once written into law, the legislation could not be revoked in any shape or form as it was subject to what was known as *the law of the Medes and the Persians* (Esther 1:19, 8:8). Failure to comply with this *lex scripta* earned the offender an evening in the den of lions, where death was a foregone conclusion.

The king granted their request and the law was written into the statute books. Daniel's colleagues, a happy bunch, left the palace brimming with confidence and exuding an air of smug temerity. Having set the trap, they now pull out all the stops to spring the trap. On the face of it, it looked as if the wicked were going to triumph (Psalm 73:2-12).

6:10-11

A stark choice: obey or disobey

When Daniel knew that the document had been signed, he went to his house where he had windows in his upper chamber open toward Jerusalem. He got down on his knees three times a day and prayed and gave thanks before his God, as he had done previously. Then these men came by agreement and found Daniel making petition and plea before his God.

Not surprisingly, the news quickly filtered through to Daniel that the king had passed a 30-day law banning all prayer to anyone but himself. That did not unnerve Daniel at all for he carried on with normal life as if nothing had happened back at the throne room in the palace; irrespective of the outcome, his obedience and loyalty to God were never in doubt (Acts 5:29). He sensed that this was a test case and that he was being used as a guinea pig, a political pawn. Exhibit A.

Daniel's mind was made up, he was adamant that he would continue to pray, law or no law. His response was instinctive because his set of values, his principles to live by, and his allegiances had been clearly marked out long before this new impediment arrived in his life. And so, when the critical hurdle needed to be stepped over, Daniel's decision was already made. In our lives, it is too late to shut the stable door when the horse has bolted. The man of God is always prepared for whatever onslaught the enemy throws at him.

It must have concerned him, however, that the king had been so easily duped by his devious, deceitful colleagues. He was hoodwinked. That he had been elevated to such a precarious height where only he could be worshipped throughout the empire was quite alarming for it contravened all that Daniel knew to be true from Scripture (Exodus 20:1-6). No man is worthy to sit on a divine pedestal. The king was on dangerous ground.

This is probably the biggest test that Daniel has ever faced in his long life of walking with God. It reminds us that the journey does not necessarily get any easier the older we are, for Daniel is well on in years at this point and here he is confronted with a ginormous challenge to his faith. Ligon Duncan writes, 'In this, the hour of his temptation, we can see Daniel savouring the opportunity to die for his Lord if necessary. I would have been wringing my hands, if this were me, but Daniel immediately senses that his whole life leads up to this moment. This is the moment that he can stand for his God. This is the moment that he can testify of his loyalty to his God, and this is the moment that God, the God of Israel, can display his glory, and Daniel cannot wait.' It was Dietrich Bonhoeffer who said, 'When Christ calls a man, he bids him come and die.' And Martin Luther King Jr. said, 'If a man hasn't discovered something that he will die for, he isn't fit to live.'

Daniel has had a terrifically long life, a God-blessed life; he has lived well for God. Now he is preparing to die well, if needs be. Are we willing to join him in displaying such reckless abandon of faith because our God is first in our affections?

Ignatius of Antioch who was martyred in AD 107 was inspired by Daniel, when he said, 'I am writing to all the churches and I enjoin all, that I am dying willingly for God's sake, if only you do not prevent it. I beg you, do not do me an untimely kindness. Allow me to be eaten by the beasts, which are my way of reaching to God. I am God's wheat, and I am to be ground by the teeth of wild beasts, so that I may become the pure bread of Christ.'

A tutorial on prayer

Daniel responded by doing what he always did when he went to his usual place for prayer. It was a no-brainer. His apartment in the royal mews was obviously an upstairs room and it was there that he maintained his sweet times of fellowship and communion with his God. This was his get-alone-with-God closet (Matthew 6:6), a sanctified corner of 'quiet rest, near to the heart of God.' A place of refuge where he could be undistracted and undisturbed.

Outside circumstances had dramatically changed, but that did not dampen his enthusiasm to converse with God as one friend with another. There were added political pressures, but that did not deter him from doing what he always did. For Daniel, it was business as usual, because his daily relationship with God was more important to him than anything else. In so doing, he is one of a long line of godly worthies from early biblical times whose walk with God is exemplary, believing men like Enoch, Noah, and Abraham (Genesis 5:21-24, 6:9; Hebrews 11:5-10). Daniel's success was not dependent on his three-a-day prayer sessions, it was rooted in his personal walk with the promise-keeping Lord and his commitment to prayer was the fruit of this dynamic intimacy (Daniel 9:4). Therein lies the challenge for us for we would all love to pray like Daniel prayed, but that will only happen when we walk with God every day like Daniel did.

Daniel was fully aware of the consequences of his actions, but that did not preclude him from having an audience with the sovereign Lord. He did not go looking for trouble nor did he pray just to provoke opposition from his peers; look at him: he just got on with it, no fuss, no moans, and prayed. Daniel was not just a prayer warrior, he was a prayer general.

He even adopted his usual position in prayer when he threw open the windows which looked westward toward the city and holy hill of Jerusalem, then he knelt down in the presence of the unseen God, and worshipped. There was nothing superstitious or nostalgic about this practice, it was simply a token reminder to

Daniel of the presence of God, the power of God, and the covenant promises of a faithful God. He was adhering to the divine commitment enshrined in Solomon's prayer at the dedication of the temple (1 Kings 8:46-51; 2 Chronicles 6:36-39; Jonah 2:4). He knelt down before the King of kings as an act of submission and humility in order to conquer. Satan must have trembled when the godly Daniel bowed before the Almighty in full-blooded prayer. Knees down, head up.

It needs to be said that kneeling is not the only posture for prayer: it can be standing (1 Kings 8:22), sitting (2 Samuel 7:18), or stretched prostrate on the ground (Mark 14:35). The good thing is that our knees do not knock when we are kneeling on them!

He did not deviate from his usual plan in prayer which was a rich blend of intercession on behalf of others that God would show them 'glimpses of his warm mercy in their thick darkness' (Dale Ralph Davis); petitioning God for help and backbone as he faced the imminent threat of being tossed to ravenous lions, maybe even using the words of Psalm 57; and thanksgiving possibly focused on Psalm 92, a song for the Sabbath day.

Even though the odds were stacked against him, he prayed on and prayed through to a prayer-hearing and prayer-answering God. Because Daniel knew his God intimately, he knew how to pray. And he did so with a grateful heart. He did not press the mute button for he was willing to risk everything, even life itself, to stay in close touch with the Most High.

Nor was he sidetracked from his usual periods of prayer. Basically, Daniel had certain time-slots marked in his calendar when he sought the Lord. Just like David, it was his time-honoured tradition to pray three times daily—morning, noon, and evening—and no one and nothing was going to interfere with that routine (Psalm 55:17). For him, those moments with majesty were sacrosanct. This was his lifestyle and he was in no mood to change it for thirty days just to appease his accusers. For Daniel, this was the norm, he was doing what he always did (Daniel 6:10); down through the years, it was an uninterrupted habit. He was plumb predictable, like clockwork.

Daniel is characterised by consistency, and sometimes that can grease the gears when we stand at the crossroads. Remember, Daniel was an incredibly busy man with a plateful of demands on his expertise, but he still found time, made time, and took time to pray. To quote a couple of old hymns, one penned by William Longstaff, Daniel took 'time to be holy, to speak often with his Lord,' and another penned by James Montgomery reminding us that prayer was Daniel's 'vital breath … his native air.'

To live is Christ, to die is gain

Not unlike Polycarp in early church history: in AD 155, he was in the eventide of life; for him, the sun was setting and the shadows lengthening on a fruitful life and ministry. One day the unthinkable happened with a dreaded knock on the front door. When he answered, he was met by the Roman authorities who promptly grabbed him and took him away. He was hauled before the courts and told to renounce Jesus Christ. He flatly refused. He never flinched or wavered. This is what he said, '86 years I have served the Lord Jesus. He never did me any harm. He has been faithful to me. How can I blaspheme my King, my Lord, and my Saviour?' The outcome? Polycarp, Bishop of Smyrna, was burned alive, and died rejoicing in the great God of heaven.

This is all so challenging. Daniel faced a crisis. But he did not pray any more than he would usually do. He certainly did not pray any less. So often in our lives when we are faced with an emergency it immediately drives us to our knees; at such times, the length and earnestness of our prayers tend to fluctuate depending on the prevailing wind. Not so Daniel. He was a man of prayer, crisis or no crisis. What does it take for us to get our prayer life started? What does it take to get it stopped?

Ernest Wadsworth, a champion of effective prayer, said, 'Pray for a faith that will not shrink when washed in the waters of affliction.' Daniel had that kind of faith. Take careful note for he did not close the windows, he did not draw the curtains, he did not lower his voice, he did not reschedule his daily appointments, he did not have a special prayer time mid-afternoon or before dawn broke. None of that. He prayed! As usual. As Herman Veldkamp notes, 'The great miracle of grace in Daniel 6 is that Daniel, the man of prayer, was able to go on praying.'

Question: If the Prime Minister of the United Kingdom, or the President of the United States of America, or whoever makes the rules in your neck of the woods, did what Darius did and banned prayer for 30 days, how would that impact on your life and mine? How many prayer times, if any, would we miss?

He prayed, they pried

When Daniel was praying, others were prying. His government colleagues, aka would-be liquidators, ramped up their efforts with military precision and began eavesdropping on Daniel's conversations with God. They heard every word the elderly saint uttered from standing on the pavement just below his open latticed window. Sneakily, some of them were probably standing outside his apartment with their ears cupped against the entrance door. They did not want to miss anything as they were there to gather hard evidence. For good measure, they probably heard Daniel pleading with God on their behalf too. Have your children or other family members ever caught you praying?

Talk about an encroachment of one man's privacy. These vilifiers, with a muck-raker mindset, did not care. Such unwarranted intrusion did not bother them one little bit. They had one goal and they were resolutely determined to get their man. And get their man they did. For these scandalmongers, it was an open-and-shut case because they caught Daniel red-handed. An unlikely revolutionary. But one, nonetheless.

6:12-18

On the horns of a dilemma

Then they came near and said before the king, concerning the injunction, 'O king! Did you not sign an injunction, that anyone who makes petition to any god or man within thirty days except to you, O king, shall be cast into the den of lions?' The king answered and said, 'The thing stands fast, according to the law of the Medes and Persians, which cannot be revoked.' Then they answered and said before the king, 'Daniel, who is one of the exiles from Judah, pays no attention to you, O king, or the injunction you have signed, but makes his petition three times a day.' Then the king, when he heard these words, was much distressed and set his mind to deliver Daniel. And he laboured till the sun went down to rescue him. Then these men came by agreement to the king and said to the king, 'Know, O king, that it is a law of the Medes and Persians that no injunction or ordinance that the king establishes can be changed.' Then the king commanded, and Daniel was brought and cast into the den of lions. The king declared to Daniel, 'May your

God, whom you serve continually, deliver you!' And a stone was brought and laid on the mouth of the den, and the king sealed it with his own signet and with the signet of his lords, that nothing might be changed concerning Daniel. Then the king went to his palace and spent the night fasting; no diversions were brought to him, and sleep fled from him.

The king finds himself in a catch-22 situation when Daniel's enemies visit with him, not once, but twice, to blurt out the racially prejudiced findings from their proactive investigation into Daniel's prayer life. As sly as a fox, these slippery satraps are Machiavellian in their behaviour. As Dale Ralph Davis says, 'Daniel's accusers hold Darius' feet to the legal fire.' No matter what the king does at this point in the drama, he cannot win. He has a monkey on his back. He was tricked. These perverted politicians have him where they want him, backed into a corner of his own making. The law was the law, period. It was set in stone and therefore it was irrevocable. No matter what the king wished, there were no legal loopholes so he could not and dare not repeal it out of deference to a trusted confidant and esteemed employee.

Back in the reign of Nebuchadnezzar it could have been so different. He regarded himself as above the law. He did what he liked and no man dared say boo to any decision that was carried through. Darius was different. His was a constitutional monarchy whereby he himself was subject to the law.

Needless to say, this episode took its toll on the pro-Daniel king for he was emotionally drained and distressed. He is angry with himself. Stupid, even. This was a royal gaffe like no other. He was a sucker having allowed his ego to entrap him. He was genuinely grieved and distraught when he realised the untenable position he found himself in. The king had huge admiration for Daniel and he certainly did not want it to turn out like this for he would lose a valued friend. In those moments, his respect for Daniel's detractors and their pernicious plan must have plummeted to an all-time low.

At the appointed hour, before nightfall, Daniel was sent to the gallows. It was unfair, unjust, and undeserved. A poignant reminder of the Lord Jesus who went all the way to Calvary for every one of us; Daniel's response to such harassment is symptomatic of the Suffering Servant of Isaiah 53:7. Someone asked C S Lewis, 'Why do the righteous suffer?' To which he replied, 'Why not? They are the only ones who can take it!' The numerous lions in the den must have been licking their lips when the iron grille was opened and God's servant was tossed unceremoniously inside. A heavy stone covered and secured the entrance and it bore the seal of the king and his nobles; for the indefatigable Daniel, there was a way in to the den, but seemingly no way out.

These words bear an uncanny resemblance to the biblical record of Jesus' burial, where we read, '"Take a guard," Pilate answered. "Go, make the tomb as secure as you know how." So they went and made the tomb secure by putting a seal on the stone and posting the guard' (Matthew 27:65-66, NIV). Daniel in a den and Jesus in a tomb were both under seal, their fate inevitable, and in both instances the human sealing led to the greater glory for God, when he brought Daniel up out of the pit and he raised Christ up out of the tomb.

Archaeologists have uncovered Near Eastern lion dens or caverns which were actually open from above. They were dug deep into the earth and could be viewed from outside. Steps led down the side to an opening through which they could deposit

a condemned prisoner—which they probably did with Daniel—
or they could throw over the edge any number of people, which
they probably did with Daniel's slanderers. Such dens were dug
in a square fashion, having a partition wall built down the centre
which divided the den in half. At the base of the partition wall
was an iron door hinged so that it could be raised and lowered
by a rope from above. In this way they could throw food into one
side and get all the lions over in that section, close the gate, and
deposit a prisoner in the other side, and once they covered that
lower doorway with a boulder they could roll into place, they
would go up the stairs to the top, raise the gate and the lions
would be free to make their way into the other section and begin
to maul the frightened-out-of-his-wits prisoner. In that den, there
was nowhere to run or hide and little time to even pray.

The unerringly faithful Daniel went to the big, hungry lions
with an encouraging whisper from the king ringing in his ears;
it was a shining tribute to Daniel's personal relationship with
God, a warm recognition of his steadfast service, and a heartfelt
plea for divine intervention, when he declared, *May your God,
whom you serve continually, deliver you!* That was a nice, touching
gesture. Daniel's fate, however, was in the hands of his sovereign
God, a God of gracious providence. Maybe, just maybe, there was
a way out, but that would take a miracle.

For Darius, it was a horrendously long night, just as it had
been with Nebuchadnezzar some years earlier (Daniel 2:1). The
dawning of a new day, with its promise of azure blue skies and
warm sunshine, seemed a long time in coming, for we read, 'Then
the king returned to his palace and spent the night fasting. He
refused his usual entertainment and couldn't sleep at all that
night' (Daniel 6:18, NLT). Poor man.

He is king but, in this loss-loss situation, he feels so helpless, inadequate, and powerless; he goes into deprivation mode when he declines his evening meal, refuses all forms of musical entertainment or whatever, and struggles to sleep. His pretentious vanity and weak-kneed will cost him his supper and his sleep. Other matters are weighing heavily on his mind, namely Daniel and his fate. Sinclair Ferguson writes that 'it is better to be a child of faith in a den of lions than a king in a palace without faith.'

6:19-23

Lockdown with lions

Then, at break of day, the king arose and went in haste to the den of lions. As he came near to the den where Daniel was, he cried out in a tone of anguish. The king declared to Daniel, 'O Daniel, servant of the living God, has your God, whom you serve continually, been able to deliver you from the lions?' Then Daniel said to the king, 'O king, live forever! My God sent his angel and shut the lions' mouths, and they have not harmed me, because I was found blameless before him; and also before you, O king, I have done no harm.' Then the king was exceedingly glad, and commanded that Daniel be taken up out of the den. So Daniel was taken up out of the den, and no kind of harm was found on him, because he had trusted in his God.

The morning after the night before dawned with the rising of the sun in the east; 'the night before' was a unique night in the land for the lions wanted to eat but could not, and the king could eat but would not. Today was a new day. With that uppermost in his mind, the fretful king made a hurried dash to the den to see what had become of Daniel. The seals were still intact.

He probably felt like an idiot as he shouted in a doleful voice, 'Daniel, did you make it through the night? Have you survived? Are you ok?' He was hoping for the best, and prepared for the worst. I mean, no one else ever lived to tell such a tale! Why should Daniel be the first? Daniel's immediate response to the king's question is the stuff of legend, when he said with composed calmness, 'My God sent his angel, and he shut the mouths of the lions' (Daniel 6:22, NIV). *Deo Gloria.*

It was solitary confinement for Daniel. With only lions for company, he must have been shrouded in a cloak of loneliness. It was pitch black. The kings of the jungle were stalking around the den, doing what lions do. He could feel them walking by. He could hear their roaring and growling. The smell was a rancid stench, enough to make any man throw up. The whole ordeal was enough to give you a coronary, but the old saint of God found it was far better to be in the dark with God than to be in the light without him.

Lions with lockjaw

Daniel enjoyed the closeness of a comforter when he found himself in a den of lions. How gracious of a merciful God to give him some company in his loneliest hour. The great God of heaven dispatched his angel to minister unto God's servant in his hour of great need. In all likelihood, this is the same angel—a Christophany—who was with Shadrach, Meshach, and Abednego in the fiery furnace. One angel, only one – there again, if one angel can take care of 185,000 Assyrian soldiers and eliminate them overnight, shutting the mouths of a pride of cooped up lions should be fairly easy. It was! The lions had lockjaw. Not one lion did Daniel any harm. Not one! He was 'rescued from the mouth of the lions' (Psalm 22:21, NIV). God did his part. Daniel did his, when he believed in the power and greatness of the Lord of all creation. Here is the God who always has our back, one who takes care of his own.

'Daniel slept like a lamb, even though he was watched over by lions,' writes David Jeremiah. The famed London preacher Charles H Spurgeon observed that it was a good thing the lions did not try to eat Daniel. They would not have enjoyed him, since he was one half grit and the other half backbone! Here is one story where the good guy wins.

Daniel was not kept from his hour of trial. He was not granted immunity from the ups and downs of real life. But he was preserved in the den of testing. Big golden beasts became like purring tabby cats! The implication is that a man of God in the will of God is immortal until his work for God on earth is finished. Daniel's task was not yet complete. Even at a ripe old age, there was more for him to do. Thank God, there always is.

It seems fairly clear that Daniel is one of those mentioned in the *Semper Fidelis* chapter of Scripture, where we read, 'How much more do I need to say? It would take too long to recount the stories of the faith of Gideon, Barak, Samson, Jephthah, David, Samuel, and all the prophets. By faith these people … shut the mouths of lions' (Hebrews 11:32-33, NLT). There are other times when the sovereign Lord ordains that his choice servants, just like his well-beloved Son, should pass through such horrific trials which ultimately end in death, only for them to arrive on the other side in a blaze of divine glory (Hebrews 11:36-38; 1 Peter 4:12-14).

There is an illustrious trio of men in the Old Testament who fought with lions – Samson (Judges 14:5-6), David (1 Samuel

17:34-35), and Benaiah (1 Chronicles 11:22). Daniel is not among that elite number because God took care of the lions for him.

Darius is jumping up and down with rapturous elation when he hears the voice of Daniel from within the den; he is even more ecstatic when he sees him in the flesh and sees for himself that he is hale and hearty. Not a scratch on his skin. Not a bruise. Not a tear on his clothing. Kenneth Gangel says, 'When God delivers, he does it completely.' A story with a happy ending.

Daniel was innocent of all charges levelled against him. He knew that. The king knew that. And, more important, God knew that. Daniel is not claiming to be sinless; he is not saying that he has never done anything wrong; he is saying that, in this circumstance, his hands are clean and his heart is pure.

A Sunday School teacher once asked her class why Daniel was not afraid when he was thrown into the den of lions. After a brief pause, one little girl spoke up and said, 'Because the Lion of the tribe of Judah was in there with him!' Sound theology.

6:24-28

A great reversal

And the king commanded, and those men who had maliciously accused Daniel were brought and cast into the den of lions – they, their children, and their wives. And before they reached the bottom of the den, the lions overpowered them and broke all their bones in pieces. Then King Darius wrote to all the peoples, nations, and languages that dwell in all the earth: 'Peace be multiplied to you. I make a decree, that in all my royal dominion people are to tremble and fear before the God of Daniel, for he is the living God, enduring forever; his kingdom shall never be destroyed, and his

*dominion shall be to the end. He delivers and rescues; he works
signs and wonders in heaven and on earth, he who has saved
Daniel from the power of the lions.' So this Daniel prospered
during the reign of Darius and the reign of Cyrus the Persian.*

Daniel is alive and well. Daniel's God is alive and well. The
ringleaders who pointed the finger at Daniel's prayer life and
apparent insubordination to the king are mincemeat. The bone-
crushing lions got them, one and all, even before they hit the dirt
bottom. They were torn to shreds. These gutless guys are not
alive, and not well! David Jeremiah portrays it with these words,
when he notes, 'The lions got their reward. Instead of one tough
old Jew, they got a lot of tender, spineless Persians for breakfast.'

Vindication for Daniel involves retribution for his enemies,
not only them as individuals, but their entire families in a form
of collective punishment (Proverbs 11:8). If this incident had
happened in Israel, the wives and children would have been
spared (Deuteronomy 24:16; Ezekiel 18:20), but this was not
Israel, this was life under a Persian regime where such judgment
was the norm. A horrific scene.

It should never cease to amaze us how God takes every situation
and turns it around to such a degree that his name is exalted,
magnified, and glorified. That is what Darius ensures when he
transmits his message to the ends of the earth which, in essence,
is a robust acknowledgment of the greatness of Daniel's God. In
one sense, this is what world mission is all about, it is sharing
glad tidings and witnessing to people about God. Everything that
Darius knew about God he learned by observing Daniel's public
life of integrity. That tells us that Daniel's actions in the public
square matched his words in private to the king.

Warren Wiersbe notes that 'the theology expressed in the

decree of Darius is as true as anything written by Moses, David, or Paul.' He affirms that Daniel's God is like no other god and he is to be reverenced at all times. He declares that Daniel's God is real, living, and eternal. He sets the record straight that Daniel's God rules and reigns and that his kingdom, unlike earthly dominions, is indestructible and unshakeable and goes on beyond time and is forever. He testifies from what he has seen with his own eyes that Daniel's God is one who rescues, saves, and delivers his people in their times of greatest trial and trauma. He proclaims that Daniel's God is one who can do whatever he wishes to do, whenever he wishes to do it because he is the unrivalled sovereign over all things in heaven and on earth.

The last sentence is a fitting finale to a memorable chapter when we are informed that Daniel prospered during the reigns of Darius and Cyrus (please remember that name Cyrus, a very important figure in history especially in relation to the Jewish people going back home after decades in exile).

Our God is the great encourager. After all Daniel experienced as a man of advanced years, he is still going strong and flourishing to the praise and glory of God (James 1:12). Faithful and fruitful. He stood for what he believed even though the stars might fall, and no king, however powerful on earth, could dissuade his focus on the King of heaven. Daniel is a model of courage, conviction, and commitment. He is a paragon of virtue who joyfully gives all the acclaim to one who sits on a higher throne, the Most High God.

John MacArthur is right when he says that 'if you see one thread through the book of Daniel, it is not the exaltation of Daniel, it is the majesty of God.'

7

A MENAGERIE
OF MONSTERS

I am definitely not a movie buff, nor am I a devotee of anything that smacks of sci-fi! Box office record-breakers like *Star Wars* and epic television series like *Star Trek* do not press any buttons for me. Big screen, small screen, I just switch off. That said, I have many great friends who are totally absorbed by such entertainment. Out of loving deference for them, I listen to their insights and watch their enthusiasm with one ear and one eye!

So, yes, I have heard all about the James Cameron sci-fi thriller, *Aliens* (1986), where a rescue team from earth engages in a confrontation with hostile alien monsters that inflict serious carnage on the team. Amazingly, a small girl named Newt (played by Carrie Henn) has lived for months on the planet as the lone survivor of an earlier mission. After a tough encounter with the aliens, Newt informs leader Ripley (played by Sigourney Weaver) that the team needs to pull out all the stops and get back to a safe place. Why?

Her response is an all-time classic and most memorable, 'We

better get back because it will be dark soon. And they mostly come at night … mostly.' Newt is right! Monsters mostly come at night … mostly. They come out at night when it is dark; they come out at night when we lie in our beds, as many of us recall from childhood nightmares. They come out at night when we sleep and have dreams with visions, as Daniel would quickly affirm (Daniel 7:1-2).

Daniel is an apocalyptic book where the curtain is drawn back and the future is unveiled; other examples are parts of Isaiah, Ezekiel, Joel, and Zechariah, along with a couple of chapters in the Gospels, and most of Revelation, aka the Apocalypse.

The book of Daniel is a ground-breaker in that its prophetic message comes through signs and symbols, vivid word pictures and visions. One picture is worth a thousand words, we are told. The genre of narrative or story-telling now gives way to a category that is comparable to movie-watching or playing video games like *FIFA 20* or *NBA 2K20*. Throughout apocalyptic literature, as we see here in Daniel, the wonderfully distinctive message remains the same that the Lord is sovereign over all things, at all times (Daniel 4:17, 7:13-14), and is still seated on the throne. He has not, he will not, he cannot abdicate his kingship.

The question is asked: Is anyone really in control? Yes, God is in full control! He has his finger on the pulse and his steady hand is on the tiller. The divine graffiti artist declares to a world of chaos and confusion that *heaven rules* (Daniel 4:26), thereby ensuring that God's despised and disheartened people are enlightened and encouraged to such an extent that we know, *really* know, *confidently* know, that we are on the winning side (Daniel 7:27).

A game of two halves

The throbbing heartbeat of the second half of Daniel is that we are kingdom people, a people of sure and certain hope, and our great God is the High King of heaven. Simply put, in the ripening purpose of God, there is coming a glorious King who will establish a glorious kingdom. For us, we know how the story ends because we have read the last chapter.

We dipped our toes in the water in the first half of the book (Daniel 1-6) when we considered the dreams and visions which Daniel interpreted on behalf of other men; now, in the second half of the book (Daniel 7-12), we are knee-deep in more of the same, but with greater detail, sharper focus, and cosmic impact. And from this moment forwards, Daniel is the one whom God wants as his audience and, indeed, the shoe is on the other foot for he is the one who now needs an interpreter (Daniel 7:19). John MacArthur spells it out helpfully when he writes that 'the first six chapters are mostly history with a little bit of prediction; the last six chapters are mostly prediction with just a little bit of history.'

As we shall see in this incredible chapter (and there is more to follow in chapter eight), some of the pictures are grotesque, scary, imaginative, bizarre, and head-scratching. To illustrate, if you do a Google search on 'Daniel 7' you get 2.05 billion hits in 0.43 of a second and, to be honest, most of it is dodgy stuff and not worth ploughing through. By way of contrast, I am told that among the scribes who assiduously copied the Old Testament, the seventh chapter of Daniel was considered the greatest chapter in all the Scriptures. Sinclair Ferguson writes, 'This section of God's Word is not meant to be an amusement for armchair theological sleuths. It is intended to give an overwhelming impression of the mysteries of God's purposes and the awful conflict that lies behind and beneath history.'

We catch a glimpse of the mission of God in the book. For example, the first half emphasised a message which God wanted to share with the world at large; it was revealed to various kings through Daniel unpacking their dreams, then declaring the unembellished truth to them. In the second half, there is a slight tweaking for the emphasis switches to one man, Daniel, receiving the dream whereupon the message is tailored to his own people, Israel, and then by application, to you and me in the global community of believers.

7:1-3

Daniel dreams

In the first year of Belshazzar king of Babylon, Daniel saw a dream and visions of his head as he lay in his bed. Then he wrote down the dream and told the sum of the matter. Daniel declared, 'I saw in my vision by night, and behold, the four winds of heaven were stirring up the great sea. And four great beasts came up out of the sea, different from one another.'

This is an exhilarating chapter of *great* things. The adjective is used at least six times to strengthen and consolidate the truth of the vision. A timely reminder that behind all the genius of man's intrigue and inventiveness lies the mighty hand of an even greater God. This faith-building chapter begins with a historical marker indicating the date in which it was given to Daniel, God's reliable servant, making it around 553 BC.

That means, this dream chapter slots in chronologically between chapters 4 and 5 in the book, and helps explain Daniel's attitude to Belshazzar on that fateful night fourteen years later in 539 BC. The evergreen Daniel was privy to inside information and, therefore, knew what was just around the next bend on the road for Belshazzar and Babylon. He was also aware that God was pulling all the strings, no matter who was sitting on an earthly throne (Daniel 7:13-14). Kenneth Gangel writes that 'this section of Daniel is a powerpack of prophecy—detailed, definitive, and determined.' Prophetic truth, properly taught and understood, gives every believer an advantageous edge over his fellow man, and at the same time, gives them a sanctified perspective on life and its challenges.

Daniel was asleep when God clearly spoke to him in a dream; for him, it was unforgettable as it impacted him there and then and left him crestfallen (Daniel 7:15, 28). He recorded the pith of the vision with his own handwriting as he did not have the luxury of a secretariat to do such menial tasks. Such words bear his stamp and signature and are fully authentic and authoritative. He tells it like it is for over and over again we read that he *saw* and he *looked*. It captivated Daniel and he is enthralled with all that he sees and hears. John Walvoord writes, 'This chapter is hailed as one of the great prophecies of the Bible and the key to the entire program of God from Babylon to the Second Coming of Christ.'

A storm at sea

The *four winds* of the compass—north, south, east, and west— are here referred to as the *winds of heaven* reminding us that this is God's sovereign work as he strives with people (Genesis 6:3; John 3:8). He is active as he breathes on the peoples who populate Planet Earth, often causing cosmic convulsions, turbulence, and turmoil (Isaiah 17:12-13; Revelation 17:15). When the howling wind of God blows upon the choppy sea there is a churning up of the waters which highlights the raging chaos, confusion, and conflict among the restless nations of earth (Job 41:31; Psalms 89:9, 93:3-4). God often uses the wind as a means to attain his ends (Genesis 8:1; Exodus 10:13-19; 1 Kings 18:45). Like those early disciples in a boat on Galilee, we exclaim, 'Even the wind and waves obey him' (Matthew 8:27, NIV). Allied to that, the sea was considered to be the natural home of giant aquatic creatures such as Leviathan, the multiheaded monster of ancient times (Job 41:1-34; Psalms 74:13-14, 104:24-26).

It is worth noting that wind is mentioned more than 120 times in the Bible (more than 90 in the Old Testament and about 30 in the New) and more than half of these point to the sovereignty and power of God. Indeed, that is the only way Daniel uses the word. Ultimately, it teaches us that God is behind the scenes directing the scenes he is behind.

A day at the zoo

The copious grace of God is shown to Daniel when God starts with what he knows and then moves to what he does not know: so the four extraordinary, no-two-alike beasts correspond to the four metals that were used in the metallic colossus of Nebuchadnezzar's dream in Daniel 2. There, we noted man's view of the kingdoms of the world for he sees them in all their majesty, pomp, and splendour and, consequently, sets them on a pedestal to be revered and worshipped.

With the arrival of four strange, surreal beasts, however, a new concept is introduced to the scenario. This is the course of global history from God's perspective as he looks upon it from the vantage point of his elevated throne: nothing glamorous, glittering, or glorious here, for these empires are brutal and bestial in character, fierce and feral in conduct. A thrice-holy God sees through the smoke and mirrors and sees them in their total depravity and utter degradation.

'The overall impression of the vision,' writes John Lennox, 'is of the dark underbelly of politics: the jockeying for power, with less and less moral qualm, until a sense of humanity and compassion disappears under the ruthless lust for domination.'

Many global superpowers in our day have animals or birds as a national symbol. For example, Britain uses the lion, China the dragon, Russia the bear, and America the eagle.

7:4-8

Jungle book

'The first was like a lion and had eagles' wings. Then as I looked its wings were plucked off, and it was lifted up from the ground and made to stand on two feet like a man, and the mind of a man was given to it. And behold, another beast, a second one, like a bear. It was raised up on one side. It had three ribs in its mouth between its teeth; and it was told, "Arise, devour much flesh." After this I looked, and behold, another, like a leopard, with four wings of a bird on its back. And the beast had four heads, and dominion was given to it. After this I saw in the night visions, and behold, a fourth beast, terrifying and dreadful and exceedingly strong. It had great iron teeth; it devoured and broke in pieces and stamped what was left with its feet. It was different from all the beasts that were before it, and it had ten horns. I considered the horns, and behold, there came up among them another horn, a little one, before which three of the first horns were plucked up by the roots.

And behold, in this horn were eyes like the eyes of a man, and a mouth speaking great things.'

#1 monster

The first monster on show is a rare hybrid in that it is an eagle-winged lion, the king of birds and king of animals combined. Actually, the traditional symbol of Babylon was a winged lion, and there are references to that in both Jeremiah and Ezekiel, two prophets, both of whom were familiar to Daniel (Jeremiah 4:7, 50:44; Ezekiel 17:3, 11-12). In fact, the Ishtar Gates, which gave access to the city's Processional Way whose ceramic glazed brick walls were lined with enamelled lions, show two winged lions guarding the gates. The same honour guard was found on the gates of all the royal palaces in Babylon.

Swiftness and strength are the distinguishing traits anticipated in this image. Nebuchadnezzar's victorious conquests were rapid and ruthless (Jeremiah 49:19-22; Habakkuk 1:6-8). He annexed country after country, and in so doing, instilled fear and dread into the populace. Aggression coupled with arrogance were symptomatic of his tyrannical leadership. The disclosure that *its wings were plucked off* is hugely significant for a bird is rendered helpless and impotent so far as flight is concerned. It may as well be caged. This appears to show the dramatic and drastic change that enveloped the empire as she began to lose her former glory. A waning empire.

When the lion was made to *stand upright* on its hind legs and then given *the mind of a man* it suggests transformation. Again, both actions are a sovereign work of God. No longer could they use their teeth and claws to overcome and overpower the enemy. Intellect was the weapon in its arsenal. How devious. This possibly refers to the fact that Nebuchadnezzar, following his period of insanity and subsequent conversion to faith in Yahweh, became more humane in his dealings with his subjects. In a sense, he had been tamed.

#2 monster

The second monster is like a bear which visually represents the second world power, namely the Medo-Persian empire. When compared with a lion, a bear is comparatively slow and ponderous in its movements. However, its innate ability is to savagely crush its opponents using ferocious force (Isaiah 13:17-18; Amos 5:19).

The bear *raised up on one side* (again, by God) indicates that ultimately Persia would gain ascendancy over Media and dominate the duo as the superior power. The history books corroborate such precise information. It is normal for a bear to feed on fruits, vegetables, and roots, but it will eat flesh when hungry and attack other animals and people. Her greedy appetite and unquenchable lust for action is seen by the *three ribs in its mouth*. This is an unambiguous reference to her conquest over Babylon in 539 BC, Lydia in 546 BC, and Egypt in 525 BC. They were swallowed up as she was hungry for power and strategic territory.

The bloodthirsty bear was far from satisfied and she continued to *devour* more nations as time ran its course (again, prompted by God). Her military prowess is reflected in the knowledge that by the end of her days her kingdom extended from the Indus River on the east to the land of Egypt and the Aegean Sea on the west.

#3 monster

The third monster looked like a leopard and depicts the Grecian empire under Alexander the Great, son of Philip II of Macedon, and his successors. This identification is further confirmed in Daniel 8:20-22 where it discloses that Persia would be overrun by Greece. The leopard is the most agile and graceful of wild animals, and although slight in its build, is famed for its phenomenal speed (Habakkuk 1:8). It is cunning and cruel, lying in wait for its prey, and its insatiable thirst for blood (Jeremiah 5:6; Hosea 13:7) accurately portrayed Alexander's all-consuming passion for global supremacy.

The *four wings* tell of the stunning pace at which Alexander subdued the world of his day in an unprecedented manner, backed by an original army of under fifty thousand fighting men. Tutored as a child by Aristotle, he accomplished some of the greatest feats of military history in a very short time. For a few years from 334 BC his armies marched irresistibly eastward until he became the master of all lands between the Mediterranean and the modern borders of Afghanistan (all this was achieved in the same life span as that of Jesus). He was unstoppable. He is the only military commander of whom it could rightly be said that he never lost a battle. Alexander is heralded as the progenitor of the military strategy called the blitzkrieg. According to the biblical record, he scored many victories, but *dominion was given to him* by the sovereign Lord. In other words, God granted it to him because all the threads of history lead to the throne room of the Most High.

When Alexander died an untimely death at 33, at the height of his success, his kingdom was eventually split into four as represented by *the four heads*. Each of the segments was under the command of a general: one, Antipater, and later Cassander, gained control of Macedon and Greece; two, Lysimachus ruled a large part of Asia Minor and Thrace; three, Seleucus I Nicator governed Syria, Babylon, and much of the Middle East (all of Asia except Asia Minor and Israel); and, four, Ptolemy I Soter controlled Egypt, Israel, and Arabia Petrea.

Take a break

Before we consider the fourth monster, all that we have seen so far in the previous three world empires is water under the bridge. However, in Daniel's day, so much of this information was penned in the future tense; it had not yet happened. In our day, we look back with amazement, delight, and immense satisfaction to the unshakeable fact that an omniscient God knows the end from the beginning. Even the tiniest, seemingly insignificant detail is known to him and history confirms the unbelievable accuracy of every prediction made in Daniel 2 and here in Daniel 7. 'And it came to pass.' Warren Wiersbe says that 'prophecy is history written beforehand.'

The rise and fall of the first three monsters is a powerful reminder to us that civilisation is not on the up; Utopia is not even on the most distant horizon when it comes to the evolution of mankind. Rather, as we discovered in Daniel 2, we are on a downward trajectory; we are hurtling fast downhill from bad to worse, and still some. Dale Ralph Davis captures the essence of such, when he writes that 'on the whole, nations and kingdoms are out for conflict and conquest and control, that empires are bent to dominate and devour, no matter how many people they mangle or how much misery they inflict.'

Daniel's vision informs us that global history is not nice, genteel, and gentlemanly, but it is ghastly, beastly, and unspeakably cruel. A cursory look through the archives of the last century will unearth many tragic stories of brutal oppression: we have seen murderous beasts like Adolf Hitler, Joseph Stalin, Idi Amin, and Kim Jong-il; during the Holocaust, we have witnessed the gas chambers of Auschwitz and Belsen; we observed the genocidal killing fields of Cambodia and Rwanda. Welcome to the real world, it is not a pretty sight!

#4 monster

The fourth monster defies description and, significantly, there is no 'like' associated with it. That suggests no one has ever seen or will ever see anything similar. It is freakishly outside the box, beyond human comprehension, almost dinosauric. Daniel notes in a consummate understatement that it was *different* to the previous three beasts, and that it certainly is. Dale Ralph Davis says that this beast is *different* in 'the terror it inspires, the havoc it wreaks, the power it possesses ... and in the ruler it produces.'

It is distastefully hideous and totally unattractive as it crushed ruthlessly and violently every last vestige of opposition. 'Here,' says Sinclair Ferguson, 'is orderly, monotonous, ruthless expansion.' Troops put down each revolt with merciless savagery killing captives by the thousands and selling them into slavery by the hundreds of thousands. Roman law was forcibly rammed down the throats of the vulnerable masses. Pagan religious superstition and the unprecedented slaughter of innocent people were the norm in her heyday (Matthew 2:16).

Both the Lord Jesus and the early Church felt the rancorous fury of her vindictive hatred and white-hot wrath. It was Rome that crucified Peter and beheaded Paul. It was Rome that banished the aged John to the Greek island of Patmos to work in the mines and quarries, and Rome that burned Christians and butchered men, women, and children. Those first believers in Jesus endured no less than ten waves of persecution under Nero (AD 54-68), Domitian (AD 81-96), and their sadistic successors, right up to Diocletian (AD 292-304).

I read of one guy who, waxing eloquent, compared it to a Tyrannosaurus Rex with ten horns like a Mohawk! As this nondescript creature follows on from Babylon, Medo-Persia, and Greece, I think we can safely assume it speaks of the expansive Roman Empire. In light of the context, however, it has to be Rome and more: Rome plus ... or something like, Rome tbc (to be continued) ... is possibly a more accurate explanation. Why do I say that? Because of verse 8 and Daniel's additional insights regarding this monster in verses 19-26.

The multiple horns correspond with the ten toes of the image in Daniel 2:42-43, and the ten kings mentioned in Revelation 13:1. A horn is frequently seen in the Bible as a symbol of strength, or depicting a ruler or royal authority (1 Samuel 2:10; Psalm 132:17). The thought here is that, in the future, ten rulers reigning as contemporaries will join hands in a loose confederation of ten nations which is really an extension of the Roman Empire. Stuart Olyott, John Walvoord, and Renald Showers are on a similar wavelength, when Showers writes that 'this indicated that the Roman Empire would experience three stages of history: first, the beast stage; second, the ten-horn or ten-kingdom stage; and third, the little horn or antichrist stage.'

A horn with plenty of honk

And then, for Daniel, while he is trying to get his head around what he has just seen in relation to the ten horns, up comes one more from among them, making eleven: *another horn, a little one.*

There is no reference to the size of the other ten horns, but this one is classed as little. Its size does not in any way imperil or endanger his ability to do what needs to be done so that he can be top dog as he quickly topples three horns (rulers) and seizes power himself.

He also has *eyes like the eyes of a man, and a mouth speaking great things*. He is someone whose intelligence and intellect puts him head and shoulders above the others around him; his mouth is a big one and that spells trouble as he toots his own horn, as we shall see later (Revelation 13:1-10). He has brains and bravado. James Boice notes that 'this seems to be the first biblical reference to the individual later described in the Bible as the antichrist. He appears in 2 Thessalonians 2:3 as "the man of lawlessness … doomed to destruction" (NIV) and is seen again in Revelation.' As antichrist (1 John 2:18), he is Satan's counterfeit of Jesus Christ, the devil's messiah. At the end of his day, Jesus will handle him (2 Thessalonians 2:8).

Before we progress, this needs to be flagged up: we must not confuse the 'little horn' of chapter 7 with the 'little horn' of chapter 8 that seems to point clearly to Antiochus Epiphanes.

7:9-10

'Behold our God'

> *'As I looked, thrones were placed, and the Ancient of Days took his seat; his clothing was white as snow, and the hair of his head like pure wool; his throne was fiery flames; its wheels were burning fire. A stream of fire issued and came out from before him; a thousand thousands served him, and ten thousand times ten thousand stood before him; the court sat in judgment, and the books were opened.'*

Daniel keeps on gazing intently as the vision continues to unfold before him; he is mesmerised with what he sees because the transition from verse 8 to verse 9 is neither smooth nor seamless. Verse 8 shuts down unexpectedly and abruptly, then there is a bit of a shudder, and we are right into the beautiful scene portrayed in verse 9. Talk about contrast, this is it. We move suddenly from something ridiculous to someone sublime, from a tough-talking no-gooder to catching a glimpse of the Most High God seated on a throne. And what an eye-catching, enduring spectacle it is. An awe-inspiring sight. Danny Akin writes that these verses are 'some of the most important verses in all of the Bible. They are important theologically, eschatologically, and Christologically.'

Born just three years after American patriarchs signed the Declaration of Independence, Sir Robert Grant became a member of the British Parliament and governor of Bombay. Kenneth Osbeck, in *101 Hymn Stories*, writes that 'Grant was a devoutly evangelical Christian who strongly supported the missionary outreach of his church and endeared himself to the people of India by establishing a medical college in Bombay.' Perhaps he is best known for his fantastic worship hymn which shines a laser beam on the greatness of our God, 'O worship the King, all-glorious above, And gratefully sing his power and his love; Our shield and defender, the Ancient of Days, Pavilioned in splendour and girded with praise.'

The heavenly court assembles, and the Ancient of Days sits in judgment as the presiding judge. There is a marvellous similarity between this vista and the one recorded by John in Revelation 4 and 5, where the spotlight shines on the throne of God and also on the other thrones round about which were occupied by the twenty-four elders. They are a heavenly hierarchy who form a jury of angelic beings who observe God's judgment being meted out. Their honoured position gives them an edge over others who may aspire to such a prestigious appointment as they watch the justice of God unfolding. They are there, and have a role to play.

'O tell of his might, O sing of his grace'

The main beam is focused on the one who is seated on the universal throne, namely God our Father (1 John 3:1), the Judge of all the earth (Genesis 18:25). He is the *Ancient of Days*—a title found only here in Daniel 7—and that is a reminder of his eternality for he always has been, he is, and he always will be. He was there before time began in eternity past and he will still be there when time is no more in eternity future. Here is one who reads the past, rides the present, and rules the future. All other kings and kingdoms are short-lived and are like grasshoppers (Isaiah 40:22), Daniel's God is eternal. Moses was right to acknowledge that he is the everlasting God (Psalm 90:2), one who is immortal, invisible, and wise (1 Timothy 1:17). Dale Ralph Davis writes that 'this title for God means that he is grand, not that he is frail; it imports ideas of dignity, not of senility.'

His white garment speaks of his purity, his holiness, and the impeccability of his character. His wool-like hair is a symbol of age and experience for here is one who is untainted, unsullied, and unblemished. He is one who cannot err. He makes no mistakes, he never has to apologise, and he never backtracks on any promise or commitment made. There are no miscarriages of justice from his throne for he is marked by fairness and equity. He gets it right first time, every time.

The fact that he is seated is massively reassuring for Daniel, and the rest of us. He is at ease with himself and in full control of all that he is doing. He sits, he does not stew (Psalm 110:1). As Sinclair Ferguson notes, 'He is never taken by surprise, never undecided, never in a panic about his world. He reigns.' There may be tumultuous chaos on earth, but there is an unflappable calmness in heaven.

'There is a higher throne'

His throne is bathed in fire and ablaze with flames reminding us that 'our God is a consuming fire' (Deuteronomy 4:24; Hebrews 12:29, NIV). As we trace salvation history from its earliest days, fire is often used to depict God's presence (Genesis 15:17; Exodus 3:2, 13:21, 19:18), even his presence in judgment (Leviticus 10:1-2; Numbers 11:1-3). Justice is administered from an environment characterised by divine glory, righteousness, and jealousy (Psalms 50:3-4, 97:3). The rotation of the wheels remind us that God is active in this capacity and that his work continues unhindered by man or nation. In every sense, he sets the wheels in motion (Ezekiel 1:13-21).

An uncountable number of holy angels serve him and stand before him, ready to do their Master's bidding (Deuteronomy 33:2). An innumerable throng are patiently waiting to execute the will of God as the sentence is handed down at the supreme court of the universe (Revelation 5:11). So, so many are there—over a hundred million—in heaven's garrison, extolling the supremacy and splendour of the Ancient of Days. And for Daniel, that must have warmed and cheered his heart to see such a huge number assembled before the throne; it was a token of grace that, in the fruition of God's plan for his life, he would no longer be alone or in a minority of one, but he will be there with a multitude that no man can number (Revelation 7:9).

As the session gets underway *the books are opened* (Revelation 20:11-15). God has at his disposal a record of the deeds of men and nations. Their words and activities are noted for posterity and in that day will be used in evidence against them. Everything is registered in his journal. Nothing has been omitted, exaggerated, or tampered with. God will set the movie on playback, then press the button, and man will be instantly aware of his failure to reach God's standard (Romans 3:23). He does everything by the book. And by the Book.

7:11-12

Good riddance, beast

'I looked then because of the sound of the great words that the horn was speaking. And as I looked, the beast was killed, and its body destroyed and given over to be burned with fire. As for the rest of the beasts, their dominion was taken away, but their lives were prolonged for a season and a time.'

With the briefest of comments, the minimum of fuss, and a feeling of anti-climax, Daniel is made aware of the judgment handed down to the fourth monster. Eradication. Extermination. Before his eyes, the last empire of man is dealt a mortal blow and forever wiped out. Justice is done, and justice is seen to be done. Ligon Duncan likens it to 'Godzilla versus Bambi!' No one is a match for the invincible God. Game over. Lights out. So quick. So simple. The end.

In contrast to the fourth beast, the others had their *dominion* removed, but in an act of generous grace and mercy they continued to chug along for a wee while longer. Even though all three empires had been vanquished, they kept on going as part of the kingdom that conquered them. They were a shadow of themselves, but they were still there, albeit in a much diminished sense. Joyce Baldwin is right on target when she suggests that 'history has not yet come to an end, despite the intervention of God's judgment, though *a season and a time* implies a limited future.'

The word *season* draws attention to the character of the period, as does our English word when we speak of the 'autumn season' or the 'winter season.' The word *time* refers to the chronology of the period as in the counting of days and weeks, months and years. Jim Allen writes that 'these nations, as such, could continue until a new season comes in with the new *dominion* of the Son of Man referred to in verse 14.'

The shockingly scandalous ramblings from the horn, aka the antichrist, caught Daniel's attention; his impertinent mouthing was a needless distraction from all that Daniel had seen in scene one. Presumably, he was promoting himself and his personal agenda, whilst openly blaspheming against the one seated on the throne. Nothing new there, it has to be said. More about him and his fate later in the chapter. The lurid details of his ignominious demise and eternal destruction are splashed across the pages of apocalyptic literature (Matthew 25:31-46; Revelation 19:19-21).

God has a unique way of doing things and we see evidence of that in this mini-section in Daniel 7:9-14, where we have two verses on the Ancient of Days, two verses on the doom of the beast, and two verses on the Son of Man. Just like a sandwich, except that the jam in the middle is not deliciously tasty. Rather, it is vile and repulsive. Dale Ralph Davis says that 'it is as if the little horn and its beast are scrunched and squeezed between the Ancient of Days and the Son of Man ... the Bible is trying to thrill you by placarding where the power and the glory, justice and kingship really reside.' Like the daily weather forecast, the outlook for the next twenty-four hours may not be too promising, but the uplook is exceedingly gorgeous and glorious.

7:13-14

'Risen and exalted one, Jesus'

'I saw in the night visions, and behold, with the clouds of heaven there came one like a son of man, and he came to the Ancient of Days and was presented before him. And to him was given dominion and glory and a kingdom, that all peoples, nations, and languages should serve him; his dominion is an everlasting dominion, which shall not pass away, and his kingdom one that shall not be destroyed.'

This is a seminal moment in the biblical revelation given to Daniel for he sees the arrival of *one like a son of man*. Of whom is he speaking? It can be none other than the Lord Jesus Christ. He often referred to himself in such terms when here on earth, as when he said to his disciples, 'For even the Son of Man did not come to be served, but to serve, and to give his life as a ransom for many' (Mark 10:45, NIV). When we align this instance with the message of Daniel 7, we discover that Jesus is not just a fully human figure, marked by purity, perfection, and nobility, but an exalted figure, one from another world, fully God. Graham Kendrick wrote in a song we often sing, 'Meekness and majesty, Manhood and deity, In perfect harmony, The man who is God.'

Actually, this was his favourite self-designation, inasmuch as he used this title around eighty times in the four gospels. John Piper notes that 'those with ears to hear [during his earthly ministry] could hear Daniel 7, in which he was claiming a very exalted role in the history of redemption. And he meant to do it.'

Here is one who alone is all-worthy to receive the approval rating granted to him from the Ancient of Days; this is a moment to outshine all others when God the Son rides on the cloud chariot and meets God the Father (Psalms 68:4, 104:3; Isaiah 19:1). What a wonderful presentation from one to the other of two distinct persons in the Godhead. John Phillips writes, 'A similar scene is set before us in Revelation 5:1-7 where Jesus, as the Lord of creation and the Lamb of Calvary, steps into the spotlight of eternity to receive from him who sits on the throne the title deeds of Planet Earth.'

And here in a beautiful choreographed response from the sovereign God, as the Son ascends to the right hand of the Father after his atoning death and sits down beside him (Acts 1:9-11; Hebrews 1:3, 12:2), he grants to his Son the nations as his inheritance (Psalm 2:8), as well as the spontaneous worship of every people group to the ends of the earth (Philippians 2:9-11). John MacArthur writes that 'this is the crucial moment in the history of eternity … the coronation of the King of kings and Lord of lords.' He is *given a kingdom* for he is one crowned and clothed with glory and honour (Hebrews 2:9); he is *given dominion* for his is the sole right to rule and reign over all (Zechariah 6:13). This is the kingdom that God had in mind when he told David that his throne would never end (2 Samuel 7:13-16). Unlike every earthly kingdom and global power as represented by the quartet of ugly beasts, there is nothing transient about his worldwide kingdom, it is never-ending, unconquerable, and indestructible (Psalm 72:8, 11, 17).

This is something we need to grasp with both hands today and every day; following Jesus in today's hostile climate is, at times, fraught with all kinds of dangers and challenges and we may feel as though we are battered so much that the bright future promised to us cannot come soon enough. Life may seem to be a confusing collage, but this secret given to Daniel should lift our spirits to a new level and serve as a constant reminder to us that our great God is sovereign and that he is running the show 24/7. To quote Dale Ralph Davis, 'These words say to hard-pressed saints, "Here is what is going to happen, heaven's kingship is firm; it may not eliminate suffering, but it will give sanity."'

Because of a stupendous vision given to Daniel back in the sixth century BC, there are two huge positives for us presently when 'the sands of time are sinking' beneath our weary feet and before 'the dawn of heaven breaks' above us: one, we are jerked out of our spiritual lethargy and complacency; two, we now know what is going to happen ahead of time. As Ligon Duncan says, 'A vision that began like a nightmare with monsters coming out of the sea, ends happily and hopefully with a Man coming out of heaven whom God crowns sovereign over the world.'

7:15-16

Animal parade

'As for me, Daniel, my spirit within me was anxious, and the visions of my head alarmed me. I approached one of those who stood there and asked him the truth concerning all this. So he told me and made known to me the interpretation of the things.'

Eric Arthur Blair was born in 1903 in Motihari, India, and at the age of nineteen began his service with the Imperial Police in Burma. Five years later he returned to England where he had been educated and lived in poverty trying to publish his first book. In

1933 he released *Down and Out in Paris and London*, describing the terribly sad conditions of the homeless poor.

But in his mind he had resolved to speak out against oppression and evil which abounded during his years in Burma. So in 1945, under his pen name George Orwell, he wrote *Animal Farm*, a scathing condemnation of that society expressed in a sweeping indictment of totalitarianism, particularly the communism of the mid-twentieth century. It describes a farm in which the animals take over, agreeing to create the perfect society in which all will have an equal voice. Sadly, their inner nature wins out, and the whole project ends in chaos. Considering the strength of communism in 1945, Orwell was something of a prophet, especially when we include his satirical novel *1984* which he produced four years later to describe the terrifying life of people under the constant surveillance of 'big brother.'

Orwell, as you will realise from reading Daniel 7, was not the first prophet to speak out against wicked animals taking over the world. 'In a very real sense,' writes Kenneth Gangel, 'this chapter describes the animal farm of earth for at least twenty-six hundred years and counting.' In this pivotal vision which God gave Daniel, the beasts appear to be running riot and causing all kinds of problems; they are roaming around like Rottweilers off the leash. But the sovereign Lord holds the reins of one and all and he is using each of them to pave the way for the coming Messiah. Gangel notes, 'The Persians will send the people of God back to their own land. The Greeks will develop a culture and construct a language by which the gospel can be communicated all over the Mediterranean world. And the Romans will build roads and write laws so that Christ's messengers may carry his Word wherever he sends them.'

That in itself is a powerful reminder that all is going according to plan. His plan (Galatians 4:4). When that plan is revealed to Daniel, he is horrified, mystified, and thoroughly perplexed. His anxiety levels rise because, in his words, he is *alarmed* with all that he has seen, and not yet fully understood. His mind is in a whirl. He is stressed out.

Many of us can identify with that reaction as we try to unravel the mystery of God's ways and make sense of God's leading in our lives. Even in moments when we are overwhelmed with a conscious sense of God's otherness and his greatness, it is easy for us to buckle under with the sheer weight of revelation resting on our sagging shoulders. Reading Daniel's experience brings much needed comfort, for it helps us realise that we are not alone when battling against such unexpected interruptions to the daily rhythm of our lives.

Thankfully, there was someone to whom Daniel could turn in his hour of need and bewilderment. We assume it was an angel that he shared his heart's concern with, as the biblical text does not explicitly say either way. This was a vision, remember, and as one writer said, 'I expect it looked much more like a Star Trek hologram in which all the characters appeared completely real, and it seemed quite normal to interact with one of them.' Some commentators feel it was Gabriel who gave him a crash course on heavenly hermeneutics thereby enabling him to come to terms with the message of the vision.

7:17-18

The main thing is the main thing

"These four great beasts are four kings who shall arise out of the earth. But the saints of the Most High shall receive the kingdom and possess the kingdom forever, forever and ever."

Daniel's informant gives him a quick résumé of the vision reassuring him that everything will turn out alright in the end, because God is in control. It was about a quadruplet of beasts—four world empires—who will play their part in global history, and when they have fulfilled their God-assigned role, they will be summarily dismissed.

When man's worldly kingdoms have come and gone, a final kingdom—the kingdom of God—will emerge (Revelation 11:15), and be divinely established for the remaining years of time and then far beyond into eternity. Without doubt, God's redeemed people—*the saints of the Most High*—have an extraordinarily bright future. Blessed forever. Safe and secure eternally in that haven of rest (Romans 8:31-39). We with him. He with us. That is why God's extravagant grace is so amazing.

The anonymous poet expressed it like this, 'Come, thou almighty King, Help us thy name to sing, Help us to praise. Father, all glorious, O'er all victorious, Come and reign over us, Ancient of Days.'

7:19-26

Joining the dots

'Then I desired to know the truth about the fourth beast, which was different from all the rest, exceedingly terrifying, with its teeth of iron and claws of bronze, and which devoured and broke in pieces and stamped what was left with its feet, and about the ten horns that were on its head, and the other horn that came up and before which three of them fell, the horn that had eyes and a mouth that spoke great things, and that seemed greater than its companions. As I looked, this horn made war with the saints

and prevailed over them, until the Ancient of Days came, and judgment was given for the saints of the Most High, and the time came when the saints possessed the kingdom. Thus he said: "As for the fourth beast, there shall be a fourth kingdom on earth, which shall be different from all the kingdoms, and it shall devour the whole earth, and trample it down, and break it to pieces. As for the ten horns, out of this kingdom ten kings shall arise, and another one shall arise after them; he shall be different from the former ones, and shall put down three kings. He shall speak words against the Most High, and shall wear out the saints of the Most High, and shall think to change the times and the law; and they shall be given into his hand for a time, times, and half a time. But the court shall sit in judgment, and his dominion shall be taken away, to be consumed and destroyed to the end."'

Daniel is partially satisfied and bolstered with the lowdown given to him, but he presses harder for a more definitive explanation surrounding the fourth beast and the little horn. The sight of such a monstrous whatever-it-was has had a colossal impact on Daniel and he is zealously determined to get to the bottom of it. We have catalogued its appallingly barbarous history elsewhere in this volume so there is no need to go over it again; suffice to say, during phase one of its regime as the ancient Roman empire (Daniel 2:40, 7:23), the iron king left its imprint on global affairs.

For the more inquisitive among us, there are still many questions that are not fully answered, and there are some important matters for which we have no crystal clear timeline or precise understanding as to how it is all going to pan out between now and the end of time. It will. Because God is God, and he can be trusted. He has the roadmap in his hand, all we have are key markers along the path. And that is where we are unreservedly committed to the providence of a faithful God and we are thrown upon the sovereignty of a God who tells us only what he wants to tell us. There are hazy moments when our awareness of what he is doing is somewhat blurred and perhaps dimmed but, again, we are dependent on him to do what he has scheduled. And he will.

Such a scenario is painted for us in this section where we grapple with the second phase of the beast's toing and froing in the ten-horn or ten-kingdom stage (Daniel 7:20, 24a). Anticipated here is the formation of a coalition of ten nations into a superpower which will ultimately become the little horn's playground.

The third phase is where he, the antichrist, comes to the fore from within this power bloc which seems to lack lasting cohesion (Daniel 7:20, 24b). Dale Ralph Davis writes that 'the iron and clay (Daniel 2:41-43) just cannot seem to bond.' Therefore, it is an ideal breeding ground for discontent and the *little horn* is fanatically keen to make hay when the sun is shining. For him, it is one of those *carpe diem* moments. Not content to be one among equals, he milks it for all that it is worth as he topples three of the ten rulers and ends up where he desperately wanted to be all along, as the dominant leader of the coalition. How he does it we do not know, as Scripture is silent on the matter; but it underlines the fact that this guy is into political subterfuge and he knows his way around. I agree with Dale Ralph Davis when he notes that 'Daniel's vision presents [the little horn] as the last leader of earth's final kingdom.'

Now that he is top dog and calling all the shots within the alliance, he shows himself up for what he really is – a power-crazed, anti-God, arrogant thug whose paymaster is the devil. He was a little horn to start with but after a while he became larger as his power is unprecedented (Daniel 7:20). And when we see the shenanigans of this hell-inspired, Satan-energised puppet it is spine-chilling and stomach-curdling to read for his blasphemy is brazen and in-your-face (Daniel 7:21, 25; Revelation 13). He has no inhibitions as he flaunts himself before a holy God; he does not appear to realise that he may push his luck too far and overstep the mark with some of his bullying and bravado.

The fact that he has eyes (Daniel 7:20) indicates that he is a man who can read the signs of the times and then respond to whatever situation he finds himself in. He is obviously a notch above his fellows within the grouping of nations, and by his bloodless coup has earned himself a name as a shrewd operator in the corridors of power. Socially gifted, he is adept at making friends in the upper echelons for his own use. He comes across as a problem-solver; this guy has all the answers, even to questions which people are not asking! No inferiority complex with him.

Daniel's vision shows that he is a man renowned for his powerfully persuasive oratory. Mr Articulate. A brilliant, golden-tongued communicator, he skilfully uses the very latest technology to get his message across to Joe Public. He easily sways the crowds and garners public opinion to his side. A man with a big mouth is a real threat, especially when he pontificates against the Most High (Daniel 7:25; Revelation 13:6). He seems to have no qualms when he engages in such verbal abuse of the God of all glory. In his heart, he fancies himself as the greatest and is at ease when he sees himself as a rival to God; his conceited aspiration is to elevate himself above God (Daniel 11:36-37; 2 Thessalonians 2:4).

Charles Swindoll writes of him that 'he will have the oratorical skill of a John Kennedy, the inspirational power of a Winston Churchill, the determination of a Joseph Stalin, the vision of a Karl Marx, the respectability of a Mahatma Gandhi, the military prowess of a Douglas MacArthur, the charm of a Will Rogers, and the genius of a King Solomon.' I mean, when all is said and done, who does this spinmeister really think he is?!

The alarm bells are ringing when we read that *he made war with the saints and prevailed over them* and that *he shall wear out the saints of the Most High*. Such is the lot for God's people who are devotedly following the Lamb and who are passing through the throes of great tribulation (Daniel 7:21, 25; Revelation 13:7). They are severely oppressed and given a rough ride. Hate-driven persecution is their experience from the hand of this demonically controlled superman. It is important to realise that the Lord grants him the authority to do what he does against the saints, but that his time is limited to what the Bible calls *a time, times, and half a time* (Daniel 7:25). He can do so much and no more, he can go so far and no further, all within the allotted timeframe. His days are numbered; his time will expire after three-and-a-half years (Revelation 11:3 speaks of it as 1,260 days, and Revelation 13:5 as forty-two months).

There is a fascinating turn of phrase in Daniel 7:25 where we read that the antichrist will *think to change the times and the law*. This is a tough one, but I think initially it refers to his attempt to repeal the laws of Judaism and to rewrite the directives surrounding the various Jewish feasts and festivals. This phrase should be seen in the light of Daniel 9:27 where he casually breaks his promise and reneges on his commitment to the Jewish people, and that is what triggers off his despicable undermining of all things related to their faith.

There is another possible application to this episode for we read that God alone 'changes times and seasons' (Daniel 2:21, NIV). The little horn may do all in his power as the lawless one to subvert the law and thus transform society into a godless mass. Basically, he may try to rewrite the statute books, and in so doing, obliterate everything that smacks of the Ten Commandments. Such intemperate arrogance flies in the face of logic and common sense. Sinclair Ferguson writes that 'it is a picture of blatant and sinister opposition to God and his rule of the world.'

He gets his comeuppance when the Most High, the Ancient of Days, calls a halt to all that he is doing. His time is up. And for him, the end is nigh. The court goes into session and judgment is swift and sure; his powerbase is wiped out, he is consigned to an eternity of everlasting punishment (Psalm 96:10-13). John Lennox writes, 'When the awesome heavenly court sits and God presides, the books will be opened, and rational, measured, and righteous judgment will be done.' The little horn will have his day. He has had his say. God deals with him in such a manner that he is banished forever. The horn has lost its toot. As Danny Akin says, 'Piddly despots come and go.' Never seen or heard of again, and praise the name of the Lord, he poses no further threat to the saints of God.

7:27-28

Thine is the kingdom

'"And the kingdom and the dominion and the greatness of the kingdoms under the whole heaven shall be given to the people of the saints of the Most High; his kingdom shall be an everlasting kingdom, and all dominions shall serve and obey him." Here is the

*end of the matter. As for me, Daniel, my thoughts greatly alarmed
me, and my colour changed, but I kept the matter in my heart.'*

In direct contrast to every political has-been and every empire
and nation from the onset of time, here is one kingdom that
outshines and outlasts them all, the kingdom of God on earth. It
will arrive with the supernatural return of Jesus Christ to oppose
the beast and his kingdom (Revelation 19:11-16). The *saints of the
Most High* are those who have been set apart by God because
they have set him apart as Lord in their own lives (1 Peter 3:15).
These are the ones who *receive* and *possess* the kingdom having
clung on to God in spite of overwhelming odds, and then go
on to share in the bounteous blessings of the kingdom of God's
dear Son. Dale Ralph Davis says, 'So the servants have no
kingdom apart from their King, and the King does not reign
without his servants. Jesus just cannot stand being separated
from his people.'

In that day, the prayer offered up by so many believers in our
day—'thy kingdom come'—will be fully answered, and in the
words of Isaac Watts, then 'Jesus shall reign where'er the sun,
doth its successive journeys run' (Zechariah 14:9).

Understandably, Daniel is massively impacted by all that
he has seen and heard in this sensational vision. It left a deep,
deep impression on him, but he, wisely, chose to meditate on its
content and bask in its overall message that God rules and reigns.
He was given a glimpse into life in his day, but he was also given
a panoramic preview of the future, his future, our future. The
great news is that the King is coming and our future is as bright
as the promises of God. Max Lucado writes that 'God's promises
are pine trees in the Rocky Mountains of Scripture: abundant,
unbending, and perennial.'

When we feel confused, even perplexed, and we struggle at times to make sense of what is going on in today's world, it is easy to lose heart and become dispirited and despondent. In such times, it is absolutely imperative that we look up and catch a vision of one who is seated on the throne and be encouraged that the Lord Jesus is sitting at his right hand. As we sing, 'When Satan tempts me to despair, And tells me of the guilt within; Upward I look and see him there, Who made an end of all my sin.' In the throne room, all is calm. Sometimes, that is all we have. Every time, that is all we need.

I appreciate the story Faith Cook shares in her book, *Lives Turned Upside Down*, about Ruth Clark, the housekeeper and cook for Vicar Henry Venn (d. 1797) and his household. Ruth was converted during her years of service with the Venn family. After Henry's death, his married children provided and cared for her. Declining health and then being hit by a speeding horse and carriage brought Ruth near her end. One of the Venn daughters asked Ruth whether she had any doubts as her earthly life was coming to a close. Ruth confessed she had 'no rapturous feelings' but still no fears or doubts, and then she explained, 'He that has loved me all my life through will not forsake me now.'

That glowing truth kept Ruth Clark from caving in when the going was tough and she was passing through a dark valley; that same truth enabled Daniel to fire on all cylinders as he wilted under the revelation of God's plan for the world; for you and me, it is that simple, changeless truth that will help us stay on the front line, no matter what the enemy fires at us. Our confidence is rooted in the Ancient of Days.

8

SUPERPOWERS ON A SLIPPERY SLOPE

American novelist, Judith Viorst, is author of the beloved *Alexander and the Terrible, Horrible, No-Good, Very Bad Day* children's story book. And many more. Here are a few snippets from the bestseller:

'I went to sleep with gum in my mouth and now there is gum in my hair when I got up this morning. I tripped on the skateboard and dropped my sweater in the sink when the water was running, and I could tell it was going to be a terrible, horrible, no-good, very bad day.'

'In the carpool, Mr Gibson let Becky have the seat by the window and Audrey and Elliot got seats by the window too. I said I was scrunched. I said I was smushed. I said, "If I don't get a seat by the window I am going to get carsick." Nobody even answered me. I could tell it was going to be a terrible, horrible, no-good, very bad day.'

'There were two cupcakes in Philip Barker's lunchbox, Howard got a Hershey bar with almonds, Paul's mother gave him a jelly roll-up that had little coconut sprinkles on the top, and guess whose mother forgot to put dessert in his lunchbox. It was a terrible, horrible, no-good, very bad day.'

'There were lima beans for dinner. I hate lima beans. My bath was too hot, I got soap in my eyes, my marble went down the drain, and I had to wear my railroad pyjamas. I hate my railroad pyjamas. And when I went to bed, Nick took back the pillow he said I could keep, and my Mickey Mouse night-light burned out and I bit my tongue. The cat wants to sleep with Anthony and not me. It has been a terrible, horrible, no-good, very bad day.'

We smile and chuckle when we read chronicles like that, but I am sure all of us know that same sagging feeling of deflation only too well. From time to time, be honest, we have experienced those terrible, horrible, no-good, very bad days! In today's culture, we often hear folks saying, 'Ah, I see so-and-so is having a bad hair day!'

Well, in this tripartite vision, there are stages of progression: first, it starts off bad; second, it then gets badder; third, it continues downhill to a nadir labelled 'baddest.' As we shall see, in this chapter, Daniel was favoured with a preview of a terrible, horrible, no-good, very bad day for the covenant people of God. Tough times. Hard days and nights. A downward spiral to an all-time low.

The ray of glossy light shining through the inky black darkness reminds us that it is not spiralling out of control because God remains firmly in charge. As Rodney Stortz says, 'No matter how long the tough times last, the Lord God is sovereign, he is in control, and he will bring deliverance in his time. He will turn those difficulties into a blessing.' Yes! Our God and Saviour has an exemplary track record of turning the worst of times (all those terrible, horrible, no-good, very bad days) into the best of times, so we need to keep looking to him and trusting in him.

There are two threads woven into the fabric of Daniel 8: a golden thread which clearly shows that, irrespective of every earth-shattering movement in society and in our lives, God's matchless glory is all that matters; and a silver thread which, regardless of whatever is going on in the world at large, focuses our thinking on his sovereignty and supremacy.

When we wrap both threads around our little finger, this is what it means: we may be the recipient of bad news at 12 noon on a Monday, and within a day or two, we can stand up and step out to face an unknown future knowing that all is in the strong hand of our eternal God who holds us fast. When his glory is at stake, his sovereignty rides to the rescue of every weary pilgrim. That is the only explanation I can offer, at this point, for Daniel's post-traumatic response in verse 27, where we read, 'I, Daniel, was exhausted and lay ill for several days. Then I got up and went about the king's business' (NIV).

8:1-2

Another day, another vision

In the third year of the reign of King Belshazzar a vision appeared to me, Daniel, after that which appeared to me at the first. And I saw in the vision; and when I saw, I was in Susa the citadel, which is in the province of Elam. And I saw in the vision, and I was at the Ulai canal.

This is Daniel's second vision in the space of two years: the first, in the previous chapter, came in the year 553 BC; this one, therefore, is around 551 BC for it was revealed *in the third year* of Belshazzar's kingship. Daniel is now in his early seventies. His previous vision happened during the hours of darkness when he was asleep; this one is different in that it occurred during daylight hours when he had an experience comparable to that of the Apostle John on Patmos (Revelation 17:3, 21:10), and Ezekiel when he was taken by the Spirit up to Jerusalem (Ezekiel 8:3, 40:1-4).

It is a reminder that the sovereign Lord communicates with his faithful servants, day and night. Such a conversation is a gift from God. And Daniel is more than a tad surprised that he is on the receiving end of another major disclosure from on high; he feels unworthy and overwhelmed by the kindness and grace of his God. Not unlike C S Lewis when he penned, 'Surprised by joy, shocked that God should be so favourable,' or like Paul's confession in 1 Timothy 1:12-14 and Ephesians 3:8. For us, we must never lose that sense of awe and wonder when we contemplate his gracious dealings in our lives.

Daniel is transported about 225 miles east of Babylon and 150 miles north of the Persian Gulf (in what is today southwestern Iran) to an entirely new location in Elam province (Genesis 14:9) and the city of Susa (aka Shushan, modern-day Shush). The name is a Hebrew word meaning 'lilies' and the city was named after the abundance of those beautiful flowers that grew in the district. In Daniel's time, Susa was out in the back of beyond, but after his time it became the royal city of the Medes and Persians. It was there that Esther sat on her throne as queen (Esther 1:19-2:8), and Nehemiah responded to God's definite call upon his life to rebuild the fallen-down walls of Jerusalem (Nehemiah 1:1-11). Beginning in 1884, the site of ancient Susa, then a large mound, has been explored and has divulged many archaeological treasures. The acclaimed Code of Hammurabi was found there in 1901. 'So,' according to John MacArthur, 'it became a very significant city later on.'

Another thought on where it all happened, for we read it was *at the Ulai canal*. The Hebrew word used for 'river' is found only here in the Bible and it has been translated 'canal' in the ESV, NIV, and NASB. Archaeologists have discovered that running through the area of Susa, on the northeast of the city, was an artificial canal built to transport water between the Choaspes and Coprates rivers that flowed north and south. This manmade waterway was around 900 feet wide. Today, all that is left of the canal is a dry riverbed. Again, we are thrilled, but not at all surprised, with the pinpoint accuracy of Scripture.

From Daniel 2:4 up to the end of chapter 7 the language was Aramaic. It was the parlance of Babylon because the main thrust of the message was to the Gentiles. Then all of a sudden, in this watershed chapter, he switches back to Hebrew because the laser beam is on the times of the Gentiles and how they specifically relate to Israel and the future of the Jewish people.

As David Jeremiah notes, 'Israel has been the nerve centre of the earth since the time of Abraham. It has been the truth centre from which a stream of divine revelation has flowed since the birth of Christ. It has been the storm centre of warring nations since the days of Joshua. And it will be the peace centre of the earth during the kingdom age.' And that is precisely the reason why, from now to the end of the book, Daniel is talking in the vernacular—the heart language—of God's ancient people.

This is paramount for it means that God's people are reliably informed as to what lies ahead for them (we caught glimpses of that in Daniel 7); it also enables them to prepare for what they will have to face along the tortuous route mapped out here in Daniel

8. John Calvin says it well, when he writes that 'the faithful were informed beforehand of these grievous and oppressive calamities to induce them to look up to God when oppressed by such extreme darkness.' The biblical principle is: to be forewarned is to be forearmed. A pertinent lesson for us because God gives us all the tools that we need to face the minor and major crises of history.

Iain Duguid is most reassuring, when he says, 'No matter how great and menacing an empire may appear to be, it is simply an actor in a play written by someone else. It plays out the role assigned to it by God on the revolving stage of world history, and then, when its lines are over, it slinks off ignominiously into the wings.' Yet another reminder that God directs the course of history on an international scale and also on a personal front as it impacts your life and mine. Earthly empires come and go in a ceaseless round; only the kingdom of God is forever.

Based on the historic timeline of Daniel, this unputdownable chapter fits chronologically immediately after chapter 7 and prior to chapter 5; therefore, the riveting narrative should be read as follows: chapters 1-2-3-4-7-8-5. And the plot thickens when we come to chapter 9.

8:3-4, 20

A butting ram becomes a battering ram

I raised my eyes and saw, and behold, a ram standing on the bank of the canal. It had two horns, and both horns were high, but one was higher than the other, and the higher one came up last. I saw the ram charging westward and northward and southward. No beast could stand before him, and there was no one who could rescue from his power. He did as he pleased and became great. "As for the ram that you saw with the two horns, these are the kings of Media and Persia."

In Daniel's first vision he saw four beasts (Daniel 7:3-7), this time around it is limited to two, a ram and a male goat. We do not need to rack our brains to work out the connection between each animal and a particular empire, as the biblical text does that for us (Daniel 8:20-21): the ram represents Medo-Persia, and the goat symbolises Greece. As before, the interpretation of the vision immediately follows the unveiling of the message to God's servant (Daniel 8:17-26).

Tradition confirms that the ram was the symbol of Persia. It was stamped on their coins and adorned the sculptured pillars of Persepolis, capital city of the Persian King Xerxes. On the battlefield, a banner displaying a ram was held aloft. The Persian king always wore the head of a ram on his head when in public. The ram was noted for its sturdy strength and its superb ability to thrust the enemy from its path – those horns were meant to be used, and they were! Like a raging bull, you did not dilly-dally when a marauding ram was coming at you. If you had any sense at all, you made a speedy exit.

There were two horns of varying size, one growing bigger after the other. Again, that depicts the twin powers of Media and Persia, but ultimately Persia under the rule of Cyrus became the stronger and more influential within the empire (Daniel 7:5). Let me give you some background: In the early years of Medo-Persian control, the Medes were the stronger power. They joined with the Babylonians and Nabopolasser in 612 BC to destroy the Assyrian Empire at Nineveh. 'But that was before Cyrus,' writes Kenneth Gangel, 'under whose leadership the Persians became masters of the dual empire. The *later* horn became the *longer* horn in 550 BC when the Medes betrayed their king into his hands.' He conquered Ekbatana, the Median capital, and became Cyrus the Great, king of Persia. Joyce Baldwin says that 'nearly two hundred years of history and political aggrandisement' are summed up in the space of nine or ten lines on your average-size Bible page column.

Talking about Cyrus, it is most interesting to discover that Isaiah wrote of him two hundred years before he appears on the world stage. God speaks through the prophet and calls Cyrus, 'my shepherd' (Isaiah 44:28) and 'his anointed' (Isaiah 45:1). 'Both references,' notes Jim Allen, 'allow us to see God at work among the nations of the world who, while they think they are doing their own will, are simply outworking the purposes of God.' As we shall see in Daniel 9, here is the king who, having captured Babylon in 539 BC, shortly afterward issued the decree that allowed the captive Jewish people to return back home to their own land (Isaiah 44:28; 2 Chronicles 36:22-23; Ezra 1:1-3, 6:2-5). This was a monumental milestone in the unfolding drama of God's everlasting purposes for his covenant people, as well as being an appreciable step in light of the advent of the Messiah (Daniel 9:24-27).

The magnificent ram seemed invincible as he trounced upon the neighbouring states and annexed them to enlarge his own kingdom. He appeared indomitable as one by one he picked off his enemies further enhancing his own reputation as an eastern warlord. Advancing from beyond the River Euphrates, an aggressive Medo-Persia conquered primarily towards the west (Babylonia, Syria, Mesopotamia, and Asia Minor), and north (Armenia, Colchis, Iberia, and regions surrounding the Caspian

Sea), and south (Egypt, Israel, Libya, and Ethiopia). Ligon Duncan says that 'the butting or the moving in all directions which the ram is described to do indicates that the Persian kingdom is expansionist ... the ram is going in every direction, gobbling up people and nations around it.'

Millions of men were conscripted into armed frontline action and so, by sheer weight of numbers, they swamped and bamboozled the panic-stricken opposition. Seemingly, none could repel the virile military muscle and nous of the Medes and Persians. The ram is conquering and unconquerable; he is impervious and untouchable. Irresistible. Standing there, on the bank of the canal, alone in majestic solitude, the ram is monarch of all he surveyed. To say there was nothing sheepish about an unbeatable Medo-Persia is an astute and accurate assessment. They were the greatest. And they knew it ... until!

8:5-8, 21-22

The galloping goat

As I was considering, behold, a male goat came from the west across the face of the whole earth, without touching the ground. And the goat had a conspicuous horn between his eyes. He came to the ram with the two horns, which I had seen standing on the bank of the canal, and he ran at him in his powerful wrath. I saw him come close to the ram, and he was enraged against him and struck the ram and broke his two horns. And the ram had no power to stand before him, but he cast him down to the ground and trampled on him. And there was no one who could rescue the ram from his power. Then the goat became exceedingly great, but when he was strong, the great horn was broken, and instead of it there came up four conspicuous horns toward the four winds of heaven. "And the goat is the king of Greece. And the great horn between his eyes is the first king. As for the horn that was broken, in place of which four others arose, four kingdoms shall arise from his nation, but not with his power."

The pictorial language used in the text is breathtakingly veracious as it perfectly describes the rapid conquests of the third world power, Greece, who hold the honour of being the first global empire of European extraction. Like a fast-moving hovercraft, out from the sunset, he crossed the Hellespont (now known as the Dardanelles) and skimmed across the surface pulverising the ram of Medo-Persia in a one-sided skirmish at the Granicus River (in modern Turkey) in May 334 BC, thereby seizing control of yet more territory.

Riding on the crest of a wave and obstinately determined to settle old scores, he pounced unexpectedly on his weakened prey, and complete victory was assured at the battles of Issus the following year and at Guagamela near Nineveh in October 331 BC. The ram is dead! Long live the goat! The world was then his oyster. In little over a decade, Alexander built an empire spread over 1.5 million square miles stretching from the River Danube, in Europe, to the Indus River, in Pakistan.

Alexander smashed and mashed the opposition to such an extent that they could do nothing but raise the white flag in surrender. They were indefatigable in their energy, often defeating forces ten times the size of his own. Students of military tactics take their hats off to Alexander for his well-drilled infantry marched forward closely tied together with shields and spears forming a knife-like force called a *phalanx*. This type of warfare was still being used 1,500 years later by the Byzantine armies that controlled Constantinople. Their amazing war machine was financed by a seemingly bottomless pit of valuable resources, most of which were treasures and riches pillaged from other countries. This shaggy goat was in a class of its own. Remember, for Daniel, this prediction was still far ahead into the future, two hundred years, and it came to pass. A gentle reminder that Alexander did not write the script, he was simply an actor on stage fulfilling the plans of the divine Director.

The goat symbol was found on the hard currency of Greece. Her ancient capital, Aegae, means 'goat city' and the sparkling blue waters of the Aegean Sea are also spoken of as 'goat sea.' Another fascinating coincidence is seen in that her zodiac sign is Capricorn, a goat. It stems from the Latin, *caper*, a goat, and *cornu*, a horn.

We note from the biblical text that there was a *conspicuous horn between his eyes*. There is no doubt that this is a specific reference to Alexander the Great who was a general in the army at age 21, and whom we have met already in our studies in Daniel 2 and Daniel 7. He was a military maestro with unique intelligence and tactical genius. A virtuoso, he was light years ahead of his contemporaries with his Einstein-flair for strategy on the battlefields of the world. And it showed. Having gone to the top of the hill, he fell. He reached the summit and then tragically it all came to an abrupt end. A brief obituary of one short sentence chronicles his death, for we read, *when he was strong, the great horn was broken*. After twelve years on the roof of the world, his demise came quickly when he died at the age of thirty-three on 10 June 323 BC.

He was the victim of a severe fever (reputedly malaria) which, humanly speaking, brought about his premature and untimely death. Other debilitating factors seem to indicate that he had strong homosexual tendencies and lived a life of drunken debauchery. Sadly, he conquered the world by age 26, but he failed to conquer himself. On that point, I'm sure there is a red warning light for each of us to seriously ponder and take on board in our own life and ministry.

One moment, he was sitting on the pinnacle of success, at his zenith; next moment, he is six feet under in a hole in the ground. Here today. Gone today. So compellingly authoritative and yet so tenuously delicate. In the hour of his death, Alexander the Great became Alexander Not-so Great. As Paul reminds us, death is man's last enemy (1 Corinthians 15:26), and as history confirms, on this occasion, Alexander lost his first and final battle at the same decisive moment.

Anthony Read, author of *The Devil's Disciples: Hitler's Inner Circle*, writes in a similar vein when he reflects on the aftermath of the Nuremberg war trials of 1946. After the executions by hanging of Nazi celebrities on 16 October, fourteen bodies including those of Goering, Ribbentrop, and Keitel, were delivered to a Munich crematorium. Later, a container holding their ashes was driven through a rain shower into the lush Bavarian countryside. After an hour's drive the vehicle stopped and the ashes were poured into a muddy ditch. That same night a drizzle of rain washed them away!

When Alexander died, with the exception of a handful of cronies, few mourned his passing and his empire descended into anarchy. As the months rolled into years, the government of the realm lapsed into a state of total disarray and chaotic mayhem. A bitter power struggle was waged spanning a little over two decades before the fragile kingdom was eventually carved up into four segments. Just as the Scriptures said it would be!

Cassander and Lysimachus took their bit gaining control of

Macedon and Greece for one, western Asia Minor and Thrace for the other; the truth is that from this point forward they are written out of the prophetic script as the lens zooms in on Israel and her neighbours. The other two generals, Ptolemy and Seleucus, had their chunk of the kingdom (Egypt for one and Syria and Mesopotamia for the other); each of these men are identified as 'the king of the south' and 'the king of the north' respectively in Daniel 11:5-6. More later. Dale Ralph Davis writes, 'And this is where the people of God have to live; this history is their address.'

Looking back, we are able to see the bigger picture: in the course of his campaigns, Alexander stemmed the tide of Oriental influence that threatened to permeate the western world. His visionary outlook and global awareness had a colossal impact on the mindset and philosophy of the ancient world. By extending Greek culture and language—Hellenism—he helped bring fragmented peoples with no sense of identity together and paved the way for common (*koine*) Greek to become the language of the New Testament.

The lesson is unerringly clear for God is never taken by surprise. He is the Sovereign Lord who knows all about the future, and the past, and present. He can see beyond today into tomorrow and the day after, and so on. Superpowers are not the safest of places to be, even more so in times of conflict, but he has the whole world in his hands. And thank God, we are there as well. It is truly marvellous that God is not only in the business of controlling the destiny of his own people, but he is in the business of controlling the destiny of those who are even against his own people.

As Iain Duguid says, 'The menacing world that is out of your control is never beyond his control. The one who raises up world conquerors and then consigns them in turn to the pages of ancient history books is the same one who controls your personal story as well.' When rams and he-goats have crossed the stage of history, God has a Lamb! He is worthy (Revelation 5:12-13). And that is how we keep our head above water in days of turbulence and upheaval, knowing that Father knows best, Jesus is exalted and praised, and nothing and no one can ever separate us from his heartfelt love (Romans 8:38-39).

8:9-14

Antiochus IV Epiphanes

Out of them came a little horn, which grew exceedingly great toward the south, toward the east, and toward the glorious land. It grew great, even to the host of heaven. And some of the host and some of the stars it threw down to the ground and trampled on them. It became great, even as great as the Prince of the host. And the regular burnt offering was taken away from him, and the place of his sanctuary was overthrown. And a host will be given over to it together with the regular burnt offering because of transgression, and it will throw truth to the ground, and it will act and prosper. Then I heard a holy one speaking, and another holy one said to the one who spoke, "For how long is the vision concerning the regular burnt offering, the transgression that makes desolate, and the giving over of the sanctuary and host to be trampled underfoot?" And he said to me, "For 2,300 evenings and mornings. Then the sanctuary shall be restored to its rightful state."

A different empire, a different horn; it is important for us to realise that distinction from the outset otherwise we end up thoroughly confused and this bad guy gets mixed up with the other badder guy from Daniel 7:8, the endtime antichrist. When this *little horn* arrives on the scene we are brought face to face with Antiochus IV Epiphanes (meaning 'illustrious'). He was eighth in line of successors from Seleucus Nicator and he reigned in Syria from 175 to 164 BC. He was the son of Antiochus III the Great. 'The little horn not only takes a position of prominence,' writes Sinclair Ferguson, 'it becomes the centrepiece of the vision, and its activity is described in great detail.' In fact, Antiochus is given top billing as he elbows Alexander into the sidings.

So within the orbit of a few words in verse 8, the prophecy skips from the historic moment when Alexander's empire was divided up to 175 BC when Antiochus ruled. Much of what transpired in the intervening epoch of over a century is recorded for us in Daniel 11:1-35 with mind-blowing accuracy.

He started off in a low-key manner for he was not the rightful heir to the throne (his nephew Demetrius was being held as a hostage in Rome), but he wormed his way into power, getting where he wanted to be by means of bribery and flattery. It was not long, however, before he began to make his presence felt in the world. He made an enormous impact through victorious conquests and the heavy-handed policies he mercilessly implemented. He attacked Egypt to the south, Armenia and Elymais to the east, before encroaching upon the *glorious land*, Israel. Other translations refer to it as the 'Beautiful Land' (NIV), of which the Sons of Korah sang, 'It is beautiful in its loftiness, the joy of the whole earth' (Psalm 48:2, NIV). Antiochus had an inbred hatred towards the Jewish people. He murdered tens of thousands of them and his notoriety spread afar. He is one of the worst examples of anti-Semitism ever seen in this world.

In the Scriptures, righteous Jews are often represented by stars

(Genesis 15:5, 22:17; Daniel 12:3; Matthew 13:43; Revelation 12:1). His wholesale slaughter of the sons of Abraham is a bold, brazen attempt to obliterate the ancient people of the covenant. Actually, in one assault on Jerusalem, forty thousand Jewish people were massacred in three days and a further ten thousand deported into captivity to face an uncertain future. This was genocide, ethnic cleansing, on a frightening scale. It is no exaggeration to say that Satan empowered and energised him to such a degree that his devilish ploy is a tool in his hand to prevent the Messiah from coming into the world. Thankfully, his plans were foiled.

He profaned the temple in the holy city of Jerusalem and carried out a deep-clean purge of every form of worship associated with Judaism. He systematically looted the temple of its priceless treasures. He even had the audacity and arrogance to remove the golden altar of incense, the table of shewbread, and the golden lampstand from within the holy place. He stripped the temple of its sacred furnishings. Nothing was off limits to him, it was one atrocity after another. 'In so doing,' as Kenneth Gangel notes, 'he did not just take [everything] away from the people, he stole it from God himself.' Asaph wrote of a similar, but perhaps less awful, situation in Psalm 79:1-4.

After Antiochus successfully plundered and defiled the temple, he had it rededicated as a place of worship for Olympian Zeus, the chief Greek god. Nebuchadnezzar, Belshazzar, and Darius had defied God, but they had never done anything like this. He had a pagan altar built over the altar of God and commanded that regular sacrifices be replaced by the offering of pigs. This came to be known as the 'abomination of desolation.' He set up his own man, Jason, followed by Menelaus, as high priest. As you can imagine, all this was anathema to the Jewish people and a base act of gross sacrilege towards the Most High. He even went so far as to have coins minted with the inscription, 'Antiochus Theos Epiphanes – The God Made Manifest.' All of this is a taster of what lies even further ahead in future days when antichrist is on the prowl (Daniel 9:26-27).

The decimated Jewish community felt a total sense of revulsion and deep loathing for every scurrilous act perpetrated by this abusive tyrant. So much so that they labelled him Epimanes, that is, Antiochus the Madman. He was all that, and more. Dale Ralph Davis describes his eccentric behaviour as that of 'a slick and godless piece of scum.'

Angel talk

Daniel overhears a conversation going on between a couple of angels as they wonder how long this blasphemous act will continue. It is encouraging to know that heaven is consciously aware of what God's people are going through down here on earth. 'How long?' is the anguished cry of God's people down the years; it is echoed in many expressions of heart-aching lament (Psalms 6:3, 74:10, 80:4, 94:3). The answer is supplied with the figure of *2,300 evenings and mornings* (Genesis 1:5, 8, 13, 19, 23, 31). That is, 2,300 literal days, just as we speak of forty days and forty nights (Genesis 7:4; Exodus 24:18; 1 Kings 19:8), and three days and three nights (Jonah 1:17; Matthew 12:40).

For Daniel, that timeframe was a glimmer of light in the darkness. It is a long time, but a limited time. The desecration of God's house and the severe persecution of God's people is always bound by a strict time deadline. The parameters are set. The lines are drawn. Praise God, he never moves the goalposts. And knowing our humanness as he does, God graciously numbers their pain in days thereby giving them a figure they can easily count and then tick off the schedule when the day is done.

When we look back and consult the calendar of this period it should not surprise us that everything dovetails beautifully into place, like pieces in a jigsaw. God rescued them from a terrible, horrible, no-good, very bad day just as he had promised. Working back from 25 December 164 BC, the published date for the restoration and cleansing of the temple under Judas Maccabeus (aka Judas the Hammer), 2,300 days brings us right up to 6 September 171 BC, the date when Antiochus kicked off his cruel oppression of the Jewish people.

To this day, in Jewish homes around the world the feast of Hanukkah is celebrated annually for eight days in December. It means 'dedication' and is sometimes called the Festival of Lights. We read of one special occasion when Jesus, Prince of princes and Light of the world, was present in Jerusalem when this feast was going on (John 10:22). John Lennox writes, 'In the very place where Antiochus had stood – a man who named himself *Epiphanes*, "God made manifest" – Jesus now stood.'

Hanukkah perpetuates the memory of the miraculous discovery of consecrated oil for the temple lamps. Jewish people celebrate that glad day by lighting a series of eight candles on the hanukkiah, one each evening, using the shamash (the servant candle), in the window of their home. A light shining in the midst of darkness.

A delightful anecdote is told when a persecutor of the Jewish people in Russia asked a Jewish man what he thought the outcome would be if the wave of persecutions continued. The man answered, 'The result will be a feast! Pharaoh tried to eradicate us, but the consequence was Passover. Haman attempted to exterminate us, but the upshot was Purim. Antiochus Epiphanes sought to eliminate us, but the corollary was Hanukkah. Just try to destroy us, and we will start another feast.'

8:15-19

A divine messenger

When I, Daniel, had seen the vision, I sought to understand it. And behold, there stood before me one having the appearance of a man. And I heard a man's voice between the banks of the Ulai, and it called, "Gabriel, make this man understand the vision." So he came near where I stood. And when he came, I was frightened and fell on my face. But he said to me, "Understand, O son of man, that the vision is for the time of the end." And when he had spoken to me, I fell into a deep sleep with my face to the ground. But he touched me and made me stand up. He said, "Behold, I will make known to you what shall be at the latter end of the indignation, for it refers to the appointed time of the end."

Some things in life we understand, some things in life we plainly do not. And that is Daniel's lot right here in this mini section. He has seen the vision and it has left him overwhelmed, with loads of questions racing through his mind. He needs help from on high to crack the code, to decipher the dream. That welcome assistance comes from an angel called Gabriel. Based on the meaning of his name, he is one of God's mighty or strong ones. This is actually the first mention in the Bible of a holy angel by name; the only other one named is Michael (Daniel 10:13, 21; 12:1; Jude 9; Revelation 12:7) and he is number one in the angelic pecking order.

There is so much about Gabriel that thrills the heart because, according to John MacArthur, 'he is God's official publicity man, the guy who makes the big announcements.' When we fast forward to the last of the synoptic gospels, we read that he broke the incredible news to Zechariah who was serving in the temple that his wife Elizabeth was going to give birth to a baby boy who would be known as John the Baptist (Luke 1:11-13). For us as new covenant people, we need to learn from Zechariah's reaction of disbelief to the angelic announcement; we would do well, therefore, to 'pay more careful attention to what we have heard' of Gabriel's words right here in Daniel 8 and elsewhere (Hebrews 2:1, NIV).

A little while later history repeated itself when Gabriel visited Mary some miles north in the town of Nazareth and broke sensational news to this young woman. It was the dream and desire of every Jewish girl to be the one who would give birth to the Messiah, the Lord Jesus Christ. That huge honour was given to Mary when 'she found favour with God' (Luke 1:26-33, NIV).

So it falls to Gabriel as God's special envoy to inform Daniel of the meaning behind the divine movie and to help him make sense of it all. As you can imagine, Daniel was completely flummoxed and it showed when he fell flat on his face. He was emotionally overcome. Fearful, too. His reaction is perfectly understandable as something similar happened to John (Revelation 19:10, 22:8). It is an entirely normal response when someone of flesh and blood has a one-to-one encounter with a supernatural being from another world. Indeed, this is something of a biblical pattern (Exodus 3:6; Isaiah 6:5; Ezekiel 1:28; Acts 9:3-4; Revelation 1:17).

For Daniel, this visitor from on high was not there to intimidate him or browbeat him or condemn him in any way, he was there to reassure him that God was in the control tower and pressing all the right buttons at just the right time. In a lovely moment, that is when the angel whispered into his ear, *Understand, O son of man, that the vision is for the time of the end*. To which, Daniel prostrated himself before the holy messenger with his face to the ground. That was an act of abject humility before the throne of the Most High and a sincere recognition of his tremendous need. That is when the angel reached out and touched him, enabling him to stand up and listen to the rest of what he had to say. The angel restored him.

How often in your life and mine have we unwittingly known the touch from another to help us get up, then stand up, and face the challenges and demands of life. We thank God for the sensitive support ministry of his unseen secret agents (Hebrews 1:14). Gabriel amplified on his opening comment to Daniel when he told him, *Behold, I will make known to you what shall be at the latter end of the indignation, for it refers to the appointed time of the end*.

These words are a timely reminder to Daniel that there are terribly dark days ahead for his people, God's people. There will be storms for them to face when the future will appear so bleak and forlorn; days and weeks on end when there is no light at the end of a long tunnel of tumultuous trial. There is a tsunami of turbulence looming and it promises to be a roller-coaster ride for all those living in Israel. For them, it will be a terrible, horrible, no-good, very bad day.

The word translated *indignation* should really be translated 'fury.' As Jim Allen writes, 'It is used in the Old Testament of those periods when God showed his anger with Israel for their sin and, in his outrage at their hurtful behaviour, allowed invaders like

Assyria and Babylon (Isaiah 10:25, 54:7-8) to move against them. It is used here of the period already set for the domination of Jerusalem by Antiochus Epiphanes and it will be used again for the terrible period of tribulation that still lies ahead for Israel and for the nations of earth (Daniel 11:36).'

From God's perspective, there is an end in his sight, a cut-off point, and that date is set in stone for it is an *appointed time*. Not a day less. Not a minute more. The key movers and shakers during this anticipated period will be revealed to Daniel as he attunes his ear to the angelic interpretation. The baseline is that Antiochus Epiphanes is no friend to the people of God, and in that capacity, he foreshadows a still future world ruler, the antichrist, whose regime is even worse (Daniel 11:36-45; 2 Thessalonians 2:1-12). In that light, it signifies that the darkest days of all will be the days just before the dawn of the new day when the Son of Man rules and reigns in splendour (Daniel 7:14). Basically, a faithful God tells Daniel what he needs to know, not necessarily all that he wants to know.

Allied to that wonderful truth is another side to the argument for there are 'secret things' which belong exclusively to the Lord (Deuteronomy 29:29). Such matters are known only to him, and we must be content to leave it like that. Why did a sovereign God allow the Holocaust to happen? Why have there been more followers of Jesus martyred in the twentieth century than in all those preceding it? We have no answer to such searching questions, but we trust one who doeth all things well and who gave his one and only Son to be our Saviour (Romans 8:32). As the hymnwriter William Cowper (1731-1800) penned, 'Judge not the Lord by feeble sense, But trust him for his grace; Behind a frowning providence, He hides a smiling face.'

8:23-26

Another look at Antiochus

> *"And at the latter end of their kingdom, when the transgressors*
> *have reached their limit, a king of bold face, one who understands*
> *riddles, shall arise. His power shall be great – but not by his*
> *own power; and he shall cause fearful destruction and shall*
> *succeed in what he does, and destroy mighty men and the people*
> *who are saints. By his cunning he shall make deceit prosper*
> *under his hand, and in his own mind he shall become great.*
> *Without warning he shall destroy many. And he shall even rise*
> *up against the Prince of princes, and he shall be broken – but by*
> *no human hand. The vision of the evenings and the mornings*
> *that has been told is true, but seal up the vision, for it refers to*
> *many days from now."*

Gabriel is straight to the point when interpreting the vision to
Daniel and leaves him in absolutely no doubt as to the extreme
emergency facing God's people in Israel. Down through the
centuries they have been hunted and hounded and driven from
pillar to post, but they have never known anything quite like this.
And that is where Antiochus makes many an earthly tyrant fade
into oblivion for this maniacal, unconscionable monster is among
the worst of a very bad bunch of rotten individuals. No wonder
Daniel feels the way he does.

Suave and savvy politician that he was, Antiochus did not
suffer fools gladly. He had a stern look about him that caused big
men to tremble in their sandals; he was not the kind of person
you would walk up to and crack a joke with or invite to your
place for a coffee and chat. If he needed you, you would know
all about it; and when he had squeezed all the juice from your

lemon and finished with you, you knew all about it then too. In our culture, we would speak of him as 'a hard-nosed man.'

Antiochus, the poster boy of cunning and deceit, is a master of intrigue with a special interest in the so-called dark arts. Because of this, he has an innate ability to sway the masses of gullible folks all around. He is economical with the truth as he spawns the language of the lie to great effect. He has the poisonous tongue of a viper and is enmeshed in a web of occultic influence. As a manipulative person, he is so twisted he could easily hide behind a corkscrew. Danny Akin says of him that 'double-faced agreements and duplicitous dealings are his calling cards.'

To all intents and purposes, he was Satan's puppet on a string; his fatally flawed policy of liquidation of all things Jewish is nothing more than a masterstroke from hell itself. We know from the archives of history that there was more than one bloodbath during his vicious tenure. Without doubt, he was a debased, diabolical, degenerate, and devilish leader of men.

Gabriel hits the nail on the head when he acknowledges that *his power shall be great* – and it was – but *not by his own power* for it is clear for all to see that he is on Satan's payroll. He finds immense pleasure in evil. He has no qualms or quibbles about elevating himself to the heady heights of deity; he reckoned he was not only equal with God, but that he was one better, and it showed in his spiteful venom especially towards the Jewish people. Such audacious insolence. Egotism, conceit, and self-deification are his unholy trinity.

Simply put, this dirtbag of a monarch was a God-detesting, implacable Jew-hater. He was antichrist in all that he said and did, and as such, he embodies most of the telltale traits of the coming antichrist as portrayed in Revelation 13:1-8. I visualise Daniel

8 like a light that shines from the foot of a statue of Antiochus Epiphanes. Because the light shines from below, it leaves a huge shadow on the wall behind the statue. That shadowy silhouette marks the career of the final antichrist.

It is true that a reckless Antiochus overstepped the mark on more than one occasion in life, but in death he had no say whatsoever (Hebrews 9:27). The information surrounding his death is chilling. After committing his villainy in Israel, he travelled east hoping to conquer more territory. While in Babylon he received word that the Jews, led by the heroic Judas Maccabeus, had retaken Jerusalem, driven out the invaders, and initiated the process of cleansing the temple. When Antiochus heard this he began to journey back to Israel, intending to wipe the floor with the troublesome Jews once and for all.

A chariot crash left him sorely wounded. While recovering, he contracted a loathsome bowel disease that caused a terrible odour to surround him. One source says that worms came out of his body as it rotted away. His life ended in a wretched fashion. He died not at the hand of man; he died by the unseen hand of God (2 Maccabees 9:5-7). He was brought to heel by supernatural intervention. An idiot, he thought he could resist God and get by with it. His little journey from the womb to the tomb was over. An inglorious end. Reformer Martin Luther said, 'The Prince of Darkness grim, We tremble not for him; His rage we can endure, For lo! His doom is sure, One little word shall fell him.'

Despite the gravity and grotesqueness of this grim image, Gabriel affirms the vision is true. There is no reason for us to doubt or question its integrity (2 Peter 1:19). Daniel's responsibility was to write it down and preserve it for those in days yet to come who will need it. The kindness of the Lord ensures that his people will have an anchor in the coming storm. Because what is in the past to us was in the future to Daniel; so this significant vision must be safeguarded for future generations. The question is: Did the Bible get it right in Daniel 8? The unequivocal answer is a resounding yes!

8:27

Getting to grips

And I, Daniel, was overcome and lay sick for some days. Then I rose and went about the king's business, but I was appalled by the vision and did not understand it.

Daniel's response to the vision and its interpretation is understandable for he has seen and heard so much. His feelings of angst mirrors Jeremiah's grief when Jerusalem fell and he penned Lamentations. Daniel is so deeply moved, even overwhelmed and shocked, that it took its toll on him emotionally and physically. It is most interesting to note that when Daniel discovers that this will not happen in his lifetime, he goes down sick for several days; when Hezekiah was told that his kingdom would be sacked, but not in his lifetime, he was enormously relieved (2 Kings 20:12-19). A stark contrast.

That gives you an inkling into Daniel's heart for he was not in the least interested in building his own wee empire. He was more concerned for God's kingdom and God's people having to endure such horrendous persecution. It broke Daniel. It seems that Daniel would have been satisfied and content to live in obscurity so long as the work of God was not obscured. His life was wrapped up in theirs and his singular desire was for God's eternal name to be magnified more than any other (1 Thessalonians 3:8). Like

Charles Spurgeon, he could say, 'Let my name perish, but let the name of Jesus Christ endure.'

I love this about Daniel for no sooner is he back on his feet when he is out the front door and straight back to work, doing *the king's business*. His priorities are right, his perspectives are right, his passions are right. The vision massively impacted him, no doubts about that, but there is life after such an encounter with the Almighty. His work on earth was not yet finished, there was still more for him to do in Belshazzar's pagan Babylon. So he got up and got on with it. Period.

While riding upcountry to a preaching engagement one day, John Wesley was stopped by a stranger who asked him what he would do if he knew that Christ was going to return at noon the next day. Wesley reached down into his saddlebag, retrieved his diary, read out his engagements for the rest of the day and for the morning of the next day, and said, 'That, dear sir, is what I would do.' That was the godly attitude of Daniel. He was living and serving today in light of God's tomorrow. Living life in the future tense. Salt and light in the wider community. May God enable us to follow in his footsteps.

9

BACK TO THE FUTURE

An old story from the Far East tells about a large and beautiful 23-ton bronze bell in the city of Rangoon, Myanmar, a distinctive pride of the great Buddhist Shwedagon pagoda. During the first Anglo-Burmese war in the early 1800s, the bell, popularly known as the Singu Min Bell, had been sunk in the Yangon river that ran through the city, and no amount of effort by British engineers could raise it.

One day, a thinking-outside-the-box priest asked permission to make an attempt at rescuing the bell on the condition that the bell would be restored to its place of honour in the pagoda. When the authorities agreed, he had his assistants gather a large number of bamboo rods—hollow, light, and very buoyant. Divers took the rods down and fastened them to the bell resting on the sandy riverbed.

After thousands of rods had been securely tied to the bell, that ponderous relic actually began to move, and as more and more rods were added, their accumulated buoyancy was so great that they actually lifted the bronze mass from the river bottom and brought it to the surface. Success.

In this key chapter, we learn timely lessons on prayer from

a man of God as Daniel leads from the front when he models for us the biblical principles behind the buoyant rods of prayer. 'We all know from experience,' writes Kenneth Gangel, 'that prayer can lift the heaviest of burdens and reach down into the muddiest and deepest rivers.' Such concentrated, focused prayer sees unbelievable displays of God's power unleashed as prayer is answered in unimaginable ways that blow the cobwebs from our lives (Ephesians 3:20-21).

For Daniel, that proved to be a sweet reality over and over again. Anne Graham Lotz in her book, *The Daniel Prayer*, notes that 'God miraculously intervened to save Daniel from the fury of Nebuchadnezzar, the folly of Belshazzar, and the fanaticism of Darius until he performed [in this chapter] the greatest miracle of all in answer to Daniel's prayer.' We need to remind ourselves, one more time, that prayer does not change things, but God changes things (and us) through the medium of fervent prayer. Positive result.

Daniel's big prayer, as we shall see, is one of those passionate, heartfelt, touching the throne, rooted in Scripture prayers; the kind of prayer that says with Jacob and Jabez, 'Lord, I will not let you go until you bless me; Lord, I am pleading with you until I get an answer' (Genesis 32:26; 1 Chronicles 4:10). There are no shortcuts to cultivating such a bountiful relationship with God, as Daniel knew his God. Prayer flowed like a refreshing stream from Daniel's heart because of his faithfulness to the God of the covenant and as such he was not performing a religious duty three times per day, but when he prayed, he was showing his love for and total dependence upon his great God.

As we discovered further back in Daniel 6, it was something he worked at tirelessly and to which he was solidly committed, rain or shine. The road to the throne of grace was well trodden by Daniel as he communed with his God daily (Hebrews 4:16). It reminds me of a most challenging comment from the seventeenth-century Puritan John Owen, when he said, 'What an individual is in secret, on his knees before God, that he is and no more.'

9:1-2

First things first

In the first year of Darius the son of Ahasuerus, by descent a Mede, who was made king over the realm of the Chaldeans – in the first year of his reign, I, Daniel, perceived in the books the number of years that, according to the word of the Lord to Jeremiah the prophet, must pass before the end of the desolations of Jerusalem, namely, seventy years.

The eagle-eyed among you will immediately notice that we are now operating under a different regime with a different king sitting on the throne, *Darius the son of Ahasuerus* (please note: this is not the same Ahasuerus who married Esther). We meet Darius in the first year of his reign, around 539-538 BC. Babylon has fallen, consigned to the dustbin of history. That means we have transitioned from one world empire to another, Medo-Persia. A new day has dawned. Such a momentous event is of major importance when it comes to the chronological structure of this amazing book. The chapter order is as follows: 1, 2, 3, 4, 7, 8, 5, 9, 6 … therefore, Daniel 9 sits in between chapters 5 and 6. That means, Daniel was in the den of lions after this prayer. No wonder he refused to stop praying.

As a point of interest, the name *Darius* is not a personal name as in a man being called Joseph, George, or William, but it is a dynastic name. There were many Medo-Persian kings who went under the name of Darius. This is the same person Daniel introduced into the biblical narrative after the fall of Babylon (Daniel 5:31, 6:1). We read that he *was made king over the realm of the Chaldeans* which is a most unusual way to describe the event in question. Truth be told, Darius had been installed by Cyrus the Great as viceroy in Babylonia, with the title of king afforded to him (Daniel 6:1, 9:1). He had no scruples appointing a Mede to an important role like this as it signalled a gesture of conciliation to the masses who could be rebellious if things did not quite work out as planned. Allied to that, why should good men be dispensed with just because they are from a different tribe or nation? For Cyrus, this was the best of both worlds.

Searching the scrolls

This was a critical hour in world history and it was imperative that the new government got it right early on in their rule. Failure to do so would result in all kinds of mayhem and potential social disorder. They needed to grasp the nettle from day one, otherwise seeds of confusion and uncertainty would be sown in the minds of ordinary folks on the street and among those doing business in the bustling marketplace. This was a brand new experience for a whole generation of real people who were walking down a real road they had never navigated before; they must have been incredibly worried, piqued, and apprehensive. They woke up each new morning on tenterhooks and went to bed at night with butterflies in their stomach. Such are the jarring realities of life in Babylon in the sixth century BC.

And that is why Daniel finds himself, again, down on his knees with an open scroll of Scripture spread out before him. For him, this was the norm. In an hour of crisis, Daniel desperately longs to hear from God with a pertinent word from above. In a frenetic world, a busy Daniel is patiently investigating timeless truth because he wants and needs to be informed. He is a student of God's Word, even though he is the age that he is. He knows the value of taking time out with God. Do we? Nonconformist pastor and author Matthew Henry (1662-1714) says that 'the greatest and best men in the world must not think themselves above their Bibles.' Daniel is prayerfully reading through the scroll of his contemporary, Jeremiah, doing what Robert Murray McCheyne practised, when he turned the Bible into prayer.

So far as Daniel is concerned, it is essential for us to realise that he considered the writings of Jeremiah to be the living Word of the living God (2 Timothy 3:16). This cogent conviction is still the secret of how to live in 'Babylon' without 'Babylon' living in you. At that point in time, the Hebrew canon was incomplete, but Jeremiah's book was an integral part of God's inspired, infallible, and inerrant Word to man. Authentic. Reliable. Credible. Believable. Bob Fyall writes in *Daniel*, 'What Scripture says is what God says, and what God says happens.'

A light bulb moment

As Daniel methodically pores over the sacred writings, he is suddenly arrested. Captivated. Like a bolt from the blue, something that seemed almost too good to be true gripped his heart. He kept his finger on the papyrus. He stopped. He reread it a time or two just to make sure he was not making it up, for this is what he read, 'This entire land will become a desolate wasteland. Israel and her neighbouring lands will serve the king of Babylon for seventy years. Then, after the seventy years of captivity are over, I will punish the king of Babylon and his people for their sins, says the Lord' (Jeremiah 25:11-12, NLT). The God who had spoken to Jeremiah years earlier had now spoken to Daniel in his apartment in the royal mews. As John Lennox writes, 'Not only had God spoken through his Word; his voice could still be heard through what he had spoken. Wonderfully, this remains the case.'

If he had kept on reading the scroll for another ten minutes, Daniel would have come across a letter penned in 597 BC to the exiles in Babylon (Jeremiah 29:10-14), a few verses which also emphasise their restoration without any preconditions. It is not saying that God will do x if they will do y. Not at all. God clearly set out his specific intention in relation to the ending of the exile.

For Daniel, now in his 80s, this is an *aide-mémoire* that we are never too old to read the Word of God. For his elderly servant, this was one of those red-letter moments when your silver hair stands on end. Because these few verses reminded him, after seven decades in exile, that the God who opened up the Red Sea would open up a way for his covenant people to return to their homeland. 'God will make a way where there seems to be no way,' enthuses Don Moen.

Daniel begins to count from when he was deported in 605 BC, in the first phase of three major banishments, and he quickly reckons that seventy years are as good as past. At the very most, there are three years still to run before the deadline expired. Their time in a foreign land is drawing to a close and they are on the verge of something sensational. Their days of weeping beside the rivers of Babylon were almost up; soon they could take their harps down from the poplar trees for they were going back home to Israel, their Promised Land (Psalm 137:1-2). The Jewish captives are standing on the threshold of a new era. Exciting. Daniel certainly thought so.

9:3

Prophet of the open window

Then I turned my face to the Lord God, seeking him by prayer and pleas for mercy with fasting and sackcloth and ashes.

The message from Jeremiah's scroll fired Daniel up to such an extent that it spurred him to prayer. There is no sense with Daniel that because it is promised in Scripture and it will, therefore, come to pass that he should just sit back and wait for it all to happen. For him, the promise was a divine nudge that sent him to prayer. He was oozing confidence in the sure promises of the Word of God so he now storms the gates of heaven itself. He has a lot on his mind, perhaps even more on his heart, so he pursues what seems the most natural thing for him to do, he prays. He does what Eugene Peterson calls 'reversed thunder' when he prays God's Word back to him. C H Spurgeon was on a similar wavelength when he said that 'prayer was like a homing pigeon. It begins in the heart of God. It is sent out and it lands in the heart of God's people who then send it back to the heart of God.' That is real prayer.

When we understand the truth of the Word of God, then we make sense of the purposes and plans of God and these combine to govern and guide our prayers. Dale Ralph Davis writes, 'It is as if God's promises have Velcro on them and our prayers are meant to "get stuck" there.' We are moved to prayer by God's Word, in accordance with the promises of his Word. To help us do that, maybe we should embrace the example of the Puritans and read the Bible on our knees. That means, our hearts and lives are then shaped by what God's heart cares most about.

The titanic challenge for us is: Do we struggle to pray as we ought because we do not know the Bible as we should? John Piper makes a valid point, when he writes, 'Where the mind is not brimming with the Bible, the heart is not generally brimming with prayer.' Even for a seasoned campaigner like Daniel who has seen so much in his life and weathered so many storms, there was no hint of complacency. Absolutely none. Having heard God speak, he is highly incentivised for it drove him to action and to his knees. Daniel clearly heard from God before God heard from him. It is hearing his divine dulcet tones that makes me want to speak to him because the Bible becomes our prayer book. As Danny Akin says, 'Immersion in Scripture will energise prayer.'

A great prayer from a great pray-er

When we unpack his lengthy prayer (spanning sixteen verses) you will see how it is bathed in the Old Testament with allusions to Leviticus 26:40, Deuteronomy 28:64, Psalm 44:14, and Jeremiah 25:11. We also observe how frequently he addresses his God as LORD for he is the covenant-making, covenant-keeping God. This is the only chapter where the personal covenantal name of God, Jehovah (Hebrew, *Yahweh*), is used in the entire book and it occurs seven times from verse 2 down to verse 20. It is the same name he used to reveal himself to Abraham, Isaac, and Jacob, and the name by which he introduced himself to Moses (Exodus 6:2-8).

People often pose the question, 'If God is a sovereign God, why should we pray?' Daniel would say in response to that enquiry, 'It is *because* God is a sovereign God that I pray!' John Calvin acknowledged that 'nothing can be better for us than to ask for what he has promised.' Let me illustrate: Has God promised that when his Word is proclaimed it will not return fruitlessly to him? He has (Isaiah 55:11). So let us pray that his Word may have an impact on all those who hear it. And it will! Has God promised that the Lord Jesus will come back again? He has (1 Thessalonians 4:16-17). That is why we join hands with the beloved John and pray, 'Amen. Come, Lord Jesus' (Revelation 22:20, NIV). He will! And we will not be disappointed. The biblical basis for this principle is enshrined in 1 John 5:14-15.

This prayer is one of three noteworthy prayers recorded in Scripture and, ironically, they are all found in chapter nine of each book: apart from here in Daniel 9, there are the Levites in Nehemiah 9:6-38 and Ezra in 9:6-15. My questions are: Did Daniel's prayer set a precedent for a new type of prayer? Did he pioneer a pattern and establish a tradition of prayer that continued past him into the God-blessed ministries of other spiritually gifted men like Ezra and Nehemiah? If so, what a wonderful legacy for any man to leave behind.

Daniel has been digging down deep into the Word of God, now with the same zeal and humility he turns his face and lifts his eyes heavenwards to the Most High. This is a deliberate action on his part; there was nothing casual or flippant about it at all. For Daniel, this was far too weighty a moment for such a lackadaisical approach. He was serious. Deadly serious. He meant business with God. So much so that he approached a holy God with a contrite heart and a spirit of penitence (Psalms 34:18, 51:17). Daniel pays more than lip-service to what Stephen, a missionary friend, called 'face-down values' for he was humble before God and men.

We read that he sought the Lord by *prayer and pleas for*

mercy. He poured out his heart in supplication, he emptied his emotions, he earnestly set his face consciously gazing upon the God of Abraham, Isaac, and Jacob. Like many a prayer warrior since, Daniel was determined to get through to God. Instead of throwing a celebration party and shouting from the rooftops that liberation was imminent, Daniel makes a beeline for the mercy seat and goes before the Lord in intercession. Every word he says is God-honouring and God-centred. Billy Graham was right when he said, 'To get nations back on their feet, we must first get down on our knees.'

Doing prayer the Daniel way

There were three useful aids to his season of waiting upon God for we read that he did so *with fasting and sackcloth and ashes.* Fasting means to go without something to make time to pray. Usually, it revolves around a denial of food intake, but it can also be applied to other pursuits. In prayer, we turn solely to God; in fasting, we turn away from all the trimmings and trappings. Such an exercise of soul meant that Daniel was sorting out his personal priorities and he was saying that God was more important than anything else. He was giving God his fullest, undivided attention.

Then he wrapped himself in a rough material normally made from goat hair or camel hair. This was not silky or soft in texture, it was coarse and hard and often proved to be an irritant next to the human skin. This signified his desperation for God to work and it was a mark of his sincere repentance. Daniel went a step further when he put ashes on his head as a profound symbol of total grief. It spoke of complete ruin as he lamented and mourned over the sins of the people. He was broken before God. The petitioner has become a penitent. How true it is in our daily walk with the

Lord and especially in our prayer lives, there are no gains without pains (James 5:16).

Daniel willingly rolls up his sleeves and assumes the garb and guise of a remorseful soul as he shows God how deeply he feels about these vitally important issues (Genesis 37:34; 2 Samuel 3:31; Jonah 3:5-8). He saw himself as the representative of the Jewish people, pleading with God on their behalf. He projects himself as a beggar hammering at the back door of God's mercy and grace. Lower he cannot go. The burden on his heart is heavy, and one that he could hardly bear. So he does what he knows best, he prays. The preacher J H Jowett (1864-1923) said that 'all vital prayer makes a drain on a man's vitality. True intercession is a sacrifice, a bleeding sacrifice.'

In fact, Daniel's prayer reminds us of a poignant scene when Jesus prayed near those ancient olive trees in the Garden of Gethsemane (Luke 22:39-44). The burden of bearing the sin of the world as God's Passover lamb (John 1:29; 1 Corinthians 5:7) and draining the last drop in God's cup caused 'his sweat [to become] like drops of blood falling to the ground' (Luke 22:44, NIV). His prayer was heard and answered as the Father strengthened him for the gruelling experience of Calvary where at midday it was midnight, and three hours later, according to Martin Luther, 'God was forsaken by God' (Psalm 22:1; Matthew 27:45-46; Mark 15:33-34). The Lord Jesus 'endured the cross' so that we might 'not grow weary and lose heart' (Hebrews 12:2-3, NIV).

9:4

Great God of wonders

I prayed to the Lord my God and made confession, saying, 'O Lord,

*the great and awesome God, who keeps covenant and steadfast
love with those who love him and keep his commandments.'*

Daniel launches into his prayer with a recognition of who
God is. Before uttering any words of heartfelt confession, he
is taken up in worshipful adoration and admiration of the
beautiful character of his faithful God. He is intimate with God,
but he does so with utmost reverence as he zooms in on the
Godhood of the Most High. Always a good place to start, as
we know from the Lord's helpful instruction in the sermon on
the mount (Matthew 6:9-13). So unlike us as we tend to rush
in with a shopping list of all that we want God to do for us!
Praise at the outset paves the way for all that follows. Warren
Wiersbe says that 'the invocation to Daniel's prayer is a primer
of biblical theology.' Daniel's heart is stirred when he perceives
that the great God of heaven is a God of might, munificence,
majesty, magnificence, and mercy. If we forget God's greatness
and grace, then our prayers will be too small. In *It Happens After
Prayer*, H B Charles writes, 'Before you tell God about how big
your problem is, tell God how big he is!'

He is a promise-keeping God who can be trusted at all times;
indeed, he warmly responds to those who seek to embrace his
statutes and obey his precepts. He is marked by firmness and
fairness when it comes to dishing out justice to those who flout
his commands and ignore his guidance. His *steadfast love* is
legendary as it reminds us that God never fails; we let him down
so often when we sin in thought, word, and deed, but he loves
us still. In the space of four lines on the page of your Bible, when
compared to the rest of his prayer which encompasses almost
eighty lines, Daniel makes every word count as he joyfully extols
the unimpeachable attributes of his sovereign Lord.

9:5-6

Calling a spade a spade

'We have sinned and done wrong and acted wickedly and rebelled, turning aside from your commandments and rules. We have not listened to your servants the prophets, who spoke in your name to our kings, our princes, and our fathers, and to all the people of the land.'

When Daniel engages with his God and begins to confess the sins of the people, it is interesting to note that at no time does he point an accusing finger or play the blame game. It is not the unwelcome scenario of them and us. He offers no excuses and never downplays the seriousness of sin. Repeatedly, he uses the first person plural pronouns of *we, us,* and *our,* even though there is no blemish or stain on his personal character. Daniel's integrity is intact; he is not sinless, but he is faultless. A paragon of virtue.

And yet, amazingly, he identifies with this generation of people in every way and that is a defining point of a godly man's intercession. His solidarity with them is most impressive for he is awash in Israel's sin. Like Nehemiah, he stands alongside them in their hour of need; he is shoulder to shoulder with a generation of people, the vast majority of whom he does not even know; and he is devastated over a problem he did not create (Nehemiah 1:5-11).

Daniel's candid honesty and frankness in admitting the grievous sins of the people is highlighted when he describes their wilful intransigence using five different expressions in a single verse. One, *we have sinned* indicates they missed the mark and fell dramatically short of God's standard (Romans 3:23). Two, *we have ... done wrong* means they are perverse and allowed the bias in their hearts to dictate the way they lived; time and time again they were crooked in their dealings and bent in their outlook. Three, *we have … acted wickedly* suggests they are lawless and ungodly and their gross impiety is seen in their restless, turbulent behaviour.

Four, *we have … rebelled* informs us that they have revolted against the Lord who redeemed them. They adopted an attitude of mutiny and, basically, wanted to do their own thing and go their own way. Five, *we have … turned aside* implies that they spurned his love and flatly rejected out of hand the divine law. Sadly, their response to his impassioned appeals for them to return to 'the old paths' was negative (Jeremiah 6:16). They were seemingly content to go in the opposite direction, and in so doing, depart further away from the Lord. They knowingly turned two deaf ears to the prophetic message.

The bottom line is, times without number, they defiantly and deliberately sinned against a holy God. They consistently snubbed every overture of divine love and grace extended to them. They gave God the cold shoulder when they silenced the prophets of old. God said so much and they listened so little. To all intents and purposes, they were living life as if God did not exist.

Does that ring a bell? Fast forward to the third millennium and Daniel's insights are a running commentary on what is happening all around us and, sadly, the waters are muddied as all of us have been caught up in such a rat race at one time or another. Have we become desensitised to sin? Perhaps we have sanitised sin and we no longer call a spade a spade but a sharp-edged gardening implement? A heartfelt prayer of confession used in the time of the Reformation says, 'Deepen the sorrow within us for our sins.'

9:7-11

God is ...

'To you, O Lord, belongs righteousness, but to us open shame, as at this day, to the men of Judah, to the inhabitants of Jerusalem, and to all Israel, those who are near and those who are far away, in all the lands to which you have driven them, because of the treachery that they have committed against you. To us, O Lord, belongs open shame, to our kings, to our princes, and to our fathers, because we have sinned against you. To the Lord our God belong mercy and forgiveness, for we have rebelled against him and have not obeyed the voice of the Lord our God by walking in his laws, which he set before us by his servants the prophets. All Israel has transgressed your law and turned aside, refusing to obey your voice. And the curse and oath that are written in the Law of Moses the servant of God have been poured out upon us, because we have sinned against him.'

So far as the people are concerned, they are enveloped in a filthy garment of total shame as Daniel shows us how far they have defected and wandered away from the Lord (Psalm 44:15). There is nowhere to hide. Daniel brings it all out into the open and it is not a pretty sight. Dale Ralph Davis says they are 'homeless waifs whom Yahweh has banished from covenant turf.' From the top down, they have pushed God's patience to the limits, and even when he has been favourable towards them, they retained the option to keep on sinning. I mean, how stupidly foolish, when all of the time, their only hope was in the Lord.

What a stark contrast between them and God when Daniel outlines a five-point affirmation of God's flawless persona in this paragraph. One, he speaks of the purity of God for he is righteous in that he is true to himself at all times, never acting out of character. He never does the wrong thing. Two, he refers to the purpose of God for he has scattered them here, there, and yonder. Three, he talks of the pity of God for he exercises an abundance of rich, tender mercy in all his dealings with them. Four, he highlights the pardon of God for he is willing to forgive them even though they have ridden roughshod over his Word. Five, he upholds the promise of God for he fulfilled his side of the agreement when he withheld his blessing from them, having previously spelt it out in explicit and unnerving detail (Leviticus 26:14-39; Deuteronomy 28:15-68).

9:12-14

Getting our just deserts

'He has confirmed his words, which he spoke against us and against our rulers who ruled us, by bringing upon us a great calamity. For under the whole heaven there has not been done anything like what has been done against Jerusalem. As it is written in the Law of Moses, all this calamity has come upon us; yet we have not entreated the favour of the Lord our God, turning from our iniquities and gaining insight by your truth. Therefore the Lord has kept ready the calamity and has brought it upon us, for the Lord our God is righteous in all the works that he has done, and we have not obeyed his voice.'

The age-old principle has not altered, it is the law of cause and effect. The people provoked God so they have no one else to blame but themselves when they look at the mess in which they find themselves. It was self-inflicted. They brought it on themselves. God did what he did because they did what they did, and in all of this, there was only going to be one winner. Not them! It all seemed to run off them like water off a duck's back, such was their woeful complacency. Shame on God's people and shame on God's city is the righteous reward they have invited on themselves. John Walvoord says 'when [God's] mercy is spurned, judgment is inevitable ... Jehovah was being faithful in keeping his word both in blessings and cursing, which must have encouraged Daniel in anticipating the end of the captivity.'

It is alarmingly worrying to read at the end of the paragraph that *we have not obeyed his voice.* The blunt reality is, they did not obey in Babylon. What are the chances of them doing it when they go back to Israel? Minimal, in all honesty. They have had a lifetime of seventy years to get their act together and they remain unchanged, unbroken, and unrepentant.

It seems to me that is a challenge for all of us to take on board: Are we guilty as charged? If we are, the best we can do is hurriedly run to the Lord, pleading for mercy and humbly admitting that we are sinful and guilty before him. Thankfully, when we mourn over our sins, our gracious God abundantly pardons (Isaiah 55:7; 1 John 1:9).

9:15-19

Lord, it is time for you to act

'And now, O Lord our God, who brought your people out of the land of Egypt with a mighty hand, and have made a name for yourself, as at this day, we have sinned, we have done wickedly. O Lord, according to all your righteous acts, let your anger and your wrath turn away from your city Jerusalem, your holy hill, because for our sins, and for the iniquities of our fathers, Jerusalem

and your people have become a byword among all who are around us. Now therefore, O our God, listen to the prayer of your servant and to his pleas for mercy, and for your own sake, O Lord, make your face shine upon your sanctuary, which is desolate. O my God, incline your ear and hear. Open your eyes and see our desolations, and the city that is called by your name. For we do not present our pleas before you because of our righteousness, but because of your great mercy. O Lord, hear; O Lord, forgive. O Lord, pay attention and act. Delay not, for your own sake, O my God, because your city and your people are called by your name.'

After a substantial, no-holds-barred confession of personal and national sin stretching to eleven verses in the biblical text, Daniel finally gets to his main petition when he says, *and now.* Over the next five verses, in this people-oriented prayer, he earnestly pleads for God to step into the dreadful situation in which they presently find themselves so that his name might be magnified and glorified. Ultimately, this is all that matters to Daniel for it is the glory and splendour of God that is at stake. Dale Ralph Davis says that 'Daniel batters heaven with appeals to God's honour.' Hezekiah prayed something similar in 2 Kings 19:14-19. It is interesting to note that in these verses there is no mention of *Yahweh*, God's covenant name; instead, he reverts back to *Adonai* and *Elohim*, as an indicator that in all these matters he bows to the sovereignty of God.

Daniel lists again some of the consequences of their heinous sin when he talks about the holy city of Jerusalem having been destroyed and the sacred places desecrated, the land being left desolate and the people being the object of scorn and derision. Bad times.

He harks back to the mists of time when God redeemed and

delivered his people from bondage in the land of Egypt. That was a show of omnipotence and a clearcut declaration that he is one who saves and rescues his people when their backs are against the wall. They did not deserve it then. They do not deserve it now. Since he has done it before, it was time for him to do it again. Then, he brought them out; now, he will bring them back.

Again, we see how God-centred Daniel's prayer is because it is soaked through with references to the matchless character of God. In a few breaths, he speaks of his righteousness, his anger, his wrath, and his mercy. Daniel knows that the great God of heaven is not deaf, yet he longs for him to open his ears to his pleadings for help. He knows that the Most High seated on the throne is not blind, yet he yearns for him to open his eyes to see all that is going on. He strongly hints at the Aaronic blessing (Numbers 6:24-26) when he urges the God of the covenant to *make [his] face shine upon [the] sanctuary* (Psalm 80:3).

Daniel never forgot his roots and he was ever mindful that every blessing he enjoyed came from the open hand of a generously kind God. He knows that he has nothing to offer because he recognises that he is the recipient of God's undeserved favour. There is absolutely nothing in him (or them) that merits any tokens of divine big-heartedness. Hence, his appeal is worded the way that it is when he acknowledges that he is not worthy. Only the Lord is!

I am reminded of an incident recorded by Pastor Richard Wurmbrand in his book, *Christ in the Communist Prisons*, where he says: It was 1945 and a Congress of Cults was convened in the Romanian Parliament building in the capital city of Bucharest. Four thousand clergy from all denominations were present. Loud applause greeted the announcement that Comrade Stalin was Patron of the Congress. Various politicians made lavish assurances of support. Then bishops and other clerics expressed their delight over a 'red' stream now flowing into the river of the Church. Men of the cloth from every side of the theological spectrum all expressed their willingness to cooperate with the Communist regime. In that assembly sat a prominent Lutheran pastor and his wife. After listening to many speeches of clerical grovelling and boot-licking, Sabina Wurmbrand had had enough; she turned to her husband Richard and exclaimed, 'Go and wash this shame from the face of Christ.' He did and went to prison for it. (On a personal note, I had the unspeakable privilege of sharing an evening meal with Mr Wurmbrand and my pastor in summer 1968.)

Like Richard and Sabina Wurmbrand, Daniel's sole concern is the glory of God's high and holy name. God's unsullied reputation is at the heart of his prayer, hence his desire for God to answer prayer so that everyone will know just who he is and what he is like. As Dale Ralph Davis says, 'Our petitions should be sprinkled with the incense of pleading his honour.'

That is precisely why Daniel rounds it all off with a crescendo of intense, staccato-like phrases, *O Lord, hear. O Lord, forgive. O Lord....* Daniel, on his knees, throws himself upon the warm mercies of the God of heaven. Ligon Duncan says that 'he touches the deep places of the heart of God and moves him in his compassion for his people.' Daniel's aspiration is summed up in the opening line of a Graham Kendrick song, 'Restore, O Lord, the honour of your name.'

He has poured his heart out in fervent prayer, he can do no more, he has given it every fibre of his being. God knows his heart and the principal reason why he sought his face. Remember,

Daniel is no spring chicken so he must have been exhausted physically, mentally, and spiritually. He was, for we read of his 'extreme weariness' (Daniel 9:21, NASB). Now the ball is in God's court and the rest is up to him. The question is: Did Daniel get to finish his prayer with a hearty amen?

Before continuing to the next section, why not take a short break, open your Bible, and read Daniel's prayer through a couple of times. In future days, based on these notes, you could even use it as a template for your own prayers. My heart longs to pray like that. Perhaps you feel the same? The good news is, we can pray like Daniel prayed when we know God and live for God as he did, to the praise and glory of his name.

9:20-23

When God comes

While I was speaking and praying, confessing my sin and the sin of my people Israel, and presenting my plea before the Lord my God for the holy hill of my God, while I was speaking in prayer, the man Gabriel, whom I had seen in the vision at the first, came to me in swift flight at the time of the evening sacrifice. He made me understand, speaking with me and saying, 'O Daniel, I have now come out to give you insight and understanding. At the beginning of your pleas for mercy a word went out, and I have come to tell it to you, for you are greatly loved. Therefore consider the word and understand the vision.'

Did you see that? Daniel prays an unfinished prayer. He never did get to the end of it for God interrupts him midsentence. Yes, God heard his prayer. Thankfully, he always does. Daniel is in full flow at the peak of his prayer when, immediately, the angel

Gabriel is again despatched from heaven in fast flight mode to minister to him (Daniel 8:15-17). There is an apparent delay in the angel's arrival, but still he came and did what God wanted him to do. The angel talked with Daniel giving him sweet assurance that his prayers will be answered. No need for him to fear or fret for even when he began to pray, the answer was already on its way (Isaiah 65:24).

Gabriel, the divine emissary, who could easily win an award for 'Most Admired Angel' approached the praying Daniel *at the time of the evening sacrifice* which is around 3pm in the afternoon. According to Jewish thinking, that was spoken of as 'the ninth hour' when believing men gathered to pray in the temple as part of their three-a-day schedule (Exodus 29:38-41; Acts 3:1, 10:30). It is a fascinating turn of phrase, bearing in mind that there had been no burnt offering sacrifices at the temple in Jerusalem for half a century since it was destroyed in 586 BC. There is a sense in which prayer is seen by God as a spiritual sacrifice to him (Psalm 141:2).

For dear old Daniel, who has not been in Jerusalem for the best part of seventy years, his heart is still there as he fondly recalls the magical moment when the angel visited with him. He pines for those extra-special occasions when he was able to feast on the old covenant 'means of grace.' The passing of time has not erased such treasured memories of precious times spent in the house of God in the holy city. He has not lost his spiritual identity and his soul thirsts for such meaningful encounters with the living God in the house of God (Psalm 84:1-4). Here in Babylon, however, it is a world away but Daniel operates on 'Jerusalem time' when it comes to his religious fervour and practice. Danny Akin succinctly notes that 'Yahweh's clock is his clock.'

Gabriel refers to Daniel as one who is *greatly loved* or 'highly esteemed' (NIV). That is quite an accolade by any stretch of the imagination, and it is one that he certainly deserves. He has a reputation in heaven. God noticed. He caught the eye and ear of his God. Daniel did not go looking for it, it came to him by royal commission from the King of heaven. He is someone who is precious to God, greatly valued by God, treasured by God, loved by God, and who matters to God. A noble testimony, because he lived his life out-and-out for God. What gracious encouragement. Those words must have thrilled him no end. Jesus referred to the Apostle John in the same way for he was known as 'the disciple whom Jesus loved' (John 20:2, 21:7, NIV). Come to think of it, Peter writes in a similar vein when he addresses us, the people of God, as 'a chosen people, a kingdom of priests, God's holy nation, his very own possession' (1 Peter 2:9, NLT).

Faith Cook tells a true story in her book, *Selina, Countess of Huntingdon*, about the English pastor and hymnwriter, Philip Doddridge. In 1751, he was nearing the end of his life and ministry. Only forty-nine years old he was dying of consumption, and his doctor suggested the only hope for some limited recovery lay in a voyage to the warmer climate of Portugal, where he died. Selina arranged for Doddridge and his wife to travel by way of Bath so that she might see and care for them before their departure for Lisbon. The morning Doddridge was to leave, Selina came unexpectedly into his room and found him weeping over the Scriptures open in front of him. The words that deeply moved him to tears were these, 'O Daniel, a man greatly beloved' (Daniel 9:23, KJV). Selina could only say, 'You are in tears, Sir.' He assured her, 'I am weeping, but they are tears of comfort and joy.' A benediction of blessing.

The American Samuel Davies (1723-61) penned a wonderful hymn, when he wrote, 'Great God of wonders! all thy ways, Are matchless, godlike, and divine; But the fair glories of thy grace, More godlike and unrivalled shine. Who is a pardoning God like thee, Or who has grace so rich and free?'

We read that 'the earnest prayer of a righteous person has great power and produces wonderful results' (James 5:16, NLT). In his epistle, James is focusing on the prayers of Elijah, he could have opted for Daniel as another brilliant example of intercession. The tremendous news in all this is that the prayer of a righteous person can change a life, a home, a marriage, a church, a school, a community, and an entire nation (such has happened in days of yore with times of heaven-sent revival). Abraham discovered that only ten men of this calibre were needed to save Sodom (Genesis 18:16-33). For you and me, we admire Elijah, but we emulate Daniel when we take on board his mindset, get down on our knees, and watch how God changes our world.

The singular message to Daniel revolves around the future of Israel when his questions with regard to her survival will be fully answered. God will draw back the curtain and give him a panoramic overview of his plan for his earthly people, the Jewish nation. The seventy years are hugely significant for Israel's immediate future, but a vision of seventy sevens (*weeks*) is of far greater importance for the longer term. Daniel asked God about the past; God was going to tell him about the future. It will shortly be revealed to God's servant and Gabriel is on hand to give him wisdom and help him grasp and appreciate it (Daniel 8:19). The angel will do his bit, and Daniel will see and hear him, but he still needs to put his own mental energy into evaluating all that the angel communicated to him in the following four verses.

As we lift the lid on this incredible disclosure, we need the aid of someone greater than Gabriel in the person of the Holy Spirit to assist us in our understanding of the prophecy (John 16:13; Ephesians 1:17-18; 2 Timothy 3:16-17).

9:24

A week is a long time in prophecy

'Seventy weeks are decreed about your people and your holy city, to finish the transgression, to put an end to sin, and to atone for iniquity, to bring in everlasting righteousness, to seal both vision and prophet, and to anoint a most holy place.'

I love the story of Leopold Cohn, a Hungarian rabbi from an orthodox Jewish family. Apparently Rabbi Cohn studied the portion before us and came to the conclusion (largely based on verse 26) that the Messiah had already come, because clearly his advent was expected before the destruction of Jerusalem in AD 70. He began to enquire among his friends where the Messiah might be. A fellow rabbi suggested to him, 'Go to New York, and you will find Messiah.' Cohn sold most of what he owned to buy passage to America and upon arrival wandered the streets of New York looking for Messiah. One day he heard bright singing coming from a building, he went in only to hear a clear gospel message. That night he received the Lord Jesus Christ as Messiah and Saviour. Shortly after Mr Cohn bought a horse stable, swept it out, set up some chairs, and began to hold evangelistic meetings, the first outreach of what was to become the American Board of Missions to the Jews – I recall my dear friend Dr Harold Sevener, former president of ABMJ, sharing with me that the acronym was the pinpoint focus of their ministry: Always Bringing Messiah to Jews. Their worldwide outreach among Jewish people continues to this day under the new name of Chosen People Ministries.

Grace encounter stories like the one above warm my heart for they are a powerful reminder that Jesus saves sinners and that the Spirit of God will use every part of Scripture to bring men into a pulsating relationship with himself.

Unfortunately, these few verses have over the years generated more heat than light because God's people are unsure what to make of them. For some, this prophecy is as illegible as the handwriting of a medical doctor on your prescription for drugs. Some of it is crystal clear and fairly easy to explain, other parts are more opaque and a tad obscure.

They were chiefly given to Daniel to bolster his faith in answer to his prayer, to encourage him that his God was still reigning on the throne, and to give him a preview of God's big picture especially as it related to his own Jewish people. They were certainly not designed to sow seeds of doubt or cynicism in his mind, nor were they devised to lead him down a dark pathway of confusion. It was never God's objective to leave Daniel (and us) in 'a morass of mush' as Dale Ralph Davis calls it. Sadly, and regrettably, we are the ones who have clouded the issue.

A definition of the 70 weeks

The six million dollar question is: How long is a week? The timespan here is for 'seventy sevens' (a literal rendering found in the NIV), implying a total of four hundred and ninety 'somethings.' These are units of time, but are they days, weeks, months, or years? The plot thickens when we carefully check out the Old Testament because Jewish people effortlessly understood this ambiguity between a week of seven days and a week of seven years! Let me explain.

In Exodus 20:8-11 we read of 'a week of days' which is a period of seven days from one Sabbath to another Sabbath. Then in Leviticus 25:1-7 there is a reference to 'a week of years' which is a stint of seven years stretching from one sabbatical year to the next sabbatical year. However, in the tangled love story of Jacob and Rachel (Genesis 29:16-30), both periods of time are used interchangeably. In that instance, one week is the same as seven years. There is another reference worthy of consideration when we read of 'seven sabbaths of years—seven times seven years' (Leviticus 25:8-17, NIV) where the forty-nine years are followed by the fiftieth year of Jubilee, when a silver trumpet is blown to herald a year of redemption, release, rejoicing, and restoration.

With those allusions in mind, for us to make any sense of the expression in Daniel's vision, it has to be seen in the context of years. Therefore, seventy weeks is the equivalent of four hundred and ninety years. Since seven and seventy are both numbers of completeness in the Bible, this is seen as the ultimate in completeness (Matthew 18:22). Iain Duguid reminds us that 'God's timescale is far bigger than Daniel imagined.'

The word *decreed* in verse 24 comes from a Hebrew root meaning 'to cut' which is most illuminating in this context. As Jim Allen notes, 'It suggests that God has acted "to cut" a certain period of time from the general stream of history, in which to accomplish a certain purpose.' It is like an entrepreneur deciding that one particular aspect of his work is so vital that he carves out a portion of his time to devote all his energies to that task until it is satisfactorily completed. Likewise, the God of Abraham, Isaac, and Jacob is going to finish a work for Israel within a structured timeframe, duly marked in his calendar—seventy weeks or seventy sevens—four hundred and ninety years.

As you will appreciate, there is a plethora of views on this subject ranging from sublime to laughable, and still some! The most convincing view is that the seventy weeks are literal years that end with Christ's second coming, but also include his first coming. Within that outer casing, there is a crucial prophetic gap between the sixty-ninth and seventieth week. As we shall see, the first sixty-nine weeks are now past, and the decisive seventieth week is still future.

The details of the 70 weeks

It is important to realise that the focal point of the vision is centred on the Jewish people and upon the city of Jerusalem, hence the biblical reference to *your people and your holy city*. This is the answer to Daniel's prayer. It has nothing to do with Gentile nations for they were dealt with in the prophecies given in Daniel 2, 7, and 8. Nor does it apply to the church of Christ for she has no relation to the city of Jerusalem, or to the promises given specifically to Israel with regard to their restoration and repossession of the land. Daniel is aware of the import of these few words for they affirm some non-negotiable truths, namely, God has not forgotten, forsaken, or failed his ancient people. Neither has he finished with them (Romans 11:1-10, 25-32).

There are four phases of 'seventy weeks' in Scripture which are affiliated to the Jewish people. Phase one begins with the birth of Abraham and ends with the Exodus. Phase two commences with the Exodus and climaxes with the building of Solomon's Temple. Phase three starts with the dedication of the Temple and finishes at the end of the Babylonian captivity. Phase four is introduced with the edict of Artaxerxes and culminates at the second advent of Jesus Christ – it is this particular phase which is alluded to in these closing verses of Daniel 9.

A summary of what is entailed is outlined in verse 24 where we discover there are six keynote features, all of which relate to the work of Jesus the Messiah. The first three of these purpose clauses focus on his sacrifice, and the second three home in on his sovereignty. Once the onerous burden of sin is efficiently and effectively dealt with and removed, then the promised Sovereign arrives to take the throne for in him all the covenant promises given to Abraham and David will be fulfilled (Genesis 12:1-3; 2 Samuel 7:8-13). John Lennox writes that 'this is a big story—the Big Story—and, in response to Daniel's prayer at a time in history where it looked as if it had all petered out, Gabriel's message takes it a quantum leap forward.'

Before we get into interpretation, have a look at the verse in *The Message*, 'Seventy sevens are set for your people and for your holy city to throttle rebellion, stop sin, wipe out crime, set things right forever, confirm what the prophet saw, and anoint The Holy of Holies.'

To finish the transgression – the underlying thought here is of rebellion. There is an intense feeling of disloyalty and disobedience, even covenant treachery attached to it. This is the root problem with Israel (and, indeed, all mankind) throughout her entire history, and to this day is still the main cause of her continued rejection of the Lord Jesus. She will not stop her inexorable opposition against God's rule until this period of time has lapsed (Romans 11:25-27). At the Lord's second coming, she will recognise him as the one whom they pierced (Zechariah 12:10), as the one who was wounded and died for her transgression (Isaiah 53:5).

To put an end to sin – this is the inevitable fruit of her rejection of God's rule and authority. This is an all-inclusive term which has the idea of failure, of falling short of a standard, of missing the target or goal (Romans 3:23). It leads to daily sins being committed and these will not end until the second coming of Christ when they repent and find 'a fountain opened to cleanse them from sin and uncleanness' (Ezekiel 37:23; Zechariah 13:1). That is when the scales will fall from blind eyes and a nation is born in a day (Isaiah 66:8).

To atone for iniquity – there is coming a day of pardon for the Jewish people who will lament over their twistedness when they see Jesus, the returning King. They will see him as the ultimate fulfilment of Yom Kippur when he became a Saviour and scapegoat for sin, and overwhelmed with remorse for their perversion, will turn to him in profound sorrow and grief (Zechariah 12:10). At that point, countless numbers of them will appropriate the reconciling death of the Lord at Calvary in their lives and be personally cleansed (Jeremiah 31:34; 2 Corinthians 5:19; Hebrews 10:11-13).

To bring in everlasting righteousness – with the arrival of the King of kings to this world a new era will be ushered in that is characterised by moral integrity, justice, godliness, and righteousness (Isaiah 11:4-5, 32:1; Jeremiah 23:5-6; Daniel 7:14). The literal kingdom of God on earth is a millennial and messianic age (Zechariah 9:10). In that day, Israel will come into the blessing of the New Covenant when God's law is indelibly written on their hearts (Jeremiah 31:33-40).

To seal both vision and prophet – all of God's predictions and prophecies for the Jewish people and nation will then be a sweet reality. Fulfilled. History will testify to that fact and God himself will stamp the divine imprimatur upon the entire prophetic page as a mark of authentication. Mission accomplished.

To anoint a most holy place – this refers to the innermost chamber, the holy of holies, in the millennial temple as anticipated by the prophet Ezekiel. It will be anointed when the presence or shekinah of God is manifest, and spoken of as Jehovah Shammah, meaning 'the Lord is there' (Ezekiel 48:35).

The first three components are aimed at cleaning up the perennial problem of sin, as is obvious when we consider the words that are used, *transgression, sin,* and *iniquity.* Dale Ralph Davis says, 'The pile-up of sin-terms in verse 24 suggests that God intends to deal finally and fully with sin in all its guises.' Exciting news. All these half-dozen strands coincide with the second advent of Jesus Christ and will be implemented there and then when his kingdom is openly established. That said, the basis for these foresights is laid in the first coming of Jesus to earth and are centralised in the cross of Calvary.

This is a truly sensational answer to Daniel's petition. Even though there is the excruciating prospect of umpteen overcast days on the horizon, it must have cheered his heart as Gabriel explained the various issues to him. Despite their catalogue of terrible failures, there is at the end a glorious future for his nation and its capital city, Jerusalem. The golden, gilt-edged promises to Abraham and David are not annulled, but simply put on the back burner, until the one already singled out as 'Jesus Christ, the son of David, the son of Abraham' (Matthew 1:1) sits upon his throne in Jerusalem.

9:25-26

The division of the 70 weeks

'Know therefore and understand that from the going out of the word to restore and build Jerusalem to the coming of an anointed

one, a prince, there shall be seven weeks. Then for sixty-two weeks it shall be built again with squares and moat, but in a troubled time. And after the sixty-two weeks, an anointed one shall be cut off and shall have nothing. And the people of the prince who is to come shall destroy the city and the sanctuary. Its end shall come with a flood, and to the end there shall be war. Desolations are decreed.'

The mystery is unravelled when we ascertain the starting point at which the divine clock begins to tick. The decree would authorise the restoration and rebuilding of the city of Jerusalem and the construction would be carried out in terrifically hard times (Ezra 9-10; Nehemiah 4, 6, 9, 13). Irrespective of the difficult moments ahead, it must have thrilled Daniel's heart to realise that the city of his boyhood and early teenage years was going to be revitalised. If he was physically able—if not, then in his heart—he must have been jumping up and down in the presence of his trustworthy God with delirious joy. Another brilliant example of answered prayer.

In response to Nehemiah's emergency prayer-enabled request, for he was scared stiff (Nehemiah 2:4), Artaxerxes approved such legislation when he tabled on the statute books that work could recommence on site. This was in the month of Nisan in the twentieth year of his reign, around March 445 BC. As a gesture of goodwill to his loyal employee, the king more or less gave him a blank cheque plus a few letters to stuff in his back pocket and granted him leave of absence from his day job in the palace. In the providence of God, Nehemiah then became the linchpin of this major refurbishment project (Nehemiah 2:1-8). He rallied the people, and in spite of the well-organised opposition and discouragement they encountered, with a combination of fantastic zeal and enthusiasm the builders completed the task of rebuilding the walls in an amazing fifty-two days (Nehemiah 6:15).

Good, but that was only the tip of the debris iceberg for there was so much more still to be done. Eventually, they did it and life returned to a new kind of normalcy. Not quite what it was, but better than it might have been. Not only was Jerusalem rebuilt during that forty-nine year period and the covenant people were home again, the temple was also established, and the canon of the Old Testament completed. Dale Ralph Davis comments, 'What is this but the unseen preservation of God? In the flow and sometimes in the fury of history God keeps his people intact.' The seven weeks of years in which the city was restored concluded in 396 BC, forty-nine years after Artaxerxes first issued the decree to rebuild it in 445 BC.

It is helpful to read about this in the NIV, where it says, 'From the issuing of the decree to restore and rebuild Jerusalem until the Anointed One, the ruler, comes, there will be seven "sevens," and sixty-two "sevens." It will be rebuilt with streets and a trench, but in times of trouble.' When we make a comparison of this verse with the ESV (quoted above in italics), you will see that a single punctuation mark can make all the difference to the text and, consequently, our understanding of it. The ESV has a full stop after seven weeks, whereas the NIV has a comma thereby linking the 'seven weeks' with the 'sixty-two weeks' making a grand total of sixty-nine weeks or four hundred and eighty-three years. As John Lennox rightly says, 'The NIV is surely the more natural reading here.'

The finishing point of this period is when Messiah is presented as the *prince* or the *Anointed One*. This is a reference to his triumphal entry in April AD 32 into the city of Jerusalem on that first Palm Sunday when the jubilant crowds gave their long-awaited Messiah the green carpet treatment. Riding on a young donkey in fulfilment of Scripture (Zechariah 9:9), the enthusiastic onlookers waved leafy palm fronds and excitedly hailed him with loud shouts of 'Hosanna! Blessed is he who comes in the name of the Lord! Blessed is the king of Israel!' (Matthew 21:8-11; Mark 11:7-10; Luke 19:35-40; John 12:12-15, NIV).

If Jewish people living in the time of Jesus had read and studied the closing paragraph of Daniel 9, they would surely have realised that prophecy was being fulfilled in front of their eyes. Sadly, the overwhelming majority of locals failed to put two and two together and get four. There were possibly a few godly people like Mary, Joseph of Arimathea, and Nicodemus who were prepared and did see the special significance of this momentous day. No wonder Jesus wept (Luke 19:41-44).

Sir Robert Anderson, former Assistant Commissioner in the Metropolitan Police, in his excellent book, *The Coming Prince*, has calculated from the first day to the last day there is a grand total of 173,880 days, based on the Hebrew calendar of 360 days per lunar year. This premise actually accords with both Babylonian and Jewish computation. As early as the book of Genesis we find it explicitly stated that from 'the seventeenth day of the second month' to 'the seventeenth day of the seventh month' it was one hundred and fifty days (Genesis 7:11, 8:3-4). One month equals thirty days; twelve months, one lunar year, equals three hundred and sixty days. Anderson's figure, therefore, of 173,880 days is equal to four hundred and eighty-three years or sixty-nine weeks. Just as the prophet said it would be.

Shortly after Palm Sunday we read that the *anointed one shall be cut off.* That is as clear a reference you will find anywhere to Calvary and the death of Jesus on a cross. The words *cut off* generally refer to the death penalty and are often translated to convey the idea of an extremely violent death (Leviticus 7:20; Nahum 3:15). The death of the Suffering Servant of Jehovah was both representative and substitutionary (Isaiah 53:8). Jesus died not for his own sin, for he was the perfect, spotless, sinless Lamb of God, but for the sin of others—yours and mine. In this phrase, we are introduced to the gospel according to Daniel. James Boice says that 'by the end of the sixty-nine weeks of years the great work of the atonement of the Lord Jesus Christ for sin should be completed.' And it was!

The expression *shall have nothing* means exactly what it says. As the Messiah, all that he was entitled to was denied him. He should have had a royal crown of gold and precious jewels, but all he had was a crown of thorns (Matthew 27:29). He should have had a royal robe, but he was stripped naked of his clothing (John 19:23-24). He should have had a royal throne, but he was given an accursed cross (John 19:17-18). He should have had the acclaim and admiration of his people, but all he knew was rejection and ridicule (John 19:14-15; Matthew 27:39-44). Indeed, the Lord Jesus was bereft of everything for he died empty-handed with no dominion, no glory, and no kingdom. Such unvarnished truth is summed up by Jim Allen when he notes that 'the cross of Calvary stands out in history as the greatest miscarriage of justice of all time.'

This must have been an alien concept for Daniel, something he probably struggled to get his head around. He could recall from memory the powerfully positive words of the vision recorded in Daniel 7:14, but this prophecy seemed light years away from that glorious prediction. The Messiah had nothing. Inexplicable. Incomprehensible. For you and me as believers, living this side of Calvary, it is so very different for we have entered into the fulness of the blessing that flows from being forgiven (Ephesians 1:3-14). We have new life, a vivacious hope, a sense of identity and belonging, a mission mandate, an international family, a faithful Saviour who succours, a great High Priest who prays for us by name, to highlight but a few of the benefits that accrue from his atoning death. And, thank God, the best is yet to be.

There are ominous signs flashing before our eyes when we read that *the people of the prince who is to come shall destroy the city and the sanctuary*. In short, this is foretelling the destruction of Jerusalem. There were times when Jesus addressed this matter in the course of his public ministry (Mark 13:1-2; Luke 19:43-44). AD 70 dawned for the rest of the world, but it spelt doom and gloom for the land of Israel and her citizens. It signalled the arrival of General Titus Flavius Vespasianus and the invading Romans. Almost forty years after Calvary the burgeoning city of Jerusalem was razed to the ground. The population was ravaged and savagely murdered. It was mass devastation and unprecedented horror caused by grossly amoral and unsparing soldiers. Renald Showers writes, 'From today's perspective, it can be understood that ... this destruction would come while the fourth kingdom of Gentile world rule (the Roman Empire represented by the legs of iron in Daniel 2 and the nondescript beast in Daniel 7) would be dominating the world.'

Sixty-five years later in AD 135, during the Bar Kochba rebellion, the mopping up operations were finished, the city was totally eradicated and the site covered with salt. The callous emperor, Hadrian, vowed total genocide and got dangerously close to success. Not one meleke stone was left standing, as predicted (Matthew 24:2). They renamed both the country and the city of Jerusalem: one as Syria Palestina, and the other Aelia Capitolina. As a further sign of hostility, they banned all Jewish people from coming anywhere near their beloved land and holy city.

The *prince who is to come* in verse 26 is the same person referred to in verse 27 where it says he shall do this, that, and the other. He is the 'little horn' of Daniel 7:8, 24-27, the 'man of lawlessness' in 2 Thessalonians 2:3-4, and the 'beast out of the sea' in Revelation 13:1-8. John speaks of him as 'the antichrist' in 1 John 2:18. More to follow.

We read at the end of verse 26 that *its end shall come with a flood, and to the end there shall be war. Desolations are decreed.* Some folks tend to link its back to Jerusalem, but this is incorrect. A closer look in the margin of your Bible may show that it could be translated *his*, thereby referring to the *prince*, aka the antichrist. His days are numbered by the Sovereign Lord and he will get his just deserts when he has ticked all the boxes in verse 27. The word translated *flood* is used in Nahum 1:8 for the outpouring of God's wrath in relation to Nineveh. Something similar is anticipated here when the reservoir of God's fury and anger bursts its banks and cascades down on the man of sin like a raging torrent. Gone. Forever.

Mind the gap

So far we have covered sixty-nine weeks, four hundred and eighty-three years, of this dramatic divine disclosure. Alas, there is one final week of seven years, the seventieth week, which is briefly covered in verse 27. There is, therefore, a hiatus—a prophetic gap—between the end of week sixty-nine and the beginning of week seventy, and in the grand scheme of things that is where we find ourselves right now at this precise moment in time.

As the redeemed people of God, under the new covenant of grace, we are an integral part of an international community of followers of Jesus Christ who look forward with bated breath to seeing the King in all his beauty. In today's world, the Spirit of God is moving among the peoples on earth and the Lord Jesus is fulfilling his cast-iron promise to build his church (Matthew 16:17-19). One living stone at a time is cemented by the Holy Spirit into the building currently under construction, one new member at a time is being added to the body of Christ. This is the age of the Spirit, an age of grace.

One day the trumpet will sound and the saints will be called up to meet the Lord in the air (1 Thessalonians 4:13-18). What a day, glorious day that will be. Immediately following that event, a seven-year period (Daniel's seventieth week) often referred to as 'the tribulation' or 'the day of the Lord' or 'the time of Jacob's trouble' (Jeremiah 30:4-7) will be ushered in when the antichrist will emerge and all kinds of terribly bad things will happen to the sons of Abraham's race (Matthew 24:4-35; Mark 13:5-31; Luke 21:8-33; 1 Thessalonians 5:1-3; 2 Thessalonians 2:1-12; Revelation 13:1-8).

9:27

A description of the 70ᵗʰ week

'And he shall make a strong covenant with many for one week, and for half of the week he shall put an end to sacrifice and offering.

And on the wing of abominations shall come one who makes desolate, until the decreed end is poured out on the desolator.'

Here we are given a discerning glimpse through a relatively small window into life and its attendant adversity and affliction during the last seven years of history on earth, just prior to the coming of God's kingdom in its full and glorious expression.

The pronoun *he* refers back to the previous verse and *the prince who is to come* which is like a *nom de plume* for the antichrist. It seems that he will present himself initially to the Jewish people as the ultimate peace-maker, a messianic figure, as the kind of person who can solve global problems (Daniel 7:8, 20, 23-25). Foreshadowed by Titus, as the little horn (Daniel 7:8) he comes across as an opportunist politician with loads of charisma who can strike a deal with other nations, like Israel in this instance (John 5:43), who since 1948 have been back in their own land as an independent nation.

Because of who he is and his influence in the corridors of world politics, they will be immensely glad to have him as a powerful ally and will welcome his diplomatic efforts on their behalf. He will offer to sign a seven-year peace pact and will apparently give them an unconditional guarantee as to the security of their land borders. The government of the day will be delighted with their new-found friend and will see it as a dream come true. God has a rather different impression for he views this *strong covenant* as a treaty with hell (Isaiah 28:15-18).

After a while, he will be seen in his true colours as the mask slips and the kid gloves are taken off, only to be replaced by a clenched fist. His intentions are not favourable to the Jewish people for he has his own agenda. Halfway through the tenure of the covenant, he tears it up. From that point onward, it is not worth the vellum it is written on as he assumes control of this last bastion of democracy in the Middle East region. The Jewish people will know all about it as they experience the rigours of 'great tribulation' (Revelation 7:14, NIV) and a nail-biting time of deprivation and distress when Jerusalem is trampled underfoot (Revelation 11:2). Broken promises. Broken people.

Daniel is certain and clear that this devil-controlled infidel is determined to banish the various sacrifices and offerings along with the annual Jewish feasts and festivals, such as Pesach, Shavuot, and Yom Kippur (Passover, Pentecost, and the Day of Atonement). He will script a new faith directive focused exclusively on himself and for the sole benefit of stroking his own ego. He further ramps up pressure on a weary population when he sets up a statue of himself in the temple and presents himself to them as one who is god, demanding their adulation in the process (Daniel 11:31, 12:11; 2 Thessalonians 2:4). Such a disgustingly vile deed is an affront to the Most High. A despicable act like this is blasphemous to the nth degree and ultimately brings about his downfall when the Judge has his say. His heinous, hellish acts will not go unchallenged.

Three-and-a-half years will seem much too long a time for those who are living at the sharp end of his foul and fiendish programme of persecution (Matthew 24:15-22). It will seem endless as individuals are left teetering on the brink of torment and torture. It will be atrocity heaped upon atrocity. A bloodbath. What Antiochus did in a small way in the second century BC will become a worldwide persecution of Jewish people. The sovereign Lord will allow these trials and troubles for he has a strategic purpose in it all for he is purging and pruning the nation of Israel and its people.

When the game is up, and the final whistle blown, the Lord as Judge will offload his anger on this satanic scoundrel. He will deal with him in a decisive manner handing down a sentence which sees him consigned to the lake of fire for his war crimes and for his untempered arrogance toward the Lord Jesus Christ (Revelation 20:10). Eliminated. The *desolator* is banished to a never-ending eternity of despair and dejection, to a hereafter of misery and memory spent in isolated desolation (Luke 16:25-26). Dale Ralph Davis succinctly says that 'a final ruler exalts himself, imposes his authority, forbids true worship, instigates idolatrous worship and runs into the meat-grinder of God's decree. Predetermined. On target. Certain.'

The king of Egypt could not diminish the Jew, the waters of the Red Sea could not drown him, Balaam could not curse him, the fiery furnace could not devour him, the gallows of Haman could not hang him, nations could not assimilate him, and dictators could not annihilate him. David Jeremiah writes that 'God has preserved their unique identity because one day his plan for his chosen people is going to be fulfilled.'

Despite being scattered to the four corners of earth and living in different cultures and eras, the Jews were never absorbed within their host nation. They were always Jews, so we talk about American Jews, Russian Jews, European Jews, British Jews, or whatever. They have survived even when the odds were stacked high against them. The history of Israel is a miracle, even as Israel is a miracle of history. That cannot be explained. Neither can it be explained away. And that is the salutary message of Daniel: behind her is the sovereign God of the patriarchs, Abraham, Isaac, and Jacob.

Daniel wrestled with two big questions as he poured out his

heart in prayer: Will Israel survive? Yes, she will. Is there a future for his people? Yes, there is. Why? Because God is God! He has not ditched them, dumped them, duped them, or deserted them. There are dark days ahead. But out of the inky blackness the Morning Star will shine heralding the prospect of a new day—a day when Jesus returns to earth to rule and reign in splendour; so her future beyond the seventieth week will be as bright as the everlasting promises of God. Because God is a promise maker, and a promise keeper. Until then, we watch, and work, and wait. We serve and we hope. The plan is in place. Heaven's timepiece is ticking. Soon the Anointed One, the Prince, the King of the ages shall come.

10

ANGELS IN COSMIC CONFLICT

Ignacy Jan Paderewski (1860-1941) was a genius, an intellectual, a statesman *par excellence*, a linguist who spoke no fewer than seven languages fluently, a great musician, a patriot, and most of all, a humanitarian who was so generous that every act of kindness to him was always returned manifold.

Through his exemplary leadership an army of volunteers of Polish descent was organised in North America to join in the fight for Poland's freedom during World War 1. Every day during roll call, when Paderewski's name was called, the entire army answered, 'Present.'

He signed the Versailles Peace Treaty in 1919 as Poland's Prime Minister and became its first delegate the year after to the League of Nations.

Substantial contributions for various worthy causes were made by him: he financed the construction of a concert hall in Switzerland and the rebuilding of a cathedral in Lausanne; funds were given to ease the plight of unemployed workers and wartime orphans; other beneficiaries were a hospital for Allied soldiers, Jewish refugees from Germany, and the American Legion for disabled veterans. His liberality knew no bounds.

By presidential decree he was buried at Arlington Cemetery in Washington, DC, laid to rest under the mast of the battleship Maine until his body could be transported to a free Poland for burial after the end of the Second World War.

Paderewski, who was discouraged from becoming a pianist by his teachers, travelled all over the world, crossed the Atlantic more than thirty times, gave more than 1,500 concerts in the USA, appeared in every US state, and drew the largest crowds in history. He was the first to give a solo recital in the newly-built Carnegie Hall with his acclaimed *Minuet in G*.

It is easy to imagine that this scenario inspired by a poster during World War 2 could have taken place: Paderewski had organised a meeting for the Polish Relief Fund and the poster featured a sketch of him next to a small boy at the piano. A story was fabricated around the picture – the boy had crept on stage and began to play, *Twinkle, Twinkle, Little Star*. The maestro appeared beside the lad and whispered, 'Don't stop, keep playing,' as he filled in the bass part with his left hand. The duo accomplished what the soloist could not – a mesmerising performance, with the help of the master pianist.

My dear friend, Dr Stephen Davey, Pastor/Teacher of Colonial Baptist Church, Cary (North Carolina), and Bible teacher on the international radio ministry, *Wisdom for the Heart*, tells that fascinating story in one of his daily online meditations. He goes on to write, 'Not one of us is truly accomplished. Not one of us has mastered life. Wrong notes are played no matter how hard we concentrate; our hands grow tired; our minds are distracted; our hearts become discouraged. But in spite of our inexperience, our ignorance, and our weakness, Jesus Christ places his sovereign fingers beside ours and whispers in our ear, "You're my child, don't stop, keep playing!" He has a way of making a simple tune sound like a beautiful melody.'

The affirming message to each of us is, do not stop ... keep playing! And that is precisely what Daniel needed to hear in this truly extraordinary tenth chapter. Keep playing! And praying 'without ceasing' (1 Thessalonians 5:17). This chapter has more than its share of 'out of this world' adventures among the angelic band. I mean, this is high octane stuff when we come to perceive something of the comings and goings in the unseen realm all around us. John Lennox writes that 'the idea of a cosmic conflict is not some peripheral notion, generated by the overheated imagination of Christian extremists.' There is, beyond any shadow of doubt, an invisible war out there, a raging conflict between the powers of good and evil, light and darkness. There are hostilities on the aerial frontline between God's good angels and Satan's bad angels.

John Piper writing in *Angels and Prayer* notes that 'there are high-ranking demonic powers over various regimes and governments of the world ... [who] strive to interrupt Christian missions and ministry as much as they can.' This brings home to each of us so powerfully the call-to-arms challenge from the Apostle Paul, a veteran soldier in the Lord's army, that 'our struggle is not against flesh and blood, but against the rulers, against the authorities, against the powers of this dark world, and against the spiritual forces of evil in the heavenly realms' (Ephesians 6:12, NIV). The apostle is emphasising in this verse the reality of spiritual warfare in high places. And that explains why he reminds us of the need to 'put on the full armour of God' so that we stand fast and firm (Ephesians 6:13-18, NIV). If we are planning to clash with the enemy, we need to wear the right gear. Suited and booted. Simple.

Daniel knew from experience that when he prayed he was entering a war zone. Similarly, we too are in the trenches on the frontline. We are not living in peacetime when it comes to engaging the enemy. Sometimes, in the heat of battle we go AWOL or, perhaps, when there is a lull in the conflict, we desert our post in the arena. Never a good sign. We miss out. And those for whom we should be praying also miss out. This is a call for every one of us to take up arms, and pray.

'Our prayers are weapons of warfare that provide ammunition for angels as they engage the demonic forces of evil in spiritual combat,' says Danny Akin. That is probably not the first thing we think about when we get down on our knees before the Lord in prayer, but that is the fact of the matter. Ask Daniel.

For some of us, such a realisation may be frightening or scary, intimidating or threatening, but it is true. I am definitely not being alarmist, but I am sounding an alarm. And that is why our prayers matter. They make a gargantuan difference. Mary Queen of Scots is reputed to have said that she feared the prayers of John Knox more than she feared an invading army. Such power should drive us to our knees.

Abraham Kuyper (1837-1920), the brilliant journalist, theologian, and prime minister of the Netherlands, once wrote, 'If once the curtain were pulled back, and the spiritual world behind it came to view, it would expose to our spiritual vision a struggle so intense, so convulsive, sweeping everything within its range, that the fiercest battle ever fought on earth would seem, by comparison, a mere game. Not here, but up there—that is where the real conflict is waged. Our earthly struggle drones in its backlash.'

This chapter enables us peer through a porthole window into the ongoing skirmishes among heavenly forces and the role that prayer plays in it. Some of what we see here may surprise you; it will certainly take the wind out of your sails. At the same time, it should quietly reassure you for there are times in all our lives when life is hard and our prayers are not answered as quickly as we think they should. This marvellous chapter gives us a behind-the-scenes glimpse into one of the main reasons why. So we need to remind ourselves on a daily basis that God's delays are not necessarily God's denials. David Jeremiah says, 'As a matter of *fact* the answer may be long in coming, but as a matter of *faith* it is ours at the time of our asking.'

Down the home straight

We have now reached the beginning of the end of this monumental book—a prophetic gem—penned by Daniel, for this trio of chapters are best seen as a single unit. Therefore, chapter 10 is a heart-thumping proem to the detailed kaleidoscope that is chapter 11. When we advance through that smorgasbord of facts and figures, wars and rumours of wars, chapter 12 then provides a superb finale to both the vision and the book.

10:1-3

To go or not to go

In the third year of Cyrus king of Persia a word was revealed to Daniel, who was named Belteshazzar. And the word was true, and it was a great conflict. And he understood the word and had understanding of the vision. In those days, I, Daniel, was mourning for three weeks. I ate no delicacies, no meat or wine entered my mouth, nor did I anoint myself at all, for the full three weeks.

Daniel is fastidious in recording dates throughout his book and that makes life so much easier for us as we seek to ascertain where and when such events of prominence transpired. The *third year of Cyrus* is around 536 BC. The defeat of Babylon three years earlier finds confirmation outside the biblical record on the *Cyrus Cylinder,* a clay cylinder with Akkadian text inscribed on it. It was unearthed in an archaeological dig in 1879 and is now housed in the British Museum.

It was two years after Cyrus had officially ended the seven decades of exile of the Jewish people in Babylon. To borrow a prison analogy, they have served their time and now they are free to go. The sovereign Lord used Cyrus, an unbeliever, whom he called 'his shepherd,' to fulfil his supreme purposes and further his cause in relation to the nation of Israel (Isaiah 44:28, NIV; 2 Chronicles 36:22-23; Ezra 1:1-2). So between the end of Daniel 9 and the beginning of Daniel 10, this has all taken place.

Daniel identifies himself here using the name that had been given to him seventy plus years earlier. He is saying something like this so as to clarify for his readers that he really is who he says he is, 'Yes, I am the very same Daniel, whom Nebuchadnezzar named Belteshazzar.'

I wonder how Daniel must have felt as he longingly watched some of the Jewish people leaving and wending their way back home. Presumably, he was too old and frail to make such a long and hazardous journey without being a burden to those around him. I imagine there were tears of joy streaming down his rugged face. We can visualise his emotional farewells to Zerubbabel, his kinsman, and to Joshua, the rightful high priest (Ezra 2:2, 3:2). After all these years living and serving together in an alien environment that was never going to be an easy cheerio, but God's way does not guarantee any one of us a soft-cushioned ride. In our humanness and vulnerability—and Daniel is made of the same material as the rest of us—partings tend to be more painful than anything else. Even more so when the likelihood of seeing one another again this side of heaven is fairly slim, as was the case with Daniel and his best friends.

There was probably more than a tinge of gut-wrenching disappointment for him as the majority of Jewish people decided to stay where they were. It was only a minority who chose to return to Jerusalem (Ezra 2:64). The remainers were comfortable and prosperous, making a very good living, enmeshed in Babylonian society. They seemed to have no real emotional attachment to the homeland. When push came to shove, they were not in the least concerned about rebuilding Jerusalem or restoring the temple. Sinclair Ferguson writes that 'those who could not sing the Lord's song in a foreign land came to the point where they had no desire either to sing it in the Lord's land.' Their harps were no longer hung on the poplars as they have become increasingly secular over the years. Zion was a fading memory, nothing more than a blur from yesteryear (Psalm 137:1-2).

That must have hit Daniel's heart like a ton of bricks falling on top of him. Even though he was an aged pilgrim, he would pull out all the stops in a valiant attempt to motivate them to think twice. He would do all in his power to shake them out of their cold complacency. And he prayed.

Bad news travels fast

Actually, he did more than just pray, for we read that he *mourned for three weeks* as well as adhering to the simplest of diets by abstaining from meat, wine, and other delicious edibles. No gourmet grub for him for his basic food intake resembled a greens-only menu, washed down with fresh water (Daniel 1:8-12). It is interesting to note in Scripture that fasting is never seen as a ritual to be observed (Matthew 6:16-18; Mark 2:19-20). Nor is it a lever designed to force the hand of God. Instead, it is a spiritual discipline whereby an individual for honourable reasons and with godly motivation enters the zone of consecration to the Lord (Deuteronomy 9:9; 2 Chronicles 20:3; Ezra 8:21-23; Nehemiah 1:4; Joel 1:14-16).

Daniel also chose not to anoint himself with essential body lotions, like skin conditioner, that would soothe and refresh his skin in such a dry, desert climate (Psalm 104:15; 2 Samuel 12:20, 14:2). After three weeks of self-denial in such hot temperatures, his skin must have been badly cracked and flaky and in desperate need of reinvigoration. A price he was willing to pay.

For Daniel, we glean from verse 4 that this was taking place around the specially sacred times of Pesach and Hag HaMatzot with Reishit in between (Feasts of Passover, Unleavened Bread, and Firstfruits). Those were seasons of celebration as Jewish people gladly recalled God's rescue mission in days of yore when he emancipated them from bondage and slavery in Egypt (Leviticus 23:4-14). Instead of indulging in all the legitimate goodies, Daniel is fasting and eating unleavened bread, 'the bread of affliction' (Deuteronomy 16:3, NIV). That takes dedication and commitment.

The question is: For whom was Daniel praying? Well, he

was certainly pleading with God for the refuseniks who opted for the 'green, green grass' of their adopted home, Babylon. Most definitely, he was interceding for those who had risen to the challenge to go back home for the news filtering back to Daniel was not particularly upbeat or encouraging. In fact, it was depressing and disheartening. No sooner had they started to clear the site, when they met huge opposition from some vocal Jerusalemites who were happy to live in the rubble and ruins rather than get their hands dirty and be involved in a major reconstruction of their city (Nehemiah 4:7-8). That explains, in part, Daniel's onerous burden and heavy heart and why he was driven into his prayer closet for such an extended period. Daniel did not complain to his friends, or gripe to his neighbours. He prayed.

It reminds me of a story I read about the inspiring prayer life of Andrew Bonar (1810-92), one of the great preachers and writers of another era. After his death, his daughter led a Welsh evangelist into the Finnieston Free Church her father pastored in the city of Glasgow. She pointed out a pew in the rear where, as a small girl, she had been asked to sit while her father went on into the empty sanctuary. After a long wait she stood up to look for him. He was seated in a pew, his head bent forward. Soon he moved to another pew, then another, and another. Sometimes she would see him carefully examine the nameplates to find the pews he desired.

When she grew older she understood what her father had been doing on that day; he had been praying for his parishioners in the very spot where each one worshipped. Bonar wrote, 'I have learned by experience that it is not much labour but much prayer that is the only means to success. I seek to keep my soul within the shadow of the throne of grace and him that sits thereon.' And so it was with Daniel. He was a man of earnest prayer with real concern and compassion for the welfare of his people.

The American revivalist A W Tozer shares that 'the Bible was written in tears, and to tears it will yield its best treasures. Daniel's long season of fasting and prayer brought an angel from heaven to tell him the secret of the centuries.' Jesus wept (John 11:35). John wept (Revelation 5:4). David wept. Daniel wept. And a host of others wept too. Ligon Duncan says that 'God speaks to us from tears, to the tears of our own hearts.' Daniel has a giant-sized heart for the people of God: for those who were faithfully serving still in Babylon and also in Jerusalem, and for those who have strayed and stayed to look only after their own interests.

In every sense, Daniel, now in his late 80s, was still a key worker who would enthusiastically invest his time and energy in the hidden but strategic work of prayer for the advance of God's mission on earth. We need men like that in today's church! E M Bounds observed that while 'the church is looking for better methods, God is looking for better men. For people are God's methods.'

On a war footing

The Lord in his tender graciousness meets again with his servant when he revealed another vision to him—something for Daniel to see. It was a *word* from on high, an authentic *word* marked by truth—something for him to hear. It would be impossible for it to be anything else but *true*, as Daniel's God is one whose integrity is not called into question and one who personifies truth in stainless purity (Numbers 23:19; Psalm 119:160; John 17:17). Jesus, speaking to his disciples, said of himself, 'I am ... the truth'

(John 14:6), and later in his Upper Room ministry, he portrays the Holy Spirit as the 'Spirit of truth' (John 16:13).

We have a juicy tidbit of information when we discover that it was about a *great conflict* or, according to the NIV, 'it concerned a great war.' That is a two-sided phrase which means, one, that Daniel would experience a level of stress and suffering in receiving the divine message and, two, it was a reminder of the severe afflictions that lay ahead for the covenant people of God (Daniel 11:29-35, 12:1). Daniel longed for his mourning to end in joy. He was puzzled at the twists and turns in the fate of his beloved nation and people. There was a lot of stuff from the previous vision (Daniel 9:24-27) that remained a blur on his mind; the seeming lack of clarity was like frosted glass. He yearned to know more. Basically, he wanted to die in peace. All this was a bitter pill for him to swallow, and there is another vision still to come. The truth is, he cannot avoid taking the medicine that God will shortly dispense.

Many of us know little or nothing of this kind of suffering for our faith in the Lord Jesus. For others, in the global family of God, it is a harsh reality as they experience almost on a daily basis incidences of mistreatment and brutal abuse for the gospel's sake. There are persecution hotspots dotted all around the world where God's cherished children are hated, hunted, and hounded from pillar to post, from dawn to dusk. Christian organisation Open Doors (in their 2020 *World Watch List*) ranks North Korea, Afghanistan, Somalia, Libya, Pakistan, Eritrea, Sudan, Yemen, Iran, and India as the top ten worst offenders where the level of persecution is said to be extreme. As Dale Ralph Davis notes, 'We need instant recall that both faith in Christ and suffering for Christ are equally gifts of grace' (Philippians 1:29). Such undisguised hostility should be seen as the norm for God's faithful servants; it is the rest of us who are living in an abnormal situation.

It is exciting and refreshing for us to discover that Daniel *understood the word and had understanding of the vision.* This came about as a direct result of Daniel doing his part when he waited on the Lord for spiritual insight and wisdom from above. It came in response to his passionate and humble prayers for he was resolute in seeking God's mind on the matter (Daniel 10:12). Not unlike the teaching of the Lord Jesus when he frankly declared that 'apart from me you can do nothing' (John 15:5, NIV). Heaven hears the heart cry of every child of the King and responds appropriately. Our God is not silent for he talks with us today through his Word by his Spirit. Back in Daniel's day, he faithfully communicated with his own as Daniel found out, one more time. A priceless blessing, something we should all be so thankful for.

10:4-9

A heavenly visitor

On the twenty-fourth day of the first month, as I was standing on the bank of the great river (that is, the Tigris) I lifted up my eyes and looked, and behold, a man clothed in linen, with a belt of fine gold from Uphaz around his waist. His body was like beryl, his face like the appearance of lightning, his eyes like flaming torches, his arms and legs like the gleam of burnished bronze, and the sound of his words like the sound of a multitude. And I, Daniel, alone saw the vision, for the men who were with me did not see the vision, but a great trembling fell upon them, and they fled to hide themselves. So I was left alone and saw this great vision, and no strength was left in me. My radiant appearance was fearfully

changed, and I retained no strength. Then I heard the sound of his
words, and as I heard the sound of his words, I fell on my face in
deep sleep with my face to the ground.

And so, ten days after the celebratory commemoration of
Pesach, Daniel finds himself down by the Tigris riverbank
(Genesis 2:14). It was a *great river*, albeit not quite as great as
the Euphrates from a biblical perspective (Genesis 15:18). Like
many strategic cities located by major waterways, Babylon is
built by the Euphrates, but the Tigris (aka Hiddekel) is about
sixty miles from the capital city. Both rivers have their sources in
the Taurus Mountains of eastern Turkey from where they travel
southeast through northern Syria and Iraq before emptying into
the Persian Gulf in the lowlands in an area known as Shatt al-
Arab. Kenneth Gangel writes, 'Some 1,150 miles long (about
500 miles less than the Euphrates), the Tigris carries more water
than the Euphrates and actually moves more rapidly.' It is aptly
called 'river of the date palm' for it flows through the richest
area of date palm cultivation in the world.

Daniel was actually on site, unlike an earlier vision where he
saw himself in the citadel of Susa (Daniel 8:2). We have no way
of knowing the precise reason why he was there: he may have
been on official government business in the eastern region, he
may have been enjoying a short vacation, or he may have gone to
encourage a group of Jewish people in the ways of the Lord.

One minute, it was a peaceful afternoon with life going on as
normal; next minute, Daniel looks up and he can hardly believe
his eyes for he is confronted by a heavenly visitor who flashes
out of the sky. You can imagine the impact it had on Daniel. As
for his friends, they did not see it, but they sensed that something
supernatural had occurred. This intrusion from outer space

terrified them so much that they clicked their heels and ran a mile into the vegetation. You could not see Daniel's assistants for dust for they were petrified. A similar experience happened to Saul on his way to Damascus when the men with him 'stood there speechless' (Acts 9:7-8, 22:9).

As for Daniel, his senses went into overload. He just fainted. He crashed out. His body went into limp mode, some kind of a trance where he passed out and lost consciousness in the presence of the one from on high (Daniel 8:18). Dale Ralph Davis says that 'he was physically and psychologically flattened.' He was drained of every ounce of his strength; ashen-faced, he looked like death warmed up. Undone. It reminds me of the prophet Isaiah who also struggled to handle a vision of God's glory (Isaiah 6:1-7). Even though he has been walking closely with his God for a lifetime of eighty plus years, nothing prepared Daniel for the awesomeness of this moment with majesty.

Ligon Duncan is right when he says that 'in the Bible, intimacy with God always leaves its mark.' Check it out. For Jacob, it was a perpetual limp (Genesis 32:24-31). For Saul, it was temporary blindness (Acts 9:3-9). For Daniel, it was a momentary tremor (Daniel 10:8-11). There was a price to pay to hear from heaven; there was a cost incurred to see the Lord. There always is. Surely, for you and me, in light of Calvary, such an amazing God is worthy of great sacrifices.

The shining man

The heavenly visitor looks like a man, but he is clearly more than a plain man. Many commentators believe he is an angel like Gabriel or Michael, and I can see where they are coming from. However, John Lennox writes that 'this is no mere human, or even an angel; here is overwhelmingly transcendent glory.' The description of this person is so strikingly similar to that of the exalted and enthroned Lord whom John saw in his spectacular vision on the Isle of Patmos (Revelation 1:12-16) that it has to be him. The features of this mysterious person indicate that it was a Christophany, a preincarnate appearance of Jesus Christ (Daniel 3:25).

Warren Wiersbe makes the point that 'frequently in the biblical account of salvation history, you find the Lord Jesus Christ appearing to his servants at special times, either to deliver a special message or to prepare them for a special ministry.' It is even more personalised when we realise that he usually appeared in a manner compatible with their circumstances or their calling. To Abraham, a pilgrim of no fixed abode, Jesus came as a traveller (Genesis 18:1). To Jacob, the devious schemer, he came as a wrestler (Genesis 32:24-30). To Joshua, before he attacked the walled city of Jericho, he came as Captain of the Lord's armies (Joshua 5:13-15). To Isaiah, faced with an empty throne on earth, he revealed himself as the King of heaven seated on a higher throne (Isaiah 6:1). But to two Jewish exiles—Daniel in Babylon and John on Patmos—Jesus appeared as the King-Priest resplendent in majesty. After both men caught a glimpse of glory in the person of the Son, they were given sensational visions of things to come involving the people of God.

Daniel is, therefore, one of only a select handful of men who have had such a rarefied encounter with one who is all-gracious and all-glorious. The sovereign Lord does not make many personal appearances to ordinary folks. But when he does, such covenant children can never be the same again. They are forever spoiled for life on earth having sampled the joyous delights of heaven.

Sinclair Ferguson writes that such people 'have a presence about them. It is the presence of God.'

The man Daniel saw was *dressed in linen*, the sacred garment of priests, and symbolic of righteousness and holiness (Exodus 28:42; Leviticus 6:10). This was the clothing worn by the high priest on the most hallowed day of the Jewish calendar, the Day of Atonement (Yom Kippur), when he offered a sacrifice for the sins of the people before sprinkling the blood seven times upon the golden mercy seat (Leviticus 16:4, 14). A magnificent token of the forgiveness of God.

He had *a belt of finest gold around his waist* representing kingly apparel and underscoring divine sovereignty. His *body was like chrysolite* or topaz, a beautiful transparent gem which shines like gold, and is suggestive of the effulgent glory of God. His *face like lightning* highlights his omnipotence for he is all-powerful, as we discover when God manifested his glory at Mount Sinai (Exodus 19:16, 20:18-19). In the New Testament, *lightning* looks forward to the coming of the Lord Jesus in power and glory (Matthew 24:27). God's people have something to look forward to. That pays tribute to the faithfulness of our great God.

His *eyes like flaming torches* remind us of omniscience for God sees and knows all things. His *arms and legs gleaming like burnished bronze* depicts the judgment and wrath of an angry and just God. His *voice like the sound of a multitude* portrays him as one who speaks, and when he does, people hear every utterance that flows from his mouth (perhaps not only in its strength, but also in its sweet-sounding, soothing tone).

The message is: Because of Jesus, we are forgiven, we have a future. A stirring piece of information for Daniel to employ in a bleak time when things did not look too promising. God was his stronghold, his security, and his sure hope. Same with us! The one who appeared to Daniel comes to each one of us and ministers grace, peace, and hope into all our hearts. Whatever our lot, we have a sufficient Jesus. An indescribable, incomparable Jesus.

10:10-14

Take your breath away stuff

And behold, a hand touched me and set me trembling on my hands and knees. And he said to me, 'O Daniel, man greatly loved, understand the words that I speak to you, and stand upright, for now I have been sent to you.' And when he had spoken this word to me, I stood up trembling. Then he said to me, 'Fear not, Daniel, for from the first day that you set your heart to understand and humbled yourself before your God, your words have been heard, and I have come because of your words. The prince of the kingdom of Persia withstood me twenty-one days, but Michael, one of the chief princes, came to help me, for I was left there with the kings of Persia, and came to make you understand what is to happen to your people in the latter days. For the vision is for days yet to come.'

Having caught a fresh vision of Jesus in verses 5-6, the Lord's faithful servant has been knocked off his feet. He bent, then buckled. Literally. To Daniel, in his hour of great weakness and fear, an anonymous angel now comes to him, touching him with his hand, meeting him at the point of his need. As 'ministering spirits' that is where angels excel, this is what they do best (Hebrews 1:14, NIV); many of us have been recipients of such kindness and thoughtfulness. This reminds us that angels lovingly ministered to the Lord Jesus after his forty days of temptation in the wilderness (Matthew 4:11; Mark 1:13), and in the garden of Gethsemane when he prayed his prayer of submission (Luke 22:41-43). Slowly but surely, Daniel responded to the gentle angelic pick-me-up by kneeling on his hands and feet; then, after a few more encouraging words, he gradually rose to his feet. Even then, he was shaking like a leaf in the presence of the heavenly messenger.

It was so intensely personal as the angel addressed an emotional Daniel by name and shared with him some beautiful words of affirmation. He told him, again, that he was a man *greatly loved* (Daniel 9:23). It signifies from other translations that Daniel was 'very precious to God' (NLT) and 'highly esteemed' (NIV). No matter how Daniel felt about himself yesterday or today, he was treasured by the Most High. The most wonderful thing any one of us can hear is that we are loved by God. Thank God, the same sense of belonging and value applies to every believer in God's family (1 Peter 2:9-10).

He also reminded Daniel that he was God's envoy to him at this juncture in his life. The angel touched him a few times in the course of their encounter, and he talked with him too sharing some astounding insights into life in the unseen realm. Essentially, Daniel's response is perfectly understandable, but there are no grounds for him to be afraid. Hence, the angel exhorted him to *'fear not.'* Familiar words in Scripture, where there are over three hundred and fifty similar exhortations (for example, Deuteronomy 31:6; Joshua 1:9; Isaiah 41:10, 43:1; Zephaniah 3:16; Matthew 28:5; John 14:27; Revelation 1:17). Bryan Chapell writes, 'When the glory of God is so great that it might obscure the love God has for his people, he always assures them that they need not fear harm from him.'

So often, like Daniel, when we are flustered, fretful, and frightened at the prospect of an unknown tomorrow, the Lord graciously sends someone along to help us see things from another perspective. Like the angel to Daniel, it is massively reassuring for us to know that the great God of heaven hears and answers our faintest cry.

By way of recap: Daniel prayed his heart out, God heard his pleading as soon as the words left his mouth, the answer to his appeal was immediately commissioned, an angel promptly left heaven with the answer safely tucked under his belt, then … a problem arose mid-air between heaven and earth.

That hitch lasted for twenty-one days, we are told. Three weeks is a long time to wait when you are anticipating an answer straightaway. Such was the experience of Daniel. To be sure, it is something that many of us will have faced in our prayer life. We have often wrestled and, indeed, agonised with the age-old question: Why the delay?

When angel work is not a piece of cake

Because a demon called *the prince of the kingdom of Persia* got in the way and delayed the answer reaching an exasperated Daniel. Extraordinary. There was a battle royal taking place as one angel tried to outwit and outdo the other. This was a real skirmish in the unseen world—an invisible war—where good and bad angels were fighting it out in order to gain supremacy and score a big victory. The angel dispatched from heaven's throne was, in all likelihood, Gabriel (Daniel 8:15-16, 9:21), but he faced a concerted onslaught from this other created being (Colossians 1:16).

Can we nail this fallen angelic prince down and identify him? It was not Cyrus, as he was perched on his throne on Planet

Earth. And no matter how good he was, or versatile he may have been, he still could not be two places at once. It must, therefore, be someone else. He is one of the devil's diplomats with special responsibility for the territory governed by Cyrus. This was his designated patch, his niche of responsibility, and he would do all in his satanic power to topple the angel of God. At this point, he appears to be winning for he and his cohorts have ganged up on God's angel and have successfully pinned him down on their turf.

Here is the struggle behind all other struggles recorded in time and etched in granite on the pages of history. This is an inside look at Satan's network of evil, spoken of by Paul as a collective incorporating 'all rule and authority, power and dominion, and every title that can be given' (Ephesians 1:21, NIV). The devil is real. Demonic activity is *bona fide*.

Satan and his minions form a vast unseeable structure working behind the scenes in the governments of the world. Day and night, they are hyperactive doing all they possibly can to perpetrate and promote Satan's dark philosophy. Their assignments are geared to influence opinion on international affairs, especially as it relates to the nation of Israel and God's covenant people. The aim of these fiends is to decimate the people of God, causing nothing but harm and havoc along the way. In their eyes, such collateral damage is a risk worth taking.

These infernal delegates are brilliantly organised, extremely well briefed, suitably equipped, and totally committed to Satan, their paymaster general. Their extra-terrestrial movements are designed to plant seeds of fear and anxiety in the human heart and sway public loyalty away from the Lord Jesus. It is vitally important for us to realise that through his sacrificial work on the cross the Lord Jesus soundly defeated Satan and his army (John 12:31; Colossians 2:15; Revelation 12:11). Jesus is Lord, and no matter who the fallen angel may be, the risen, exalted Jesus reigns over one and all, and their ultimate doom will be carried through at the appointed hour (Isaiah 24:21).

There is obviously a fallen angel specifically assigned to Persia, and one to Greece (Daniel 10:20). The implication is that there is one operating where you and I live and work. Think prayerfully about that chilling fact for a few minutes and when the reality of it has sunk in, why not take a moment and insert your locality into this statement: there is a prince from hell hovering over (*the place where you live*). Then pray. Dear reader, this is deadly serious stuff. We dare not treat this indisputable fact lightly or handle it flippantly.

A former missionary to Cambodia was upfront when she wrote, 'I spent years witnessing the power and reality of spiritual warfare. But I talk to people here at home about the need for confronting spiritual powers and their eyes just go vacant or suspicious. It is like the spiritual world does not even count or is not real. But I will tell you, it is very real.' Some of us could tell similar stories of such demonic influence in hindering and hampering gospel work in various parts of the world. But Satan's reach will exceed his grasp because God's purposes will prevail. Spiritual warfare is real, but so too is the power of our all-conquering Saviour (1 John 4:4).

This phenomenon may help explain the mystery surrounding some of the tardy responses to our prayers. However, there may be other contributory factors to heaven's apparent silence. Maybe our relationship with the Lord is not what it should be because of unconfessed sin lurking in our hearts (Psalm 66:18). We may be asking for the wrong thing or requesting something with the wrong motive (James 4:3). There may even be a breakdown in marital harmony between husband and wife (1 Peter 3:1-7). These are practical issues which need to be dealt with before the Lord if we are to expect positive answers to prayer. And there is another, for F B Meyer reminds us that 'the great tragedy of life is not unanswered prayer, it is unoffered prayer.'

I love the phrase *Michael, one of the chief princes, came to help me* for it confirms that good triumphed over evil and light prevailed over darkness. He is an archangel and is number one in the angelic pecking order, a superangel. We read of him elsewhere in Scripture (Daniel 10:21, 12:1; Jude 9; Revelation 12:7) where his main focus is linked to Israel and the protection of the Jewish people. Simply put, Michael is Israel's guardian angel whose name means, 'Who is like God?' The answer to that question is, of course, no one. Nobody compares to God, not even the mighty captain of the angelic host. Regardless of his influence and track record over many seasons of conflict and ministry, Michael would be first to recognise that 'the Lord *alone* does marvellous deeds' (Psalm 72:18, NIV).

Stephen Miller writes in his commentary that 'Israel has a mighty angelic supporter in the heavenly realm. Therefore, regardless of Israel's political, military, and economic weaknesses, its existence is assured because no earthly power can resist their great prince.' Right on cue, Michael, a royal champion of God's elect, secures a landmark victory for God's angel when he routs the enemy and shoos them off elsewhere. The enemy's interception is foiled and ends in blissful failure when Israel's warrior-advocate, Michael, delivers a knockout punch. Twenty-one days it took for the angel to arrive to Daniel by the Tigris, but better late than never!

10:15-21

He touched me

When he had spoken to me according to these words, I turned my face toward the ground and was mute. And behold, one in the likeness of the children of man touched my lips. Then I opened my mouth and spoke. I said to him who stood before me, 'O my lord, by reason of the vision pains have come upon me, and I retain no strength. How can my lord's servant talk with my lord? For now no strength remains in me, and no breath is left in me.' Again one having the appearance of a man touched me and strengthened me. And he said, 'O man greatly loved, fear not, peace be with you; be strong and of good courage.' And as he spoke to me, I was strengthened and said, 'Let my lord speak, for you have strengthened me.' Then he said, 'Do you know why I have come to you? But now I will return to fight against the prince of Persia; and when I go out, behold, the prince of Greece will come. But I will tell you what is inscribed in the book of truth: there is none who contends by my side against these except Michael, your prince.'

Daniel is gobsmacked when he hears the angelic message regarding the nation of Israel and her people. He is speechless, staring down at the ground. Bamboozled. All at sea. Spiritual warfare is not for the faint-hearted or weak-kneed. Even spiritual giants like Daniel can be overcome and overwhelmed. Dale Ralph Davis says, 'One might wonder if this helpless, sleeping, shaking, speechless, breathless man will ever be in shape to receive the angel's revelation.' Well, after a double touch from the hand of the angel, he was able to both speak and stand. His voice returns. His vitality is restored.

So far as the angel is concerned, his work was still not over as he must engage in further conflict with the princes of Persia and Greece. Life goes on. The hidden war carries on. He was immensely grateful too for the support of Michael when the battle was fiercest. And Michael's role continues to this day. A powerful reminder that the devil does not work part-time or confine his nefarious schedule to office hours. Certainly not! John Phillips writes that 'the world's best protection against these extra-terrestrials is a praying believer, Bible in hand, indwelt by the Holy Spirit of God.' In our lives, it is important to realise that when we say no to the devil and mean it, it is just like kryptonite to Superman.

Before bidding Daniel farewell, the angel divulges to him the contents of *the book of truth* and that is what we shall explore together in the next two chapters.

11

AN UNCIVIL WAR: NORTH AND SOUTH

Henry Ford (1863-1947), American industrialist and big business magnate, founder of the Ford Motor Company in 1903, spent most of his life making headlines, good, bad, but never indifferent. He was celebrated as a visionary genius, a folk hero, a go-getter, and the creative force behind the automobile industry. Within five years of establishing the Ford Motor Company, he rolled out the first Model T. A decade later, his innovation skills showed when he introduced the world's first moving assembly line for cars. As production increased, demand for the Tin Lizzie remained consistently high, and by 1918, half of all cars in America were Model Ts. Near the end of the 1920s the Ford Motor Company was the largest car manufacturer in the world.

Some of his sayings are unforgettable and via social media have travelled around the world: 'Failure is simply an opportunity to begin again, this time more intelligently.' 'Quality means doing it right when no one else is looking.' 'When everything seems to be going against you, remember that the aeroplane takes off against the wind, not with it.' One of his all-time classics was, 'Any colour, so long as it is black.' Another dictum ascribed to him that 'history is more or less bunk' is exceptionally well known.

Ford's lack of appreciation of history is based on his view that it gets in the way of living life in the here and now. For him, nothing in the past was of any practical use to living in the present. Basically, he felt that history was an irrelevance. Many people find history dull and boring, something which holds no fascination for them at all. For some, it probably reflects the fact that they had a seriously bad history teacher in high school! Miss Catherine Morland, one of the characters in Jane Austen's novel *Northanger Abbey*, says it best, 'History, real solemn history, I cannot be interested in…. I read it a little as a duty; but it tells me nothing that does not either vex or weary me. The quarrels of popes and kings, with wars and pestilences on every page; the men all so good for nothing, and hardly any women at all—it is very tiresome.'

A first run through Daniel 11, assuming you read the entire chapter, could easily lead you to the same conclusion as Mr Ford or Miss Morland on matters of history. If so, that is where you need to prayerfully read it again, and again, in bite-size chunks, preferably with the help of a good commentary by your side. You will not be disappointed. It really is worth the effort, I promise. Iain Duguid writes that 'it presents a dizzying and confusing array of alliances and conflicts, of wars and rumours of wars, the kind that could easily seem to have been simply ripped from a trash bag of random coincidences.' Unlike Henry Ford's aphorism, I believe there are ace lessons for us to learn from this quite remarkable chapter which is Daniel's equivalent to the first four chapters of 1 Chronicles!

Even though this lengthy chapter is famed for its machinations of man, it is essential for us to appreciate that it is no less inspired than, say, the Pauline epistles or the book of Psalms (2 Peter 1:19-21). I concede that it may not be as inspirational or as motivational as them; however, still it remains the living Word of the living God and is hugely beneficial to our spiritual development and growth in grace (2 Timothy 3:16-17).

As I mentioned in the previous chapter, these final three chapters are best seen as a single entity. Danny Akin summarises them crisply when he writes that 'chapter 10 provides the context, chapter 11 contains the content, and chapter 12 is the conclusion.' Through the gracious providence of one who reigns on high and who rules all of history we are given a fascinating glimpse into the comings and goings apposite to the so-called four hundred silent years between the Old and New Testaments. There is a perceived silence because God did not say anything new to his people through his servants, the prophets, during the intertestamental period; in that sense, things were quiet on the biblical revelation front. That said, things were not quite so quiet down here on *terra firma* for here we have a panoramic picture of potentates in prophetic perspective. It seems to me that no other chapter in the Bible gives us such an awesome demonstration of God's ability to foretell the future; for example, in verses 2-35 it is estimated that there is a minimum of one hundred and thirty five specific predictions that have already been fulfilled!

This aspect of prophetic truth is exciting and comforting, not only for us in the twenty-first century, but especially for that godly remnant among God's ancient people who lived through those terribly dark days between Malachi and Matthew. They could put their index finger on the open scroll and say to one another, 'Ah, this is where we are,' thereby enabling them to track and trace their journey thus far. John Phillips says that 'those silent centuries were not without echoes, and those echoes sound loudly in this impressive chapter. This chapter was written to be a lamp to the feet of God's people and a light on their path in the intertestamental period.' In his second epistle, the Apostle Peter advises us that prophecy is analogous to 'a light shining in a dark place' (2 Peter 1:19, NIV).

For us, most of it is history as we are looking back, courtesy of a rear-view mirror; for Daniel, it was prophecy as he was looking forward through a telescope to the unborn ages ahead. When we speak of biblical prophecy, it is not only talking about major events or key moments before they materialise; prophecy is the omniscient God's interpretation of that history. Ligon Duncan wisely counsels, 'It is God telling you how he wants you to think about those events.'

Chuck Colson in his book, *Kingdoms in Conflict*, tells about his days in the White House. He said, 'One of the things about us is that we thought we were running the world.' He reflected on a meeting he held with President Nixon, Henry Kissinger, and other special advisors, when Kissinger quipped, 'Gentlemen, what we do today will determine the future history of the world.' Speaking personally, Colson said, 'While I was sitting there, goose pimples ran up my back and I thought, "I'm really important. I'm determining the future history of the world."' Later, he penned, 'Looking back on that assumption from a prison cell, I realised how utterly arrogant and wrong it was. We were not determining the future history of the world. That was in God's hands.'

It so important for us to grasp the same message when we watch events unfolding in the drama of global history. Daniel

11 is a brilliant illustration of that principle. That means, we see each milestone from the vantage point of an eternal throne which can never be shaken (Psalm 45:6; Lamentations 5:19), and through the glowing eyes of one who has a vested interest in his covenant peoples because of redemption's storyline (Isaiah 43:1; Acts 20:28).

11:1-4

Setting the stage

'And as for me, in the first year of Darius the Mede, I stood up to confirm and strengthen him. And now I will show you the truth. Behold, three more kings shall arise in Persia, and a fourth shall be far richer than all of them. And when he has become strong through his riches, he shall stir up all against the kingdom of Greece. Then a mighty king shall arise, who shall rule with great dominion and do as he wills. And as soon as he has arisen, his kingdom shall be broken and divided toward the four winds of heaven, but not to his posterity, nor according to the authority with which he ruled, for his kingdom shall be plucked up and go to others besides these.'

In this opening hinge verse connecting chapters 10 and 11, the same angel (possibly Gabriel) continues his conversation where he left off at the end of the previous chapter by informing Daniel of the support role that he played in relation to Darius in his first year on the throne, 539 BC, two years prior to the big vision of chapters 10-12. In answer to Daniel's persistent prayers, and in order to fulfil the strategic purpose of God, the angel nudged Darius along in the right direction in terms of freeing God's people to journey home.

God has a unique way of doing things, and if he chooses to use a good angel and an unbelieving monarch to initiate their return from exile, then that is the divine prerogative. Who are we to question the sovereign workings of God? God does what he does because he is who he is. God. The same criterion holds true in our lives, especially when we try to understand the leading of the Lord with regard to some of life's major choices. Even when things do not work out the way we hoped or prayed, as the disciples discovered when they sailed into an unexpected squall on the Galilee, we can still trust him for he knows all about today and tomorrow (Mark 4:35-41; Romans 8:28). The abiding truth is that God will not lead us where his grace cannot keep us.

Having cleared the air on that vitally important issue, the angel goes on to give Daniel a word of affirmation, when he says, *and now I will show you the truth*. Up to this point, not surprisingly, it has been the truth, the whole truth, and nothing but the plain truth. From now on, the angel confirmed, same again. Truth unchanged. Truth unchanging. He was reassuring Daniel, at the outset of this inconceivably long history lesson on future proceedings, that the gold standard of probity is the plumbline. The angel's intention is to outline a sequence of unembellished facts from the *book of truth* (Daniel 10:21) to assist all those who will live through perilous times. For Daniel, nearing the end of life's pilgrimage, it is ammunition for prayer; for future generations, it is a thumbs-up to the sovereignty of God in the midst of tough times.

Life after Darius

You will recall from Daniel 2 and Daniel 7 that four vast global empires were described in relation to Israel and the Jewish people: Babylon, Medo-Persia, Greece, and Rome. Then, in Daniel 8, the focus narrowed to two: Medo-Persia and Greece. It is those same two empires which the angel zooms in on here in Daniel 11, but this time around they are allocated only a few lines of biblical text, three verses in a single paragraph. They have been given the shrink wrap treatment and we shall soon discover the reason why.

In succession to Darius, the three kings were: one, Cambyses, eldest son of Cyrus (530-522 BC), not mentioned in the Old Testament; two, Pseudo-Smerdis (522-521 BC), a usurper who only lasted six months; three, Darius I Hystapes (521-486 BC), an able ruler mentioned in Ezra 5-6. Number four is presented as one who *shall be far richer than all of them* and who will set the cat among the pigeons in his hostile attitude towards Greece. His name, Xerxes I Ahasuerus (486-465 BC), whom we read of in the books of Ezra and Esther.

From his numerous military altercations, he amassed enormous wealth and accumulated a horde of priceless treasures. Xerxes wisely consolidated his position at home before moving with a massive army towards Greece; the famous one hundred and eighty days banquet for the good and great followed by a week-long garden party for lesser lights describes the grandeur of preparation for that campaign (Esther 1:2-5). As it turned out, his invasion was nothing more than a damp squib, even though he deployed hundreds of thousands of fighting men. He was first humiliated at the pass at Thermopylae by a tiny force of Spartan warriors, then crushed and torn to shreds by the Greek navy at the battle of Salamis in 480 BC. He limped back home like a whimpering dog. For him, and for Persia, this was the beginning of the end.

So far as Persia was concerned, its job was done for it was

instrumental in giving the green light to God's exiled people to venture back home. A minority did. The majority did not. Danny Akin says that Persia was assigned 'to the dustbin of history.... God supported and protected it to accomplish his chosen purpose.' Since Daniel died in 530 BC, just months before Cyrus was killed in a minor infringement, he may have had a sprinkling of knowledge of Cambyses, but not the others. The prophetic word to Daniel was fulfilled in history to the letter. Again.

Knee-deep in Greece

There is a time lapse of about one hundred and fifty years between verses 2 and 3. All that transpired during those intervening years is left unsaid as it is not relevant or important to the evolving storyline in the vision. The *mighty king* of verse 3 is none other than Alexander the Great (336-323 BC). His meteoric rise and fall is well documented in the annals of history, but within a dozen or so years, he had conquered the known world of his day. Because of his lust for control, he ruled his expansive empire with unbridled power. Woe betide any man who spoke out of turn. He did not suffer fools gladly. Basically, he called all the shots, and as predicted in the vision, he did whatever he wanted to do. Jim Allen notes that 'it would be very difficult to find another man in history exhibiting such self-will. Thus the prophetic Scripture marks out a man; history points to its accuracy.'

When Alexander died in June 323 BC at age thirty-three, the prophecy of verse 4 was implemented with phenomenal exactitude. After many years of acrimonious bickering, political intrigue, treachery, and assassinations, the kingdom was *divided toward the four winds of heaven*. Alexander's sons were murdered in-between times meaning that no part of the empire went to his bloodline. That signalled the end for Alexander who is whisked off the page in just twenty-seven Hebrew words. He walked on to the world stage in robust health, he was carried off it a broken man (Daniel 8:22). The truth is, in God's grand scheme as it relates to Israel and the chosen people, he does not really matter that much. Unwittingly, he served God's purposes in life, and now he is gone. Another clear indication to us that whopping empires and illustrious emperors of history are as a drop in the bucket to God (Isaiah 40:15). The lesson is that all of us need to work towards a biblically-oriented mindset whereby we see current affairs through the unfiltered lens of Scripture (Isaiah 40:22-23).

The empire was carved up into four parts and given to four generals from among the Macedonian veterans, none of whom wielded a fraction of the authority enjoyed by Alexander and who were often viewed as inferior men ruling large provincial fiefdoms. The north—Babylon, Syria, and much of the Middle East—went to Seleucus I Nicator; the south—Egypt, Israel, and Arabia Petrea—went to Ptolemy I Soter; the west—Macedon and Greece—went to Cassander; and the east—Thrace and a large part of Asia Minor—went to Lysimachus (Daniel 7:6, 8:22). 'It will be observed,' writes Jim Allen, 'that the centre of the geographic direction is taken from neither Babylon (capital of the Babylonian Empire and the *de facto* capital for the Grecian Empire) nor Susa (capital of the Persian Empire), but Jerusalem. God, through Daniel, is focusing upon his people and their capital city, Jerusalem, which he uses as God's geographic centre of earth.'

Making sense of ancient history

Two of the four kingdoms that emanated out of Alexander's splintered empire were the southern kingdom of the Ptolemies, based in Egypt, and the northern kingdom of the Seleucids, based in Syria. It was during the third and second centuries BC that the kings of the south and the kings of the north played political ping-pong with each other leaving Israel to play piggy-in-the-middle. All of this toing and froing is anticipated in the vision given to Daniel.

Dale Ralph Davis writes that 'the reason for the zoom lens on the kings of the south and north is because the people of God (a substantial number of them) will be back in the land of Israel, living on that sliver of land at the east end of the Mediterranean, that crossroads where Africa, Asia, and Europe come together, where they will be scrunched between and subject to the whims of these opposing dynasties.'

John Calvin devotes some forty pages to a full analysis of this chapter; I have no intention of following his example as it could easily become tedious and confusing, unless you are a fanatical history buff. As we patiently work our way through this fairly detailed section, you will be elated and thrilled to see the precision of the predictions as the divine thumbprint is stamped all over them. Astonishing. Mind-blowing.

It may be helpful if I give you a list of the kings from the Seleucid dynasty in Syria and the Ptolemy dynasty in Egypt who appear in verses 5-35. There may be a slight discrepancy in a couple of the dates (different historians give different data), but they are accurate to within one year. They are:

The kings of the north
Seleucus I (Nicator) 312-280 BC
Antiochus I (Soter) 280-261 BC
Antiochus II (Theos) 261-246 BC

Seleucus II (Callinicus) 246-226 BC

Seleucus III (Ceraunus) 226-223 BC

Antiochus III (Magnus) 223-187 BC

Seleucus IV (Philopator) 187-175 BC

Antiochus IV (Epiphanes) 175-164 BC

The kings of the south

Ptolemy I (Soter) 323-285 BC

Ptolemy II (Philadelphus) 285-246 BC

Ptolemy III (Euergetes) 246-221 BC

Ptolemy IV (Philopator) 221-204 BC

Ptolemy V (Epiphanes) 204-181 BC

Ptolemy VI (Philometor) 181-145 BC

When we unpack the events surrounding each of these characters we shall find that there is nothing dull or boring about history. As you would expect, every piece fits perfectly in the jigsaw puzzle of prophecy. For a passionate dissectologist, there is nothing more annoying and frustrating than finding one piece missing before the puzzle is complete; that does not happen in this case for every piece is accounted for. Here below are the first few pieces for us to put together, with lots more to follow.

11:5-6

The blunt truth about sharp practice

'Then the king of the south shall be strong, but one of his princes shall be stronger than he and shall rule, and his authority shall be a great authority. After some years they shall make an alliance, and the daughter of the king of the south shall come to the king

of the north to make an agreement. But she shall not retain the strength of her arm, and he and his arm shall not endure, but she shall be given up, and her attendants, he who fathered her, and he who supported her in those times.'

Beginning here in verse 5 the struggle between the kings of the south and the kings of the north kicks off. From the outset up to the arrival of Antiochus Epiphanes there is a timeframe of about one hundred and fifty years.

The ball starts rolling with Ptolemy I Soter, the king of the South, who finds himself in a very strong position as ruler. The one referred to as *stronger than he* is Seleucus I Nicator. There is more than a hint of intrigue in this for after a bloodless coup Seleucus fled south from Antigonus of Babylon and temporarily joined hands with Ptolemy. He had ulterior motives in so doing and that was obvious when they combined their strengths and roundly defeated Antigonus in 312 BC, thus opening the door for Seleucus to ultimately gain control of the entire area from the Hellespont to India; and as predicted at the end of verse 5, the king of the north eventually became stronger than his southern friend Ptolemy, ruler of Egypt. Inevitably, having started out as friends, they soon became rivals.

Ptolemy I died in 285 BC, and war continued under his son Ptolemy II Philadelphus. Danny Akin says that 'according to tradition he commissioned the translation of the Hebrew Bible into Greek—called the Septuagint (abbreviated LXX).' *After some years* hints at a time lapse of several years and points us to an era of bitter animosity between the north and south when they waged war after war against each other.

Fed up with all this acrimony, Ptolemy II was keen to make a peace treaty with the Seleucid ruler, Antiochus II Theos, grandson of Seleucus, around 250 BC. As an example of romantic diplomacy, Berenice, Ptolemy's daughter (*the daughter of the king of the south*), was arranged to marry Antiochus II (*the king of the north*) to *make an agreement* between the two kingdoms. Marriages for political expediency have been going on for a long time; it was a policy adopted by Solomon (1 Kings 3:1). This seems to be fulfilled in the bigamous marriage between Antiochus II and Berenice.

Not long after, Ptolemy II died, leaving Berenice powerless to broker a degree of unity between the opposing factions. Within weeks of his father-in-law dying, Antiochus II seized his moment and divorced Berenice, returning to his former wife, Laodice. She was less than confident about the resumed relationship; once jilted, twice shy. Rightly or wrongly, she felt there was a third person in their marriage so she poisoned Antiochus and actively encouraged her son, Seleucus Callinicus, to eliminate Berenice and her infant child, thus leaving the way clear for him to inherit the throne. Needless to say, it is all a bit messy, but as foretold in verse 6, those are the bare facts of a sordid story. This brings the timeline down to 246 BC.

11:7-9

Getting your own back

'And from a branch from her roots one shall arise in his place. He shall come against the army and enter the fortress of the king of the north, and he shall deal with them and shall prevail. He shall also carry off to Egypt their gods with their metal images and their precious vessels of silver and gold, and for some years he shall refrain from attacking the king of the north. Then the latter shall come into the realm of the king of the south but shall return to his own land.'

'All this blood-letting, however, was not smart,' notes Dale Ralph Davis. Berenice's brother, Ptolemy III Euergetes, *a branch from her roots*, succeeded his father as king of Egypt. To avenge his sister's liquidation and to defend her honour, he marched north, resoundingly defeated the Syrian army, captured and executed the vindictive Laodice. Revenge was swift and sweet, bloody and brutal (verse 7). He pillaged Antioch, the fortified capital city, and carried back to Egypt an estimated 4,000 talents of gold, 40,000 talents of silver, and 2,500 molten images. In his booty stockpile, there were a number of treasures and sacred idols that had been taken by the Persian monarch Cambyses in 524 BC. Invariably, he remained a more potent force than the Syrians for a protracted time (verse 8).

In commemoration of his overwhelming military achievement, a proud Euergetes erected a monument *Marmor Adulitanum* boasting that he flattened the enemy. About 240 BC the new Syrian king, Seleucus Callinicus, made a retaliatory strike against Egypt. He was clobbered. Humiliated, he beat a hasty retreat with his tail between his legs (verse 9).

John Walvoord writes that 'this was the beginning of the seesaw battle between the two nations. The inclusion of this background material leads up to the important point, the burden of the prophecy in verses 10-19, which is the ascendancy of Syria over Egypt and the return of the Holy Land to Syrian control. This set the stage for the persecutions of Israel under Antiochus Epiphanes, which is the major concern of verses 21-35 of this prophecy.'

11:10-12

Two men's war machines

'His sons shall wage war and assemble a multitude of great

forces, which shall keep coming and overflow and pass through, and again shall carry the war as far as his fortress. Then the king of the south, moved with rage, shall come out and fight against the king of the north. And he shall raise a great multitude, but it shall be given into his hand. And when the multitude is taken away, his heart shall be exalted, and he shall cast down tens of thousands, but he shall not prevail.'

A new wrinkle is introduced in verse 10 with the arrival of the two sons of Callinicus, Seleucus III Ceraunus and Antiochus III Magnus. As a duo, they gathered enormous forces and charged south to wipe out the Egyptians. Ceraunus, however, came to an untimely end, having perished in battle in Asia Minor before the invasion, so his late-teens brother Antiochus the Great (Magnus) took up the reins of power. He overran Phoenicia and Israel, as far south as Gaza, until he came up against the Egyptians at the Battle of Raphia, on the frontier between Israel and Egypt, where he was thrashed by the playboy and pervert Ptolemy IV Philopator, who was accompanied by his sister-wife, Arsinoe, about 218 BC. Antiochus III sustained a catastrophic loss of at least 17,000 troops, the Egyptians only 2,200 (verse 11). The same verse appears to suggest that the sovereign God granted Ptolemy the victory over his archenemy, for we read *it shall be given into his hand*. Kenneth Gangel writes that 'Ptolemy owed no allegiance to the Geneva Convention, of course, so he slaughtered most of the troops he captured.' That explains the phrase, *he shall cast down tens of thousands* (verse 12).

The ascendancy of Ptolemy IV was short-lived. Marked by indolence and indulgence, he was puffed up with pride, and thinking he was untouchable, he failed to press home his advantage. And possibly because of his profligate lifestyle, hinted at in verse

12, he was living a luxurious life on extra time. We all know how God deals with proud men and women (James 4:6). Ptolemy IV Philopator and his queen died mysteriously in 203 BC and were succeeded by their young son, four-year-old Ptolemy V Epiphanes.

It is worth noting that Philopator was not the nicest guy to have in your company. Gleason Archer, in *The Expositor's Bible Commentary*, writes of him: 'He was a cruel debauchee who began his reign by murdering his own mother, Berenice of Cyrene, and then his wife, his sister, and his brother. He then gave himself over to a degenerate dissipation with male and female sex partners and finally succumbed to a disease in 203 BC.'

11:13-17

The comeback king

'For the king of the north shall again raise a multitude, greater than the first. And after some years he shall come on with a great army and abundant supplies. In those times many shall rise against the king of the south, and the violent among your own people shall lift themselves up in order to fulfil the vision, but they shall fail. Then the king of the north shall come and throw up siegeworks and take a well-fortified city. And the forces of the south shall not stand, or even his best troops, for there shall be no strength to stand. But he who comes against him shall do as he wills, and none shall stand before him. And he shall stand in the glorious land, with destruction in his hand. He shall set his face to come with the strength of his whole kingdom, and he shall bring terms of an agreement and perform them. He shall give him the daughter of women to destroy the kingdom, but it shall not stand or be to his advantage.'

Something like fourteen years later, Antiochus III made a comeback. One of the lessons of history is that you can never write any man off, especially one who was hammered on the battlefield. On this occasion he marched south with a larger, better equipped, and better trained army which he had mustered through a series of memorable eastern campaigns since Raphia, some years earlier (verse 13). He was also keen to take advantage of the boy king. As Jim Allen points out, 'This is where Israel comes again into the world picture.'

There is a compelling morsel of information in verse 14 which almost points to something like an insurrection of sorts. We read that *many shall rise against the king of the south.* Those who did were Philip V of Macedon and a band of other revolutionaries within Egypt. There were also *violent [ones] among your own people*, which refers to those Jewish bullyboys who aided and abetted Antiochus. They were united in their fierce opposition to the boy king as well as bitterly resenting Egypt's influence in Israel. Their guerrilla tactics were intended to help Antiochus release Israel from the clutch of Egypt. They had a goal for they were zealous to *fulfil the vision* (Isaiah 19:1-17). Unknown to them, the vision God gave Daniel made it crystal clear that they would fail, and fail they did.

Their defeat came at the hands of the eminent Egyptian General Scopas. However, he himself was eventually defeated. This is how it happened: Antiochus and his Syrian forces advanced against Egypt at the Battle of Panium (near to Paneas in the area of Caesarea Philippi mentioned in the Gospels) in 199 BC and won a terrific victory. They then pursued the Egyptians further south and besieged, then captured, the *well-fortified city* of Sidon (verse 15), where Scopas finally surrendered in 198 BC.

The allusion to *the forces of the south shall not stand* in verse 15 is to the unsuccessful attempt by three Egyptian leaders, Eropas, Menacles, and Damoyenus, to rescue the besieged Scopas from Sidon. The South were pummelled into a decisive defeat at the hands of the north.

That walloping victory secured complete control for Antiochus III over Israel and Phoenicia enabling him *to do as he wills, and none shall stand before him* (verse 16). Sinclair Ferguson notes that his attitude 'betrayed the hubris that characterises great men without God in the book of Daniel.' A stonking victory. Stinking pride. It must have hit Daniel hard when he discovered that Antiochus III is in *the glorious land,* suitably named, as it resonates with the testimony of the Sons of Korah (Psalm 48:1-2). Chillingly, Daniel's vision says he has *destruction in his hand* (Daniel 8:9; Ezekiel 20:6). The bottom line is that no one messed around with the king of the north. Failure to toe his party line was equivalent to signing your own death warrant.

Danny Akin notes the significance of this development when he writes, 'This is important because it sets the stage for the reign of terror to follow under the Syrian Greek ruler Antiochus IV Epiphanes (175-164 BC).'

By this time the rising power of Rome was beginning to threaten Syria's expansionist agenda. In that light, the north was in no mood to placate the feelings of loss felt by the south so they made hay while the sun was shining. Terms of peace were imposed on the losers, and in order to seal the deal, gave his beautiful early-teenage daughter Cleopatra (not the Cleopatra who married Mark Antony over a hundred years later) to nine-year-old Ptolemy as a wife (verse 17). Understandably, the marriage was not consummated for another few years. Needless to say, Antiochus was hoping for a more than favourable outcome to this arrangement. He reckoned Cleopatra would be a fifth column, working for her 'daddy' against her husband. She was supposed to work from the inside to ruin Egypt as an opponent of Syria. But he ended up with an omelette on his face when Cleopatra did not loyally support her father; instead, she dearly loved her husband and backed him to the hilt. One more time, that stance was predicted in the vision given to Daniel (verse 17).

11:18-19

Too big for his boots

> 'Afterward he shall turn his face to the coastlands and shall capture many of them, but a commander shall put an end to his insolence. Indeed, he shall turn his insolence back upon him. Then he shall turn his face back toward the fortresses of his own land, but he shall stumble and fall, and shall not be found.'

For many years Antiochus III had a penchant to invade the Mediterranean area, *the coastlands*. This was a passion for him, something he always wanted to do for his ambition was to rule where his hero Alexander the Great had ruled. Even though he had a measure of success, his desire to annex this region was seriously misguided. The Romans warned him to stay out of Greece. Dale Ralph Davis writes that 'he nevertheless invaded Greece in 192 BC, and the Romans, perhaps wondering what part of "No" Antiochus did not understand, defeated him at Thermopylae [north of Athens] in 191 BC.' Smelling blood, the Romans at a pace pursued him into Asia and under the leadership of *a commander*, General Lucius Cornelius Scipio Asiaticus, secured a superlative victory at Magnesia on the Meander River southeast of Ephesus in 190 BC. This was notably amazing because Antiochus had the Romans outnumbered more than two-to-one (70,000 to 30,000), and still lost.

The almost anonymous *commander* above, Scipio Asiaticus (verse 18), was hardly unknown in secular history. He was the brother of the general who defeated Hannibal in 202 BC. In the deflating treaty of Apamea (188 BC), Antiochus lost all claims to Europe and most of Asia Minor, and agreed to stay east of the Taurus range. His compliance was guaranteed when twenty hostages were carted off to Rome. One of these was the king's second son, who will become Antiochus Epiphanes, the notorious persecutor of the Jewish people, giving us a direct link to the next section of the chapter (Daniel 11:21-35). Warren Wiersbe writes, 'At an earlier meeting, [an *insolent*] Antiochus had insulted the Roman general, but the Romans had the last word.' History confirms that was a taster of things to come for, in God's timing, the leopard beast will be superseded by the nondescript monster (Daniel 7:6-7), and the bronze will give way to the iron in Nebuchadnezzar's metallic statue (Daniel 2:39-40).

Aside from the serious loss of life, there was another heavy price to pay for the Romans laid such an indemnity on Antiochus that he was in dire straits in urgent need of resources. In a sense, he found himself in a cul-de-sac with nowhere to go, except *toward the fortresses of his own land*. He yielded to temptation when he robbed temples to pay his massive debt to Rome. While he was looting the Temple of Zeus in Elymas in 187 BC, an incensed mob of local Zeus zealots got rid of him once and for all, thus fulfilling the words, *he shall stumble and fall* (verse 19). A man with mausolean plans bites the dust and lies forgotten in a mausoleum, location unknown. He was succeeded by his son, Seleucus IV, also known as Philopator.

Antiochus III Magnus (the Great), who could have gone down in history as one of the eminent conquerors of the ancient world if he had been content to leave Greece alone, instead fulfilled the prophecy in that he had to return to his own land, outplayed and on his knees (except it was not in prayer). The last ten years of his life brought disaster, defeat, disappointment, despair, and eventually a mortifying death. John Walvoord writes, 'In these prophecies, properly interpreted, is an accurate prophetic picture of this period, which would be remarkable even if it was history. As prophecy, it bears the unmistakeable imprint of divine inspiration.'

11:20

Two certainties: death and taxes

'Then shall arise in his place one who shall send an exactor of tribute for the glory of the kingdom. But within a few days he shall be broken, neither in anger nor in battle.'

Antiochus the Great may bite the dust and be instantly replaced by his son, but Rome still wants its annual tribute of one thousand talents of silver paid on time. They also want the backlog of some twenty thousand talents cleared immediately. Like father, like son: Seleucus IV lifts a couple of pages from his father's game-plan and sends a revenue agent (*an exactor of tribune*), his prime minister Heliodorus, to do a smash and grab raid from the temple treasury in Jerusalem. At the same time he levied a burdensome tax on his citizens. Unlike his father, he preferred a quiet life of peace and tranquillity as he had no interest at all in playing wargames and pursuing expansionist policies.

An apocryphal book, 2 Maccabees 3:7-17, tells us that the sacrilege of Heliodorus was stymied by a scary supernatural apparition of attacking angels as he was on the verge of unlocking the vaults. Not long after this wild goose chase incident, it is presumed that Heliodorus poisoned Seleucus IV and so he was *broken, neither in anger* (like his father, Antiochus III) *nor in battle* (like his grandfather, Seleucus III). He died with his boots on. A decade or so after adorning a jewelled crown and sitting down on a gilded throne, yet another king enters 'the royal landfill,' as Dale Ralph Davis calls it. With the very sudden and painful death of Seleucus IV Philopator, the timeline of the chapter is brought down to 175 BC.

Halftime lessons to learn

In the section, from verse 5 down to verse 20, where the focus has been on the kings of the north and the kings of the south strutting their stuff and doing war with each other, there is one three-lettered word which pops up all over the place, *but*. Eleven times it appears in the ESV, always with an explicit intention in view. Check it out in verses 6, 9, 11, 12, 14, 16, 17, 18, 19, 20, then highlight each one with a yellow marker, and go back for a second read. You will be lost for words for it often occurs when one plan is made by a king from either side, then we read, '*but* this happened or that happened.' A classic case of supernatural scuppering.

These texts point us in the direction of a great God who brings judgment not only at the end of time, at the climax of history, but also today within the parameters of all that is taking place around us in the world. Sometimes we are not spiritually savvy or discerning enough to see it, but the unseen hand of God is sovereignly moving in every situation. These limelight-hugging superpowers (people and nations) think they are in control; they are not. God is. The tide ebbs and flows only with divine permission. These globetrotters are here today, gone tomorrow. Their schemes and sub-plots end in shambles. God lives on. And so do his purposes and his people.

With that in mind, you will not fail to notice that the Most High is not mentioned by name in any of these instances, but as Stuart Olyott reminds us, 'God is still God, even when he is nowhere to be seen.' See the book of Esther for something similar. An ancient pearl of wisdom, attributed to Thomas à Kempis (1380-1471) says, *Homo proponit, sed Deus disponit*. Man proposes, God disposes. In other words, we make our plans and fill our diary with things to do, people to see, and places to visit, but the Lord is sovereign and he always has the last word (Proverbs 19:21; James 4:13-15). *Deo volente*.

Surely this is a principle for us to take on board as we seek to honour the Lord in every decision we make and in all that we do for the growth and blessing of his kingdom. All that matters this side of eternity for you and me, for every weary traveller on the pilgrim pathway, and for those of us facing all kinds of trial and personal upheaval is to recognise, in the words of David Helm, that 'God's king and his kingdom are our future and our everlasting treasure.' Peter was on the same wavelength (1 Peter 1:3-9).

It is also imperative for us to appreciate that the ground so far examined is not just plain history with all its implications and innuendo, of wars and rumours of wars, of successes and setbacks, of murder and mayhem, it is more than that. Much more. This is prophecy. When the vision was initially given to Daniel, the bulk of this material was brand new to him, most of which he would not live to see. It foretells the future in quite a remarkable manner.

When we grasp that fact, our hearts will be filled with an overwhelming sense of wonder and reverence for our God knows all about tomorrow, and the day after. We read these verses and we are staggered, not surprised, with the phenomenal pinpoint accuracy of biblical truth. These kings, northern and southern, are like pawns on a Middle Eastern chess board because God is directing their every move. Sure, they have a mind of their own and they are answerable for all that they do, but the sovereign Lord is pulling all the strings.

After every fulfilled prediction, and they are numerous, we should with thankfulness add a couple of exclamation marks to every sentence and pay tribute to the unerring omniscience of God (Isaiah 44:6-7). God knows. God foreknows. Because history is his story. In spite of the evil acts of men and women done in the name of government and religion, the Lord of history is seated on the throne and one day 'the earth will be filled with the knowledge of the glory of the Lord, as the waters cover the sea' (Habakkuk 2:14, NIV).

11:21-23

The dirty tricks maestro

'In his place shall arise a contemptible person to whom royal majesty has not been given. He shall come in without warning and obtain the kingdom by flatteries. Armies shall be utterly swept away before him and broken, even the prince of the covenant. And from the time an alliance is made with him he shall act deceitfully, and he shall become strong with a small people.'

The turbulent period we have just covered above spans nearly one hundred and fifty years and involves a list of over a dozen rulers from the north and south. In verses 21-35, the pace slows to a canter and we view just one decade, 175 BC to around 164 BC, and zoom in on a single ruler, Antiochus IV Epiphanes. We bumped into him in an earlier chapter where he is alluded to as the *little horn* and perceived to be the antichrist of the Old Testament (Daniel 8:9-14, 23-25), and an exemplar of the future antichrist of Daniel's seventieth week, the seven-year tribulation period (Daniel 9:26-27, 11:36-45).

This individual does not get a good press, and rightly so. To be tagged as a *contemptible person* is most certainly not a backhanded compliment. But that is precisely what he is in his true colours. Detestable. Not a nice guy, at all. And the more we find out about him, the chances of us liking anything about him rapidly diminish. His rating in the popularity stakes is well below zero. A more despicable character it would be hard to meet anywhere. If you had a daughter at home, he is the last person you would want to see her dating. So what does Scripture have to say about Antiochus IV Epiphanes?

As a loathsome individual, Antiochus was seen by the Jewish community as an odious monster and a raving, loony madman. He was the scourge of not a few because of his eccentric and erratic manner; the locals were unsure what to make of him as it all seemed to depend which side of the hammock he fell out of in the morning and if his coffee was brewed to its proper strength. John Walvoord notes that 'his life was characterised by intrigue, expediency, and lust for power in which honour was always secondary.'

Truth be told, he acquired the monarchy because, like a

snake on its belly, he slithered in through the palace back door. He was not the rightful heir to the throne. The regal position of *royal majesty* belonged to his nephew, Demetrius I Soter, son of Seleucus IV (verse 21), who was still a hostage in Rome. Not a shot was fired in anger, as Uncle Antiochus got where he always wanted to be by *flatteries* and unscrupulous behaviour. He conned them, he hoodwinked them. With promises and pleasantries, an overdose of cunning and oodles of charisma, he subtly secured the endorsement of the powers that be. Danny Akin comments that 'political skills wedded to an evil heart are a dangerous combination.' In fact, that serves as a warning to us for anything aligned to a sinful heart is a lethal mix, a double whammy (Jeremiah 17:9).

The Egyptian Ptolemy VI Philometor (181-145 BC) attacked Antiochus in 170 BC with a sizeable contingent of military personnel, but he was outmatched, outmanoeuvred, and easily repelled (*broken*) in a battle that occurred between Mount Casius and Pelusium, an area halfway between Gaza and the Nile delta on the Mediterranean coastline. Philometor, still a teenager, suffered the indignity and shame of being taken captive, faced an uncertain future at the hands of one who would use him for his own ends.

During this season, an audacious Antiochus successfully ousted Onias III, the rightful high priest—aka *the prince of the covenant* (so-called because it was his responsibility to see that Israel kept its covenant with God)—in Jerusalem, when he was assassinated in 172 BC. He was replaced by his ungodly brother, Jason, a yes-man who wanted Greek culture established in Israel, but Onias blocked it as he was not happy with an encroachment of Hellenic influence (more about this in 2 Maccabees 4:7-15). He paid the price for his actions (verse 22). When Jason ultimately fell out of favour, Menelaus, who had a bigger bank balance, was appointed.

Antiochus stretched out an olive branch to Egypt, the king of the south, in an attempt to lull it into a false sense of security. Having secured his goal by this pernicious beachhead, he went a step further as he sought to acquire control of Egypt. Every trick in the book and every deceptive tactic was used at the bargaining table so that he might gain ascendancy. He succeeded, and he began to rise from the relative obscurity into which the Romans had earlier driven Syria (verse 23) in that *he became strong with a small people.* In spite of the wheeler-dealing carried out in the name of negotiation, the Lord is still in control and watching every date circled on the calendar. Warren Wiersbe writes that the Lord 'has his appointed times and he is always on time.'

11:24-26

A day for royal handouts

'Without warning he shall come into the richest parts of the province, and he shall do what neither his fathers nor his fathers' fathers have done, scattering among them plunder, spoil, and goods. He shall devise plans against strongholds, but only for a time. And he shall stir up his power and his heart against the king of the south with a great army. And the king of the south shall wage war with an exceedingly great and mighty army, but he shall not stand, for plots shall be devised against him. Even those who eat his food shall break him. His army shall be swept away, and many shall fall down slain.'

The not-so-daft Antiochus employed a Robin Hood policy by attacking and plundering wealthy provinces and distributing the takings among his own armed forces and kowtowing cronies, as well as the poorer families in the wider community (1 Maccabees 3:27-31). Unlike his predecessors, he did not squander the wealth on himself or stash it away for a rainy day, earning him a few more brownie points in the process. In so doing, he strengthened his control over the empire (verse 24). There were two prongs to this apparent gesture of goodwill: one, it enabled him to buy friends and, two, it meant he could bribe his foes.

Alongside his benevolent handouts, he was formulating some secret plans to seize the major fortress cities of Egypt. He was chiefly interested in Pelusium, Naucratis, Alexandria, and Memphis. The sovereign Lord had other ideas, however. The text, *only for a time*, underscores the fact that God drew a line in the desert sand beyond which he would not be allowed to go. Like a dog on a leash, Antiochus could sniff around here and there, but he was forced to stay within his God-set boundary. Beyond the Middle East there were ominous signs flashing on the horizon for God was raising up mighty Rome, and Antiochus would be no match for this indescribable beast that is 'terrifying and frightening and very powerful [with] large iron teeth' (Daniel 7:7, NIV).

Flattery and deceit, in which Antiochus excelled, only get you so far in life. 'They are sinful characteristics God will not bless. They are also no match for the plans of a sovereign God,' writes Danny Akin. In our lives, as the redeemed people of God, we should resist using such devious schemes at all times. As a godly principle, irrespective of what is on the table, we must never resort to the devil's tactics. Both tacky devices dishonour the peerless name of our great God and discredit his global family and gospel ministry.

Among his military endeavours were several forays against Egypt, which are indicated en bloc in verse 25, and in all likelihood include the one referred to earlier. Basically, there was no love lost between the kings of the north and the kings of the south. There was an innate hatred that festered after every military escapade, dependent on who lost the conflict.

It is evident that some of Egypt's top brass had their eyes on higher things and were involved in all kinds of conniving plots and seamy scandals to undermine Ptolemy. Some of his closest confidantes and advisers—Eulaeus, Lenaeus, and others—who sat around the top table eating and drinking with him could not be trusted, as they were Janus-faced. As history confirms, it blew up in front of their eyes when one treacherous ruse after another backfired on a disunited, disloyal nation (verses 25-26). Like a surging tidal wave washing away all before it, the southern army was drowned with a catastrophic loss of life. Total disaster. The baseline: in every sphere of life, you cannot sin and win.

11:27-28

A crash course on how not to negotiate

'And as for the two kings, their hearts shall be bent on doing evil. They shall speak lies at the same table, but to no avail, for the end is yet to be at the time appointed. And he shall return to his land with great wealth, but his heart shall be set against the holy covenant. And he shall work his will and return to his own land.'

Two monarchs, one ruling, one deposed, have the status of kingship, but their hearts are rotten to the core. They have the trimmings and trappings of power, but they are dyed-in-the-wool sinners. They are well-dressed evildoers with a predilection for reprehensible deeds (James 3:5-8). Such nefarious acts characterised royalty in the second century BC. That trait was evident when they sat down together and were unable to speak with even a smattering of integrity. Skulduggery. We read that *they [spoke] lies at the same table* (verse 27). To an eastern mind, to indulge in such blatant deception while eating at the same table is nothing short of despicable. Outrageously unforgiveable.

Invariably, the talks break down without any real agreement. Stalemate. Sure, there is compromise on both sides but none that either man is entirely satisfied with. In the final outcome, Antiochus was left in control of Memphis, the old capital, which he sub-contracted to Philometor to run on his behalf, while his rebellious younger brother was granted control of the elusive city of Alexandria. His name, Ptolemy VIII Euergetes. The sovereign Lord was using these wars as part of his indignation against Israel which at this point in time was nothing more than a buffer zone. Renald Showers observes, 'Since Israel was located between these two Gentile powers, it suffered greatly during the course of these wars.' Into the bargain, a slightly humbled king of the north, Antiochus, left for home with a prodigious booty of *great wealth* from a ravished land, a salve for his wounded pride.

Heaven's verdict is a resounding thumbs-down for we read it is *to no avail* (verse 27). Both leaders are whistling in the wind for they will never achieve their goal of peace in the nation (Egypt) and peace between the nations (Egypt and Syria). The biblical text continues with a no-holds-barred declaration that *the end is yet to be at the time appointed*. A pertinent reminder that things will move forward on God's timetable, not the timetable of mere monarchs whose forte seems to be malpractice. The aspiration of true peace would only come *at the time appointed*, that is, in God's time, under God's man, the Prince of peace. 'Thus,' writes Jim Allen, 'prophetic anticipation is written into these statements that now are clearly history.'

As I mentioned earlier, before this major offensive against the Egyptians, Antiochus had removed Jason as high priest of Israel and replaced him with Menelaus, a man who offered him more tribute money. For Antiochus, money talks. While he was down south on the battlefield, a disgruntled Jason heard a false rumour that Antiochus had been fatally wounded in battle. Jason's immediate response was to raise an army of one thousand Jewish mercenaries with the express purpose of attacking Jerusalem and overthrowing Menelaus. He wanted his old job back! Somehow, Menelaus beat off the attackers, but on his way back home through the land of Israel, Antiochus was determined to teach the rebel Jews a lesson they would never forget.

And he did, for he mercilessly slaughtered eighty thousand Jewish men, women, and children, sold many more into slavery, stripped the temple of its valuable artefacts such as the gold and silver vessels and utensils, and carried some of the sacred furnishings like the golden altar back up north to his Antioch hideaway in Syria. (There is a fuller account of this abhorrent act in the apocryphal writings of 1 Maccabees 1:20-24 and 2 Maccabees 5:15-21.) This showed his implacable hatred for the Jewish people and his utter contempt for the thrice-holy God of their fathers (verse 28). Stephen Miller says that 'the persecution of the Jews by this evil tyrant had now escalated to calamitous proportions.' Right.

11:29-31

Eating humble pie never tastes good

> *'At the time appointed he shall return and come into the south, but it shall not be this time as it was before. For ships of Kittim shall come against him, and he shall be afraid and withdraw, and shall turn back and be enraged and take action against the holy covenant. He shall turn back and pay attention to those who forsake the holy covenant. Forces from him shall appear and profane the temple and fortress, and shall take away the regular burnt offering. And they shall set up the abomination that makes desolate.'*

The opening phrase, *at the time appointed,* indicates the overruling hand of God in the history of the nations. The year was 168 BC. I think for Daniel listening in to all this he must have found a measure of comfort and relief with the pronouncement that God was in full control of a seemingly out of control world. Like Daniel, we need to appreciate that the God of history continues to orchestrate his plan for his covenant people. He starts it, he drives it along, and he finishes it off. Everything happens in his time, and on his terms. Dale Ralph Davis says, 'It is as if Antiochus marches to God's calendar.'

Behind the broad back of Antiochus, the two Ptolemy brothers agreed to patch up their differences and tentatively form a coalition. They were still not the best of buddies, but they were united in their disdain and scorn for the king of the north. That was sufficient to mould them together as they put their chequered past firmly behind them and faced the future as a team. This new-found cooperation was too much for Antiochus to stomach so, again, he called in the troops and they single-mindedly marched south to Egypt. He was resolute in his determination to trounce them and he called for the surrender of Memphis, Pelusium, Cyprus, and other territories. One by one the dominos toppled, until he came to Alexandria.

A telltale phrase shows itself at the end of verse 29 where we read, *but it shall not be this time as it was before*. This time it would be different. And it was. The Roman navy of trireme ships (*ships of Kittim*) had anchored in the bay. These galleys with three banks of rowers were waiting in the wings ready to pounce. The fleet had sailed to Egypt after the Roman victory over Perseus of Macedon near Pydna south of Thessalonica (22 June 168 BC).

Four miles out from the great city of Alexandria the king of the north was given a no punches pulled ultimatum from the Roman senate ordering him to cease and desist without delay. Needless to say, Antiochus stalled for time. He wished to consult with his advisors. The Roman consul, a long-time friend, Gaius Popilius Laenas, having a vine stick in his hand, drew a circle in the sand around a bemused Antiochus and let him know in no uncertain terms that this was make up your mind time. There and then, at Eleusis, he had to decide what he was going to do before he stepped outside the circle: option one, leave Egypt pronto; option two, stay and fight Rome. A mortified Antiochus, conscious of past history and aware of the menacing capacity of Rome to demolish him, caved in under intense pressure and decided to head back north. Antiochus was no stranger to the toxic power of Rome, having spent his childhood in Rome as a political hostage. On this occasion, in the desert, the iron fist of Rome stopped the big bully in his tracks while the doleful music of Daniel 2 and Daniel 7 hummed away in the background. Humiliated. Embarrassed. Enraged. It was not his finest day.

He pulled himself together and implemented Plan B whereby he would vent his spleen in maniacal fury on the tiny nation of Israel and the Jewish people. Again. He needed to save face and they would be the ideal scapegoat. The history of this period is given with remarkable insight and candour in the books of First and Second Maccabees. Antiochus wreaked substantial havoc within Jerusalem and its environs and spread terror among the communities who opposed his efforts to enforce Greek culture upon the nation. He dished out special favours and sweeteners to Menelaus and his apostate followers who had turned their backs on pure Judaism and warmly embraced the Hellenising process. To speed up the sterilisation of the area, he sent in 20,000 war veterans under the command of Apollonius.

He gave the mistaken impression that he was disposed peacefully toward the Jewish people by handing out freebies, but on the Sabbath he paraded his fully armed men and then proceeded to brutally massacre those Jews who stood by as spectators. An incandescent Antiochus systematically ransacked the city and when he was done it was war-wasted. He pulled out all the stops to extinguish the faith of the people of God. No stone was left unturned. The sanctuary was defiled, the daily sacrifices abolished, an altar or image of Zeus Olympus, the supreme Greek god, was set up, and pagan rites were celebrated on the altar of burnt offering. A dastardly deed. Reprehensible. In that single act, Antiochus and his sidekicks fulfilled the prophetic scriptures with regard to *the abomination that makes desolate* (Daniel 8:9-12, 23-25, 11:31).

It is profoundly helpful to note that our Lord's only reference to Daniel and his prophecies uses this phrase, 'the abomination that causes desolation' (Matthew 24:15; Mark 13:14; Daniel 12:11,

NIV). In other words, Antiochus is a forerunner, a scale model, of the antichrist, and all that he did foreshadows life under the future man of sin (2 Thessalonians 2:3-4; Revelation 13). Dale Ralph Davis summarises his actions by noting that 'Antiochus stripped [the Jewish people] of sacrament, sacrifice, Sabbath, and Scripture. In his reign of terror it seemed the only choice was to be a live pagan or a dead Israelite.'

All these foul deeds perpetrated by Antiochus precipitated the Maccabean revolt that was cruelly suppressed by him with tens of thousands of Jewish people perishing.

11:32-35

Hammered by Judas the Hammer

'He shall seduce with flattery those who violate the covenant, but the people who know their God shall stand firm and take action. And the wise among the people shall make many understand, though for some days they shall stumble by sword and flame, by captivity and plunder. When they stumble, they shall receive a little help. And many shall join themselves to them with flattery, and some of the wise shall stumble, so that they may be refined, purified, and made white, until the time of the end, for it still awaits the appointed time.'

Antiochus has no qualms or quibbles about using *flattery* to win the hearts of Joe Public in the not-so-holy city of Jerusalem, and elsewhere in the land. He will do all he possibly can to woo them and win them over to his side. In fact, it would be in their best interests long-term to do so; failure to follow his ideology and support his policies could get rather messy, as his track record shows. The inevitable happened when a significant number capitulated and in the process abandoned the precepts of Scripture rejecting every ounce of their distinctive Jewish faith and worship.

Still—and this is so encouraging—even in this terribly dark period, there were faithful followers of the true God, believers in the Most High. They are aptly described as *the people who know their God* (verse 32). A godly remnant who took their faith seriously and who would not sanction a ranting heathen king dictating Greek philosophy to them. They were a God-fearing minority, men and women who knew God experientially, not just intellectually. They were known as the Maschilim (*the wise*). They were familiar with the scrolls of biblical truth and could see how these hard times had been foretold by their prophets. They knew they were living in the days about which Daniel had written (verse 33). John Phillips notes, 'As line by line, word by word, the prophecy was fulfilled, they could put a finger on a page and say, "We are right here, right now."' With an element of faith, they looked forward to an anticipated better day as they prayerfully longed for the advent of Jesus Christ.

The dissident Jews were blessed with the sterling leadership of the saintly Mattathias Maccabeus, a priest living at Modin, together with his five sons, three of whom—Judas, Jonathan, and Simon—became known as the Maccabees. With a spirit of solidarity they clung tightly to the covenant of God. Like the men of Isaachar, they understood the issues of the day and could distinguish clearly between truth and error (1 Chronicles 12:32). The crunch came when Mattathias refused to offer a pagan sacrifice and duly killed the lackey who ordered him to do it. He and his sons then forsook their personal possessions and fled to the desert. The resistance movement was born.

As an aside, the Maccabees became the centrepiece of the pushback, not only against Antiochus IV and his successors, but also against pro-Syrian Jewish apostates. Kenneth Gangel informs us, 'From this group later arose the Pharisees and the Essenes. The former we encounter frequently in the New Testament, and the latter became the people of Qumran who gave us the famous Dead Sea scrolls.'

Others joined hands with them in their concerted insurrection against the repressive regime of Antiochus. This was the beginning of the Maccabean revolt. These loyal individuals paid a high price for their devotion to Jehovah and love for their beloved city. As a consequence, many were mutilated and murdered by the bloodthirsty Syrian militia (verse 33). Others were captured for slaves or had their property confiscated. Those were horrendously hard times, an intense fiery trial of persecution, but it would last only for a short time. It seems likely that some of these faithful heroes are listed anonymously in Hebrews 11:34. Unknown to us. Known to him.

There were many instances when small groups of gallant men would join forces with the Maccabees to enable them score direct hits upon the unwary Syrian forces (verse 34). They were staunch in their resolve to unseat the oppressive Syrian government and so they fired salvo after salvo in a blistering barrage of words and guerrilla warfare.

Sadly, as Scripture indicates, there were those nominally committed Jews who were two-faced and who aligned themselves with the heroic Maccabees. Hypocrites. Expediency was their rationale. When they saw the Maccabees were winning, they sided with them in order to save their own skin. And particularly so, when the Maccabean forces were bolstered by the Hasidim (a word meaning 'pious ones') and methodically began to eliminate those who had collaborated with the Seleucids (1 Maccabees 2:42-48). To all intents and purposes, they were motivated by fear of reprisal and were wishy-washy in their commitment to the cause.

At the end of the day, the Maccabees were victorious as they stormed the city of Jerusalem and regained control of their temple and its sacred environs. They repaired, cleansed, and rededicated the house of God amid scenes of joy and gladness. A brand new feast, the Feast of Dedication or Lights, was instituted and duly incorporated into Israel's annual religious calendar (John 10:22). When all is said and done, the purpose of this time of persecution was to refine, purify, and cleanse the covenant people of God, as well as the nation (verse 35). And the good news is, there was a fixed time limit as to its duration. Stephen Miller writes that 'those suffering in the second century BC would have been greatly comforted by the promise of an end to their suffering.'

'Just as in Psalm 23 the way through the "valley of deep darkness" is yet one of the paths of righteousness, so here, mysteriously, even chaotic time is *appointed time*. Antiochus will not be footloose and fancy-free as he may seem, for God determines even the terms of tyrannies and they are tethered to the dates on God's calendar,' notes Dale Ralph Davis.

As a footnote, Antiochus IV Epiphanes died a horrible death in 164 BC, bringing to a finale both his depraved life and his numberless atrocities against God's people (Daniel 8:25). An inglorious end. The king of the north was. The king of the north is no more. Because all bad things must come to an end.

Fulltime lessons to learn

Throughout this exposition of Daniel 11:1-35 reference has

been made to the books of First and Second Maccabees in the Apocrypha. They are not Spirit-inspired and, therefore, are not an integral part of the canon of Scripture (2 Timothy 3:16; 2 Peter 1:20-21). They are, however, a most useful resource for cataloguing so much of what transpired during this period of time. First Maccabees is a historical account of the struggle of the Maccabee family and their loyal followers for Jewish independence from 167 to 134 BC. Second Maccabees covers the same terrain, but dramatises the accounts and makes a number of moral observations. 'They are,' writes Jim Allen, 'a valuable, eye-opening, and heart-stirring account of what the faithful ones suffered under the rule of Antiochus Epiphanes.' Should you wish to dig down deeper, these books are a useful investment and a good read.

Looking at the experiences of the faithful in the land during the reign of Antiochus is deeply challenging for it reminds us that following God's way is not the easy option. Tough times. Trying times. Turbulent times. Whatever adjectives we use, we take heart because the sovereign Lord is working his good purpose out in each of our lives. These verses are a powerful illustration of Romans 8:28 in our daily walk and a beautiful reminder that our God is one of gracious providence. James Boice is right when he says that 'God is not afraid to make promises to his people because he knows that he can and will keep them.' Even in the midst of severe trials, our great God and loving Father has our best interests at heart. He rules. And overrules. Over all.

We have seen the vacillating actions of big men and little people, the rise and fall of earthly kingdoms, the evilness of sin, a handful or two genuine acts of goodness, the folly of life lived without God, the faithful testimony of those who were willing to honour their Lord at all times; all this in the space of a few verses on a single page of Scripture. That is the way it was back then in BC days! The truth is, we may have moved on in terms of years to AD, but life is not that much different when it comes to society, culture, and attitudes in the twenty-first century. May we be numbered among those people who know their God then go forward to do exploits in his name (Daniel 11:32).

There are three optimistic lessons for us to learn about God in this section: one, God *knows* the future; two, God *plans* the future; and, three, God *tells* the future. So, dear reader, when it comes to your future and mine, we have nothing to worry about as God has it all sorted.

Mind the gap

There is a chink of indeterminate time between the full stop at the end of verse 35 and the opening capital letter in verse 36. Nothing unusual there, for the same prophetic leap happens between the sixty-ninth and seventieth week of Daniel's prophecy (Daniel 9:26-27). Something similar occurs in Isaiah 61:1-2, and further back in Isaiah 9:6-7. At this juncture, we switch from history to eschatology. We all know what history is, but this five-syllable word is not often on the lips of ordinary people when conversing about Scripture. It is a branch of theology that specifically deals with 'last things' or the end times.

There is a change in language too for we have moved from using *the time appointed* (Daniel 11:27, 29, 35) to addressing *the time of the end* (Daniel 11:40, 12:4, 6-7, 9, 13). Notwithstanding how plug-ugly and arrogant he was, Antiochus IV Epiphanes never did *exalt himself and magnify himself above every god* (Daniel 11:36). Right up to the moment of his death, Antiochus was an enthusiastic devotee of the Greek pantheon, even building an altar and offering sacrifices to Zeus in the Jerusalem temple precincts.

More than two thousand years have slipped into eternity since Antiochus popped his clogs, that means we are closer today than we were yesterday to the realisation of these, as yet unfulfilled, prophetic truths at the end of Daniel 11. We are, with every passing hour, a day's march nearer home.

The person we meet in this closing section is a major endtime personality, and the antichrist, the archenemy and final opponent of God's people, fits the bill to perfection. Sinclair Ferguson acknowledges that '… the reference [in these verses] is to the final antichrist. The king in view clearly transcends in wickedness any figure in history.'

11:36

Nuances of narcissism

'And the king shall do as he wills. He shall exalt himself and magnify himself above every god, and shall speak astonishing things against the God of gods. He shall prosper till the indignation is accomplished; for what is decreed shall be done.'

If we thought Antiochus IV Epiphanes was bad, and he was, *the king* we meet here is a million times worse, if that were possible. He makes Antiochus look like a Boy Scout. The individual in view is the still-future, egomaniacal antichrist first described as the little horn that emerges from the ten horns (Daniel 7:24). He is, notes Dale Ralph Davis, 'the final scourge of history.' Satan's superman. The devil's masterpiece. The last world dictator.

It is patently obvious that the antichrist has a mind of his own, and with a streak of ruthlessness, he will do whatever it takes to get his way (Daniel 7:23-25). Such a contrast to our blessed Lord Jesus who always submitted to the will of his Father (Mark 14:36). Nothing and no one will stand in the way of him achieving his goals and objectives. He has no scruples and no moral compass as he steers his way through the choppy waters of the tribulation. He is a man of lawlessness who rides roughshod over whoever and whatever by ignoring legal statutes or taking the law into his own hands (2 Thessalonians 2:3). This attitude to life permeates so many of the characters we have already met in the book (Daniel 3:15, 4:30, 8:25, 11:3, 12, 16). Sinclair Ferguson writes that 'it does so because it is the crux of the conflict. Its foundations run back into the origins of history and beyond into the mists of eternity.'

As a spellbinding orator, he revels in his verbosity and thrives on his inflated ego. He sees himself as a troubleshooter on global issues and is totally happy to offer himself as an international saviour, which he does to the nation of Israel (Daniel 7:25, 9:27). He is the quintessence of the 'me' generation as he constantly pushes himself to the fore where the spotlight is focused exclusively on him. As the centre of attention, he loves every minute for it fuels his sense of self-importance. Consumed with all the pride of a preening peacock, he has an overwhelming desire to swagger centre stage.

Worryingly, he brags and boasts as he establishes himself as a god. He fancies himself so much that he cannot resist the temptation to encourage the average punter to worship and revere him as a divine man on two legs (Daniel 9:27; 2 Thessalonians 2:4). When he seizes control of the Jerusalem temple he assumes the role and position of deity. Woe betide those who fail to give him the acclaim and adulation he feels he deserves (Revelation 13:15).

He goes on a downward spiral from pride, to presumption, to profanity. Actually, the air turns blue for he comes across as a compulsive, habitual blasphemer. We often hear people making rash, raucous statements designed to belittle and denigrate the Most High, but these will fade into oblivion and comparative insignificance in light of the searing challenges he makes to the unshakeable throne of God. He is one hundred percent anti-God, a mindset that goes back to when a wily serpent first whispered to Eve in the Garden of Eden, 'you will be like God' (Genesis 3:5, NIV). And even further back to Lucifer who had grandiose ideas about himself—five times he said, 'I will'—and the position he craved when he wanted to be on a par with God (Isaiah 14:12-14; Ezekiel 28:12-17). Lucifer, the son of the morning, became Satan, the father of the night.

His days are numbered. God has designated an hour when his downfall will be complete, *for what is decreed shall be done*. The reality of that event is signed, sealed, and settled (Daniel 8:19). Until then, he will be eminently successful and enjoy a level of prosperity, popularity, and power, heretofore unknown. He will surface as the Number One pin-up in society and will experience victory after victory, by fair means or foul. To casual onlookers, he appears unassailable and unconquerable. But it is all short-lived. Because the die is cast.

11:37-39

An atheist who worships one god

'He shall pay no attention to the gods of his fathers, or to the one beloved by women. He shall not pay attention to any other god, for he shall magnify himself above all. He shall honour the

god of fortresses instead of these. A god whom his fathers did not know he shall honour with gold and silver, with precious stones and costly gifts. He shall deal with the strongest fortresses with the help of a foreign god. Those who acknowledge him he shall load with honour. He shall make them rulers over many and shall divide the land for a price.'

The antichrist has little or no time for organised religion showing total disregard for *the gods* that his ancestors worshipped. He has no respect for his own religious heritage, whatever it might be. The only religion he is interested in, and fully committed to, is the one that bears his name. Likewise, he is not enamoured with *the one beloved by women.* A most unusual phrase, it appears to refer to the heartfelt desire and prayer of every godly Jewish woman to become the mother of the Messiah (Luke 1:28, 46-55), the seed of the woman promised in Genesis 3:15. His birth was *beloved* by these pious mothers of Israel. As John Walvoord notes, 'The expression then becomes a symbol of the messianic hope in general.'

When we set both facts side by side, it is clear that this king derides the God of his fathers and mocks the desire of any young woman in Israel. His religious outlook is simply defined for *he shall not pay attention to any other god.* When it comes down to issues of faith, this guy is an unashamed, card-carrying atheist. If man's chief end is to glorify God, as the Westminster divines have taught, his supremely singular goal in life is to worship himself and for others to do the same. Jim Allen writes that 'he expects to be viewed through the magnifying glass of his own self-importance.'

For a man who does not do religion, this anti-God menace is most happy to *honour the god of fortresses,* the god in whom he trusts. His confidence is in military power and proficiency for he wholeheartedly embraces the 'might is right' philosophy. This deity, unknown to his illustrious predecessors, was the beneficiary of antichrist's generosity as he lavished *gold and silver, precious stones and costly gifts* upon it. He is so power-driven that he honours the benefits that war can give him (verse 38). With immense power at his disposal he will ruthlessly crush every vestige of opposition and in the process he will reward those boot-lickers who join his expanding coalition, *making them rulers over many* and distributing land as a reward (verse 39). As the consummate politician, he knows how to manipulate people by rewards and political payoffs.

The angel has given Daniel an insight into three traits of the final world ruler for he is a combo of materialism, militarism, and man-centred religion. Danny Akin observes that 'this is a Nietzschean world come to full fruition. The vision of a Hitler-like leader and his Nietzschean Nazism will arrive in all of its infamy, and the world will not be able to stop it.'

11:40-43

War and no peace

'At the time of the end, the king of the south shall attack him, but the king of the north shall rush upon him like a whirlwind, with chariots and horsemen, and with many ships. And he shall come into countries and shall overflow and pass through. He shall come into the glorious land. And tens of thousands shall fall, but these shall be delivered out of this hand: Edom and Moab and the main part of the Ammonites. He shall stretch out his hand against the countries, and the land of Egypt shall not escape. He shall become

ruler of the treasures of gold and of silver, and all the precious things of Egypt, and the Libyans and the Cushites shall follow in his train.'

In the second half of the tribulation, after the antichrist breaks off his peace treaty with Israel (Daniel 9:27), there will be an attack from the *king of the south* and the *king of the north*. The two bitter rivals and their allies: Egypt and her friends from south of the Holy Land, and Syria along with her friends from north of the Holy Land, are locked in conflict with the antichrist and the focal point, invariably, is *the glorious land*, Israel. The fallout in terms of casualties is huge for we read that *tens of thousands shall fall*.

In light of the previous context, where the antichrist is set forth as a world ruler, coinciding with other texts picturing a world government at this time (Daniel 7:23; Revelation 13:7), John Walvoord writes that 'the war in Daniel 11:40 is a rebellion against his leadership and signifies the breaking up of the world government that previously had been in power.' Even though things are fraying around the edges on a global front, and this serious outbreak of unrest is indicative of such, the antichrist is not a soft touch for he repels all those who have attacked him, for we read that *he shall overflow and pass through*. Even though he remains a dominant figure and force it appears that he may not have totally restored the situation, as it is stated that those nations to the east of the Jordan escape; they are named as *Edom and Moab and the main part of the Ammonites* (verse 41), who are the descendants of Esau and Lot.

His pursuit of those he sees as the enemy continues with a sortie into Egypt where he claims another scalp amassing a vast amount of treasures and wealth in so doing, is followed by military incursions further south into North Africa (verse 43). In these victorious skirmishes he is adding to his power base in the run-up to the final conflict at Armageddon (Revelation 16:16).

11:44-45

The tipping point

'But news from the east and the north shall alarm him, and he shall go out with great fury to destroy and devote many to destruction. And he shall pitch his palatial tents between the sea and the glorious holy mountain. Yet he shall come to his end, with none to help him.'

Bad news travels fast, we are told. Antichrist discovers that too. We have no idea what this disturbing news entailed, except that it originated in the east and north. It may refer to the invasion described in Revelation 16:12 where the Euphrates river dries up 'to prepare the way for the kings from the east.' Whatever, it set off the alarm bells and resulted in him making one last foray towards the enemy. His ambition was to obliterate all those who opposed him.

His tented headquarters (*palatial tents*) are located *between the sea and the glorious holy mountain*, that is, between the Mediterranean and Mount Zion where the temple stood. It seems that Daniel is indicating that the final war will be fought in Israel, as outlined elsewhere in Scripture (Ezekiel 39:2-29; Joel 3:2-16; Zechariah 12:2-9; 14:1-21). John, writing in the Revelation, is more specific when he narrows it down to the valley of Megiddo, one of the most natural battlefields on earth (Revelation 16:16). Winston Churchill called it 'the cockpit of the Middle East.'

At the appointed hour, Jesus Christ, the King of kings, Lord of lords, and Prince of princes will break through the clouds.

The heavens shall glow with splendour. The royal entourage is making its way from the highest heights of Glory down to Planet Earth. As soon as he touches down on the Mount of Olives the Armageddon conflict will be finished in a split second (Zechariah 14:3-5). And the antichrist will be hauled by the scruff of the neck and hurled into the lake of fire (Daniel 7:11-14, 25-26; 2 Thessalonians 2:8; Revelation 19:11-21). Sinclair Ferguson writes that 'his defeat will be as inauspicious as his rise to power was meteoric.' It is climactic, sure, but in another sense it is an anti-climax for the all-powerful Lord Jesus will simply blow him away. Helpless. Alone. He goes out of this world with barely a whimper.

Dale Ralph Davis says that the antichrist 'is wiped off the stage of history in a mere six Hebrew words.' His obituary is so terse, so brief, so abrupt, it is almost appended to the end of the chapter as a footnote.

Takeaway truth

At the end of a tough portion of Scripture, for us and for Daniel, it is important that we do what Daniel did and keep on praying. Much of what has been said is water under the bridge, but these last ten verses are scheduled for fulfilment at a future date. And that date may be sooner than we realise. That, dear reader, behoves us to passionately pray for people whom we know, and those we do not know, who are not yet believers in the Lord Jesus. People need the Lord, especially in light of dark days fast approaching. Our mandate is to tell the world about Jesus; today, we face a task unfinished that should drive us to our knees. And to action. Because time is fast running out.

12

LIVING WELL, DYING WELL

The Dead Sea Scrolls were written between 200 BC and AD 70. You can see copies of them in the brilliantly designed Shrine of the Book museum in Israel's capital city, Jerusalem. The original scrolls were found in 1947 by a Bedouin shepherd known as Muhammed the Wolf of the Ta'amireh tribe. The teenage el-Hamed was looking after his flock of sheep and goats in the desert near the northwestern corner of the Dead Sea (the lowest point on earth), around the site of Qumran, when one of them wandered off and disappeared.

The young man climbed the steep rocky hillside to search for it and came upon a cave in a crevice of the limestone cliffs. Hoping to scare the animal out of the dark interior, he threw in a stone and was surprised to hear the clink of breaking pottery. An unmistakeable sound which echoed around the world. Hmm, he wondered.

When an inquisitive Muhammed returned later with a few of his friends they discovered a mysterious collection of several large clay jars containing ancient scrolls, some wrapped in linen and blackened with age. Unknown to him, these mainly parchment manuscripts were inscribed with about two hundred and thirty texts of every book in the Hebrew Bible, except Esther, and a lot more besides. The young man, unwittingly, had stumbled across the greatest treasure-trove of the century; indeed, his find is universally acclaimed as one of the most noteworthy archaeological discoveries of all time.

The hundreds of texts were preserved by the Essene community arising from Mattathias and the Maccabean family. A significant plank of Essenian theology centred on their keen anticipation of the Messiah's coming. Jewish people all over the Mediterranean world knew the Messiah would be born in Bethlehem from David's line and that he would bring peace to the world (Micah 5:2; Matthew 1:16; Luke 2:14). Kenneth Gangel writes, 'As we come to Daniel 12, we see again the hope and expectation of the Messiah's coming.'

This bright and cheery messianic hope was the kernel of the Essene faith experience. For us, in the twenty-first century, that cherished hope still burns brightly in our hearts (1 John 3:2-3). Scottish pastor William Arnot (1808-75) wrote that 'hope is a pure bright star fixed high in heaven, it reaches with its rays the uplifted eye of the weary pilgrim.' When the Lord next returns to earth at the climax of the tribulation, it will be trumpeted as his second advent when many amazing phenomena will take place.

Some of them we come across right here in this final portion of Daniel, which is the closing part of the chapter trilogy which began back in chapter 10. David Jeremiah writes that 'the first part of the chapter tells us about the prophecies of the end, and the second part tells us about the end of the prophecies.' The first three verses in chapter 12 pick up the thread from where we left off in the last section (which shut down at Daniel 11:45) with an electrifying disclosure of four major predictions with regard to the future of Israel, here referred to as *your people* (Daniel 9:15-16, 19, 24, 10:14, 11:14).

Between now and then, today and that day, we want to do life like Daniel did life. Here is one man whose entire ministry was marked by fruitfulness and whose character reflected a life of faithfulness to his faithful God through good times and bad times. Stuart Olyott writes that 'he who walked with the Lord in the morning of his life walks even more closely with him in the evening.' Yes, we want to live well so that when the end comes we shall die well. Daniel did.

Christian physician John Dunlop, who has had long clinical experience of caring for dying people, wrote in his book, *Finishing Well to the Glory of God*, 'One thing I have learned is that dying well is rarely a coincidence. Rather, it results from choices made throughout life. After all, dying well is nothing more than living well right up to the end.' In other words, what I will be in the future will mould and shape how I live today. It is all about living life in the future tense. Looking ahead. Looking up.

In this chapter we discover anew how we ought to live as faithful exiles in a world which is not really our home, never mind our final destination. Danny Akin says that 'it helps us answer the question, How can we live as kingdom citizens, dedicated disciples, in a land that is strange and even hostile toward us?'

12:1a

Israel will be ransacked

'At that time shall arise Michael, the great prince who has charge of your people. And there shall be a time of trouble, such as never has been since there was a nation till that time.'

The master key to unlocking the significance of these prophetic truths is found in the opening few words, *at that time*. The obvious question is, What time is he talking about? Because our answer to that rudimentary poser will determine how we proceed in our exposition of the upcoming verses. These words follow on very nicely and neatly from the close of the previous chapter; in fact, if the chapter break was not present in our English translation, it would flow perfectly naturally.

As we noted earlier, a series of battles has been pitched between the northern and southern armies and their allies, with the antichrist, Israel's consummate oppressor, also involved. The conflict is brutal, barbaric, and bloody. That sets the tone for the so-called peace-loving diplomat, aka the devil's messiah, to renege on his promise to the land of Israel. He severs his commitment to them and begins a concerted campaign of persecution against the Jewish people (Daniel 9:27). Almost overnight, his benevolence turns to malevolence as he drives nail after nail into the Israeli coffin. All hell is let loose as Satan, through his henchman, is on the warpath.

The Jewish people will find themselves in a hot furnace of affliction. The awfulness of such a season is seen in that it is unprecedented and unparalleled in the history of mankind, hence the comment, *such as never has been since there was a nation till that time*. There is nothing hyperbolic in this statement. Not at all, for this is the language of extremity and uniqueness. A one-off.

The time of Antiochus IV Epiphanes was horrendous, as was the extended period around the later fall of Jerusalem. The indescribable ghastliness of the Holocaust beggars description and pales in perspective in the cold light of what still awaits the tiny nation of Israel. I mean, how anything could be worse than the Holocaust, when the genocidal policy of Nazism led six million Jews to the gas chambers of Auschwitz and Buchenwald, is impossible for you and me to understand. John Phillips writes, 'All that fallen men or raging demons could devise, all have been used against the Jewish people.' That was bad. Very bad. This is worse. Much worse.

The vision anticipates an hour of severest trial and deepening crisis. They are in for a rough ride when they will experience a rollercoaster of emotions. Days of absolute despair when calloused hands are raised in futile surrender. The darkness blackens as the nation is bludgeoned into a tight corner where, humanly speaking, there is no exit, no way of escape. All seems lost. The gut instinct for survival will slowly evaporate. The tenacious struggle to exist, so typical of Israelis in their own land since the late 1940s, will flicker as the harsh winds of adversity and oppression blow like a boisterous gale in their craggy faces (Jeremiah 30:4-7; Zechariah 12:2-3).

That is when the superangel Michael, *the great prince*, arises and arrives on the scene. He is, we are told, the protector of God's ancient people. They are his unique responsibility and that is a role which he takes most seriously (Daniel 10:13, 21). Dale Ralph Davis says that 'Michael, the warrior-advocate of Israel, takes up the cudgels on their behalf. There are unseen legions (Matthew 26:53; Hebrews 1:14) standing behind the wobbly people of God in their darkest trouble.' As the guardian of God's people, Michael is one of those highlighted in Psalm 91:11-12 whose continuing ministry must never be understated. There are other instances in Scripture where we see angelic involvement on Israel's behalf, which may or may not involve Michael the archangel (Joshua 5:13-15; 2 Kings 6:15-17; Isaiah 37:35-36).

To get a handle on this and what it means, we need to turn from Daniel 12 to what John penned more than six hundred years later in Revelation 12, where we do read of Michael's involvement, 'And there was war in heaven. Michael and his angels fought against the dragon, and the dragon and his angels fought back. But he was not strong enough, and they lost their place in heaven. The great dragon was cast down—that ancient serpent called the devil, or Satan, who leads the whole world astray. He was hurled to the earth, and his angels with him' (Revelation 12:7-9, NIV).

Scary. This is what awaits Satan and deservedly so; but for the nation of Israel and the Jewish people, their future at that point is forebodingly bleak. This is when we move from the first half of the tribulation into the second half, commonly known as the great tribulation. Thankfully, it will not last, albeit three and one half years is long enough to encounter such vexatious travail (Daniel 9:27).

The devil knows that his days are numbered and his time is short so he makes the most of it with a livid onslaught against the people of God, using the antichrist as his foremost protagonist (Revelation 12:12). Such unheard-of grief and suffering is spoken of in other portions of Scripture (Jeremiah 30:5-7; Zechariah 14:2; Matthew 24:21-22; Mark 13:19). The worst of times will come with a vengeance. (See my book *All Hail The Lamb! Revelation Made Simple* for more on this.)

Cynical people tend to pooh-pooh the idea of such a scenario unfolding in the cauldron that is the Middle East. They treat such a glum forecast with ridicule and contempt and say it is impossible in today's enlightened world. The facts are not in their favour as in the twenty-six centuries since Daniel penned his book, it is the last century that has seen more bloodshed than any other. As John Lennox writes, 'The Battle of the Somme occurred in the twentieth century, not the second.'

When Daniel says *at that time* he is referring to this period of war, famine, darkness, disease, and demons. Even in such dangerous times, heaven has not relinquished control of what happens here on earth for the reigning sovereign Lord holds the reins of all that takes place. David Jeremiah says that 'it will be an era the likes of which our world has never seen and cannot comprehend. Horrors will be unleashed on the earth in the breaking of the seals, the blowing of the trumpets, and the emptying of the bowls of judgment described in Revelation 6-19.'

12:1b

Israel will be rescued

'But at that time your people shall be delivered, everyone whose name shall be found written in the book.'

The same phrase, *at that time*, as mentioned above, appears a second time. In other words, even though it all appears so stark and ominous for the Jewish people and nation, there is a headline of hope. Real hope. What a staggering commitment on God's part towards his own people. A precious promise. A sensational divine pledge. It is always darkest just before the dawn. Ravaged and ransacked, but redeemed. One thing is certain, you can count on God to rescue his people (Jeremiah 30:7, 11, 17; Ezekiel 20:33-38).

When the very real threat of extermination is looming larger by the hour, the prophetic vision given to Daniel draws attention to the glittering prospect of emancipation. Freedom. Yes, just when they need him most, the divine liberator is there. Great news! I am quite sure that many of us can vouch for his on-time intervention and deliverance in our own lives.

The hymn reminds us that 'God works in mysterious ways.' And he does. Irrespective of how inexplicable his dealings are, all that counts is that the Lord is actively engaged in fulfilling his eternal purposes. Israel's dire straits are intentionally designed by a sovereign Lord to prepare her for the second coming of Jesus Christ and the kingdom to come (Daniel 7:18, 27; Malachi 3:16-18).

In the closing days of this terrible time of trial, many surviving Jews will apparently search the Scriptures seeking a reason for their bitter experiences. They want to know the logic behind all that is happening. They want answers to their questions. They cannot fathom why they are singled out for such excruciating pain and sorrow (Daniel 12:4). Alas, they will discover that it is because they rejected their Messiah Jesus. When he appears a second time, many of them will pour out their hearts in a solemn confession of personal sin based on Isaiah 53. The details of their repentance (Zechariah 12:10-14) and reconciliation (Zechariah 13:9) are mapped out for us by the prophets of old. Deliverance, in this context, sees the returning King as one who rescues and saves his ancient people. In May 1948 a nation was born politically in a single day; in a coming day, the nation will be reborn spiritually (Isaiah 66:8).

The *book* refers to the famed book of life which is mentioned numerous times in the Bible (Exodus 32:32-33; Psalm 69:28; Luke 10:20; Philippians 4:3; Revelation 3:5, 13:8, 17:8, 21:27, 22:19). Back then the local authority had a register that listed the names of every citizen who lived in a particular city; an electoral roll, or something similar. If a person committed crimes or otherwise defiled his standing in the city, he could be called before a tribunal and his name removed—literally, blotted out—from the city's registry. Such a named and shamed individual would no longer be considered a citizen of that city and would be forced to move on elsewhere. Basically, they are seen as a *persona non grata.*

So among the names *written in the book* are included those of godly Jews, *the holy people* (Daniel 12:7); they are a believing, righteous remnant on earth at the end of the tribulation who will be ready to greet their Messiah when he returns (Zechariah 12:10, 13:8-9). Presumably, this number includes the 144,000 Jewish people who are sealed by the Lord and who have come in equal numbers from each of the twelve tribes (Revelation 7:1-8), the elect who are gathered from Matthew 24:22-31, and the contingent of those who are wondrously saved from Romans 11:26. It is fair to say that quite a number of names are inscribed on this roll of ransomed citizens; each one destined for the millennial kingdom as a welcome stopover before enjoying eternally the delights of heaven itself. Henry Alford's (1810-71) famously beautiful hymn, *Ten Thousand Times Ten Thousand*, speaks of them as 'the roll of thine elect.'

This is exceedingly special for it drives home a message to battle-weary, footsore pilgrims, them and us, the blessed reality that each one is personally known to the Most High. Dale Ralph Davis suggests that 'in a time when God's people will be viewed as trash, scum, and faceless protoplasm, they are assured that their names are known and precious to God.' Nothing and no one can erase the names written in indelible ink in God's book. Those names are also inscribed on the palms of his hands and etched on his heart (Isaiah 49:16). Praise God.

12:2

Israel will be resurrected

'And many of those who sleep in the dust of the earth shall awake, some to everlasting life, and some to shame and everlasting contempt.'

The focus here is on an upcoming bodily resurrection when those who have died will be raised to face the reality of an eternity with only two options for, as Stuart Olyott points out, 'resurrection day will also be division day.' One option is *to everlasting life* (this is the first occurrence of this expression in the Old Testament); the other option is *to shame and everlasting contempt*. For some, it promises endless bliss; for the rest, when it happens, it promises eternal banishment which, as Sinclair Ferguson writes, '[Such people] will be forever excluded from the city of God. The annihilation of the wicked is not envisaged here, but rather a perpetual state of guilt and separation from God.' As you can see, there is a line of demarcation drawn.

Try as you might, you will be hard pressed to find a reference in the Bible to sustain the argument for a general resurrection. In fact, the opposite is the case. The reality is there are two resurrections: one before the millennium as described here in Daniel 12:2 for those who *awake to everlasting life*, and one at the end of the millennium for unbelievers who face *shame and everlasting contempt* when summarily dealt with at the great white throne and sentenced to 'the second death' (Revelation 20:11-15). As Renald Showers says, 'The fact that [he] said "many" rather than *all* indicates that he was not teaching a general resurrection of all the dead at the same time.'

When we fast forward to Revelation 20:5 where it speaks of

'the first resurrection' we need to remember that it is one event in three distinct stages, each one associated with the culture of the Jewish harvest (Leviticus 23): the firstfruits, followed by the main harvest, and concluded with the gleanings.

The initial stage is a reference to Jesus Christ as the 'firstfruits of them that slept' (1 Corinthians 15:20, NIV). The second phase is addressed by Paul in 1 Thessalonians 4:16-17 where 'the dead in Christ' are linked to the phrase, 'then, when [Jesus] comes, those who belong to him' (1 Corinthians 15:23, NIV). The third tier is the one spoken of here which applies to all those tribulation saints and Old Testament saints *who sleep in the dust of the earth*; both groups will share in the joys of the kingdom of God on earth (Isaiah 26:19). After the trial and the tears comes the triumph—resurrection!

You can imagine what this message must have meant to Daniel. After all the maelstrom of misery and persecution which his people will face, this is a breath of fresh air to his soul, truly magnificent news. He now learns straight from the lips of the angelic messenger that deliverance will come at the end of a very long road. And when it comes, it will be worth waiting for as it is permanent and final. It promises the exhilarating prospect of everlasting life in an environment where Jesus rules and reigns in splendour and majesty. As John Lennox observes, 'There have been many disappointments, dashed hopes, vanished dreams, and utter despair. There will yet be more, but can it really be true that one day it will all come to an end, for ever? Yes....'

Such a wonderful hope shone throughout the Old Testament era when it acted as a mainstay for those old covenant believers who looked forward in faith to the first advent of the Lord Jesus Christ. Abraham certainly had a steely confidence in a resurrection from the dead when he offered up Isaac on Moriah (Genesis 22:5; Hebrews 11:19). Job, who was probably around before Moses, asserted his faith in those familiar words, 'I know that my Redeemer lives, and that in the end he will stand upon the earth. And after my skin has been destroyed, yet in my flesh I will see God' (Job 19:25-26, NIV). Such glorious anticipation was shared by the writers of the psalms (17:15, 49:15, 71:20). Isaiah, who lived more than a century before Daniel, predicted that the dead would live again and that their bodies would rise (Isaiah 26:19). The prophet Hosea, a contemporary of Isaiah, was singing from the same page in the song book (Hosea 13:14). Saints, most likely those of Maccabean times, 'were tortured and refused to be released, so that they might gain a better resurrection' (Hebrews 11:35, NIV). Even the resurrection of the Lord Jesus is foretold in the words of David, the shepherd king, in Psalm 16:9-10. As John Walvoord reminds us, 'Daniel was not revealing something new, but what has always been the hope of the saints.'

12:3

Israel will be rewarded

'And those who are wise shall shine like the brightness of the sky above; and those who turn many to righteousness, like the stars forever and ever.'

These words of immense encouragement hold out the prospect of eternal compensation for those dear saints who have weathered many storms and who have remained steadfastly faithful to their calling and to their God (Romans 8:18; 2 Corinthians 4:7-18). They are numbered among those *who are wise* and that is reflected in the vibrant and vigorous ministry which they exercised under tremendous duress in the worst of times. We are not talking here about smart people, but about those who are prudent and perceptive.

We came across these men of wisdom earlier where they are known as the Maschilim (Daniel 11:32-35). Because they lived an exemplary life under enormous pressure and stayed loyal and true to the God of their fathers, others in the wider community were attracted to them and to their gracious God. There were many ripples emanating from their everyday lives insomuch that others were so astounded with the genuineness of their story that they too turned from the wrong path of sin to the right way of following the righteous God. Such red-hot commitment to the Most High is a huge fillip for those who need their faltering faith bolstered. These believers not only talked the talk, they walked the walk.

This is illustrated by Thomas McCrie in *The Story of the Scottish Church* when he writes about a day in 1540 when two young Scotsmen, Alexander Kennedy and Jerome Russell, were condemned to burn at the stake for their faith. As they plodded to the execution site, Russell noticed some signs of depression in his companion and so heartened him with, 'Brother, fear not; greater is he that is in us, than he that is in the world. The pain that we are to suffer is short, and shall be light, but our joy and consolation shall never have an end. Let us, therefore, strive to enter in to our Master and Saviour by the same strait way which he has trod before us. Death cannot destroy us, for it is already destroyed by him for whose sake we suffer.' And so they walked on to the stake, heads held high. Dale Ralph Davis makes the valid point, 'What a help it can be to have one of the *wise* come along beside you and keep you on your feet.'

And the God who sees all and knows all is the one who has

undertaken to amply reward them in a future day (Psalm 126:5-6; 1 Corinthians 15:58). Against a woefully dark background is a gleaming, diamond-like promise that God never shortchanges his people. As endtime soul-winners and disciple-makers, they will shine like the sun and display a shimmering splendour like the stars. These boringly ordinary believers are beaming brightly forever with a lustrous glory not their own, but his (Daniel 7:13-14; 2 Corinthians 3:18; 1 John 3:1-3). The worst of times behind them, the best of times stretching before them. Jim Allen says that 'these stars will never be eclipsed. It is a well-established principle in Scripture that fidelity to God will always be rewarded; the glory of the future will reflect the loyalty of the past.'

As John Newton affirmed, 'When we've been there ten thousand years, Bright shining as the sun, We've no less days to sing God's praise, Than when we first begun.' I love the beautifully focused paraphrase of Eugene Peterson in *The Message*, when he writes, 'Those who put others on the right path to life will glow like stars forever.' Stars that never burn out in God's galaxy. This has nothing at all to do with celebrity or cult status for we talk about pop stars, football stars, and whatever. But it has everything to do with servant status, for such people are the real stars in God's eyes. Along with them, Danny Akin asks, 'Do you want to be an all-star for King Jesus?'

12:4

'There is a time for everything ...'

'But you, Daniel, shut up the words and seal the book, until the time of the end. Many shall run to and fro, and knowledge shall increase.'

Daniel is exhorted to *shut* the book and *seal* it; he is to leave it sitting on the shelf for the time being. In light of all that he has seen and heard in the entire series of visions, this seems a strange command. It suggests, however, that these words, marked by authenticity, are to be preserved until a certain day dawns (Isaiah 8:16; Jeremiah 32:9-15). Then it will be a massive source of comfort and enrichment to the faithful in Israel's darkest hour. It will be their lifeline when they seem to be sinking fast. It will provide them with an anchor when the sands of time are shifting around them.

As they treasure the truth, it will gently remind them that everything will work out alright in the end because the sovereign God is in full control. And for us, Ligon Duncan writes that 'God is concerned about us. He is concerned that we benefit from this message of hope and so he tells Daniel to keep it safe.'

The final phrase, *many shall run to and fro, and knowledge shall increase*, has been a red herring for many years among Bible students. So many hold to the view that this is a reference to global travel and the ease with which man can commute to the four corners of earth. If that is a correct interpretation of the text, then it is being fulfilled before our eyes!

I feel, as I implied earlier in the chapter, that it refers to enquiring men and women investigating the Word of God. They will search the Scriptures, looking for light on the perilous times in which they are living. As they give diligent attention to the Word of God through Daniel (and others), they will become increasingly aware of what God is specifically saying to them in their particular situation. As they grasp with clarity the relevance of biblical truth, their knowledge will increase. Dale Ralph Davis says that 'it is immersion [in the Word of God] that brings insight.'

Israel is now in a state of blindness, but one day in the providence of God the veil will be removed and her eyes will be opened. That means the book of Daniel has the potential to become one of the most widely read books of all time in the final countdown to zero hour and the second advent of Jesus Christ. It will be reopened by the people of God and they will understand it as clearly as if they were reading or watching the daily news updates online because all of the detailed events will come to pass. In that day, Daniel's book will give seeking and searching souls a running commentary on current affairs during the tribulation.

Truths for life

When we assimilate all that has happened in the previous four verses, there are three timeless principles which should be applied to your life and mine. One, man has his poster boys, his megastars, and within a generation they are normally forgotten, but our eternal God honours every faithful servant, many of whom are unknown or unrecognised by others, and he never forgets them. Two, man expects his bumper pay-off in this life, but God generously rewards his trusty people in the next life. Three, man lives and works within the orbit of time, but God's purposes and plans are geared towards eternity.

12:5-8

How long ...?

Then I, Daniel, looked, and behold, two others stood, one on this bank of the stream and one on that bank of the stream. And someone said to the man clothed in linen, who was above the waters of the stream, 'How long shall it be till the end of these

*wonders?' And I heard the man clothed in linen, who was above
the waters of the stream; he raised his right hand and his left hand
toward heaven and swore by him who lives forever that it would
be for a time, times, and half a time, and that when the shattering
of the power of the holy people comes to an end all these things
would be finished. I heard, but I did not understand. Then I said,
'O my lord, what shall be the outcome of these things?'*

Daniel is privileged to eavesdrop on an angelic conversation on
the banks of the Tigris. The heavenly messengers, one on either
side of the river, are keenly interested in human affairs as they
watch the unfolding drama on earth (Daniel 10:4). Their legitimate
question is a poignant one, *How long shall it be till the end of these
wonders?* They want more information on the specific timeframe
for these truly extraordinary events; when they start, how long
will it be before they finish? There is a real sense of urgency in
their impassioned appeal and, perhaps, a sense of frustration too
as they do not have any idea of the divine timetable (Mark 13:32).

Again, Daniel is conscious of the presence of *the man clothed in
linen, who was above the waters of the stream*. He is the same person
whom Daniel encountered earlier, none other than the glorified
Lord Jesus Christ, robed in his priestly purity (Daniel 10:5-6). In
a scene reminiscent of Psalm 29:10, he sees the Lord who 'sits
enthroned upon the flood.' He was there at the outset and he is
still there when the last punctuation mark has been added to the
disclosure. Faithful One, so unchanging.

Danny Akin writes, 'In a display of amazing solemnity and
seriousness, the Son of God raises both hands to heaven' (Genesis
14:22; Deuteronomy 32:40). This is a most unusual stance for him
to take, but it underlines the sheer weight of what is entailed.
It confirms the veracity and dependability of the message that

will be given. Bryan Chapell writes that 'the oath means that the truths revealed are sure, guaranteed by the integrity of God.' Even more so, when the immortal one invokes an oath and swears by himself, as *one who lives forever* (1 Timothy 6:16; Hebrews 6:13). This is God calling upon God to do what is needed. The fact that two angels were present is in keeping with the concept of requiring two witnesses to establish a point (Deuteronomy 19:15, 31:28; 2 Corinthians 13:1).

The answer is twofold and it is unmistakably clear what God's intentions are. First, the length of time is said to be for a *time, times, and half a time*. We came across this cryptic comment earlier in the book (Daniel 7:25) and it refers to a period of three and one half years or 42 months which corresponds with the second half of the tribulation (Revelation 11:2, 12:14, 13:5). Second, this *time of trouble* (Daniel 12:1) will conclude when God says enough is enough and it will not be a day longer than it should be (Matthew 24:22). The fantastic truth is that God is never running late. He is right on schedule. His schedule. Not necessarily ours.

Ligon Duncan is spot-on when he says, 'When evil has done its worst and the hopes of the people of God seem shattered, then God will act. The grim work of the oppressors will roll on and on and on. But, at the appropriate moment, God will intervene.' There is nothing on yonder horizon to even remotely suggest that things are going to get better with every passing year and that we can eventually Christianise the world. Instead of life becoming sweeter and more serene for God's covenant people, it becomes increasingly sour and screwed-up. The harsh reality is that God's people will be crushed and crunched to the point of crumbling, the strength of which reveals the undertow of this epic revelation.

By any flight of fancy, that was quite a message for Daniel to process in his own heart and mind. Truth be told, as we read his candid confession in verse 8, *I heard, but I did not understand.* There was so much stuff that the angel disclosed to him; basically, it was far too much for him to handle in one go. He simply could not get his head around all the ins and outs, ups and downs of the prophetic vision. His head was spinning. Since Daniel felt like that, many of us can take heart and be quietly reassured for there are many times in our lives when we know exactly how he feels. We have loads of questions and far fewer answers. But God knows. That helps explain Daniel's further query, *O my lord, what shall be the outcome of these things?*

12:9

Time to move on, Daniel

He said, 'Go your way, Daniel, for the words are shut up and sealed until the time of the end.'

Understandably, Daniel wanted more snippets of information to satisfy his curiosity and satiate his thirst for knowledge. Sounds familiar, does it not? The response from on high was less than he bargained for as he was more or less told to forget it. All done in a most respectful manner, of course, as dear old Daniel was well on in advanced years at this point. Tenderly, lovingly, and firmly he was reminded that God's covenant purposes would ripen and come to fruition and there was no need for him to climb the walls. He did not need to lie awake at night panicking over the future as God was in total control of the situation. Even when it came to the road ahead for his beloved people and homeland, all were in God's safe and strong hands.

God was telling him no more; he told him all that he needed

to know at that moment. There are things we know and things we do not know and cannot know because God has chosen not to reveal them to us. Such was Daniel's experience. Time now for him to get on with the rest of his life and leave the outcome of the vision in the lap of the sovereign Lord. As Sinclair Ferguson notes, all of this will become more clear only 'as God unravels history in the unseen future.' Simply put, the times were set, the truth was sealed, and the triumph was sure.

12:10

Some get it, some do not

'Many shall purify themselves and make themselves white and be refined, but the wicked shall act wickedly. And none of the wicked shall understand, but those who are wise shall understand.'

There are two classes of people spoken of here: the wise and the wicked, the seed of the woman and the seed of the serpent (Genesis 3:15). The former will have a deep awareness and appreciation of what God is doing and will stay close to him. When the crisis pummels them, they will know what to do and where to go. For the *many*, it will be a painfully traumatic time, likely to the point of martyrdom, but through it all they will be refined like silver in their faith and become more rounded in their character (Zechariah 13:8-9; James 1:2-4; 1 Peter 1:7). They will reflect the beauty and glory of the Lord Jesus to such a degree that they stand out among their peers. Because of all they have come through in life and in death, they are better placed to serve their God during the upcoming millennium. John MacArthur says, 'Then the *many* of Daniel becomes the "all" of Paul in Romans 11:26. They constitute the redeemed nation.'

In contrast, God's enemies will go from bad to worse. In spite of the utter devastation and carnage all around them they obstinately refuse to believe gospel truth (Revelation 9:20). Man is defiant as he persistently snubs God. The wicked will do what the wicked do. With hearts harder than granite, they choose to maintain the status quo and assume an aura of normality as they become ever more ensnared in their not so blissful ignorance. The tragic truth is that it is a 2-1 majority of them who give the real Jesus Christ a slap in the face and end up eternally lost; in fact, the prophet informs us that it will be as many as 'two-thirds [who] will be struck down and perish' (Zechariah 13:8, NIV).

12:11-12

Worth waiting for

'And from the time that the regular burnt offering is taken away and the abomination that makes desolate is set up, there shall be 1,290 days. Blessed is he who waits and arrives at the 1,335 days.'

The opening sentence in this not-easy-to-understand couple of verses takes us back to the midway point in the tribulation period. It speaks of the epoch-making moment when true worship is repressed and then immediately replaced by false worship, that is, *when the regular burnt offering is taken away and the abomination that makes desolate is set up*. One was acceptable to God, the other is abhorrent to him. As we noted, Antiochus Epiphanes did it during his reign of rebellion (8:11-13, 11:31), but the antichrist will take it to a whole new level under the aegis of this final thorn in the side of history. Dale Ralph Davis writes that 'Jesus has Daniel 9:27 and 12:11 in view when he refers to the "abomination of desolation" in Mark 13:14.'

But what are we to make of the 1,290 days of verse 11, and the beatitude and further time extension to 1,335 days in verse 12? We know that the second half of the tribulation expires after 1,260 days (42 months) with the return of the Lord Jesus Christ, touchdown being the Mount of Olives (Zechariah 12:3-9; Acts 1:10-12; Revelation 19:11-16). That leaves an extra 30 days, followed by another 45 days, for certain developments to take place. What?

It is during these extra days when that which is evil and offensive will be purged out from the city of Jerusalem and its environs in preparation for the kingdom. After all that has transpired, the temple area will need a deep-clean treatment. It will also take time to clear up the mess in the aftermath of the Armageddon campaign (Revelation 14:19-20, 19:17-21). It may also be when the Gentile nations are judged and the sheep and goats are separated (Matthew 25:31-46), and the hour when Jewish people are regathered and judgment is meted out (Ezekiel 20:34-38).

It is a period of transition from the terrible day of the Lord to the peaceful and prosperous day of Christ. John Walvoord says, 'By the end of the 1,335 days, or seventy-five days after the second advent, these great judgments will have been accomplished and the millennial kingdom formally launched.' In all honesty, after 1,260 days of brutal treatment from a brutish antichrist, where they have outlasted the pressure, the persecution, and the pain, another 75 days before being warmly welcomed into the golden age of the kingdom of God on earth is nothing too much to worry about. There is a need to persevere with an enduring spirit to the finish line; with the end in sight, this is not the time to wilt or wane. There is sunshine light at the end of the tunnel. It will be well worth the wait. No doubts there, because 'blessings abound where'er he reigns.' A sad beginning, but a supremely happy ending!

12:13

The best is yet to come

'But go your way till the end. And you shall rest and shall stand in your allotted place at the end of the days.'

The final sentiments are a deliciously personal note to Daniel. The aged prophet-cum-historian is told to go on his way. For him, this was a path of dedication, surrender, prayer, and study. Ultimately, it was the royal route to blessing, the prized blessing of being with his God forever. He was to hold on a wee while longer for death was inevitable and soon approaching.

For Daniel, after a lifetime of unflagging service it would be a welcome rest and a well-earned break away from the rigours of life in the public eye and the demands of a wider ministry in the community and to the exiles (Job 3:17; Isaiah 57:2; Revelation 14:13). There is also the exciting prospect of resurrection and reward when he would stand up in his *allotted place* and share in the majestic glories of the Lord for the countless aeons of eternity.

As an aside, the word translated as *allotted place* is used over twenty-five times in Joshua 14-21. Dale Ralph Davis notes that 'it refers both to the *lot* that is cast and to the allotment that the lot determines, so that it frequently designates the turf or the towns assigned to a tribe or group.' That suggests to us that our friend Daniel has his wee bit of turf, his patch—an *allotted place*, an assigned space—with his name printed on the attached label (Colossians 1:12).

Joachim Neander (1650-80) penned these appropriate sentiments, 'Praise to the Lord, who o'er all things so wondrously reigneth, Shieldeth thee gently from harm, or when fainting sustaineth; Hast thou not seen, How thy heart's wishes have been, Granted in what he ordaineth?'

An unimaginably bright future and a personalised inheritance await him, along with every believer in the Lord Jesus, with the dawning of God's eternal day. And, dear reader, for him and for us, such an endowment is imperishable, incorruptible, indestructible, and immortal (1 Peter 1:4). What an exhilarating prospect for every faithful servant of the Most High God. Enough to lift the spirit of pilgrims who are still on the trail towards their heavenly home. All because for Daniel, throughout his entire life, he walked closely with his God—the great God of highest heaven—the lead actor in the evolving drama of salvation history.

Some lyrics penned by Aaron Keyes and Pete James sum up the tenor of the book of Daniel so terrifically well:

> God the uncreated one, the author of salvation;
> who wrote the laws of space and time,
> who fashioned worlds to his design.
> The one whom angel hosts revere,
> hung the stars like chandeliers,
> numbered every grain of sand,
> knows the heart of every man.
> He is king forever, he is king forevermore.

God our fortress and our strength,
the rock on which we can depend;
matchless in his majesty,
his power and authority.
Unshaken by the schemes of man,
never changing, great I am,
kingdoms rise and kingdoms fall,
he is faithful through it all.
Crown him king forever, crown him king forevermore.